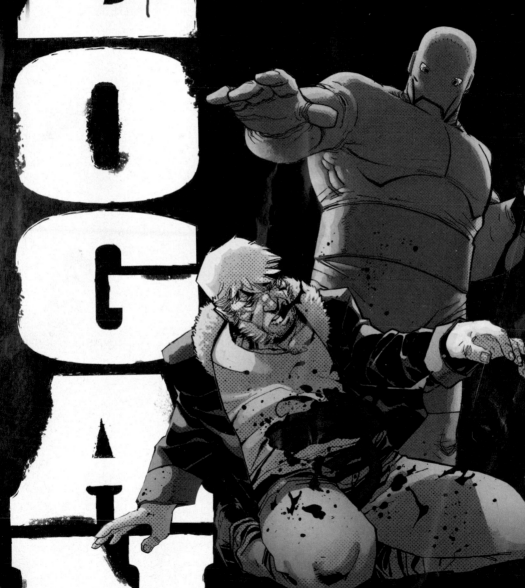

DEAD MAN LOGAN

WELCOME BACK, LOGAN

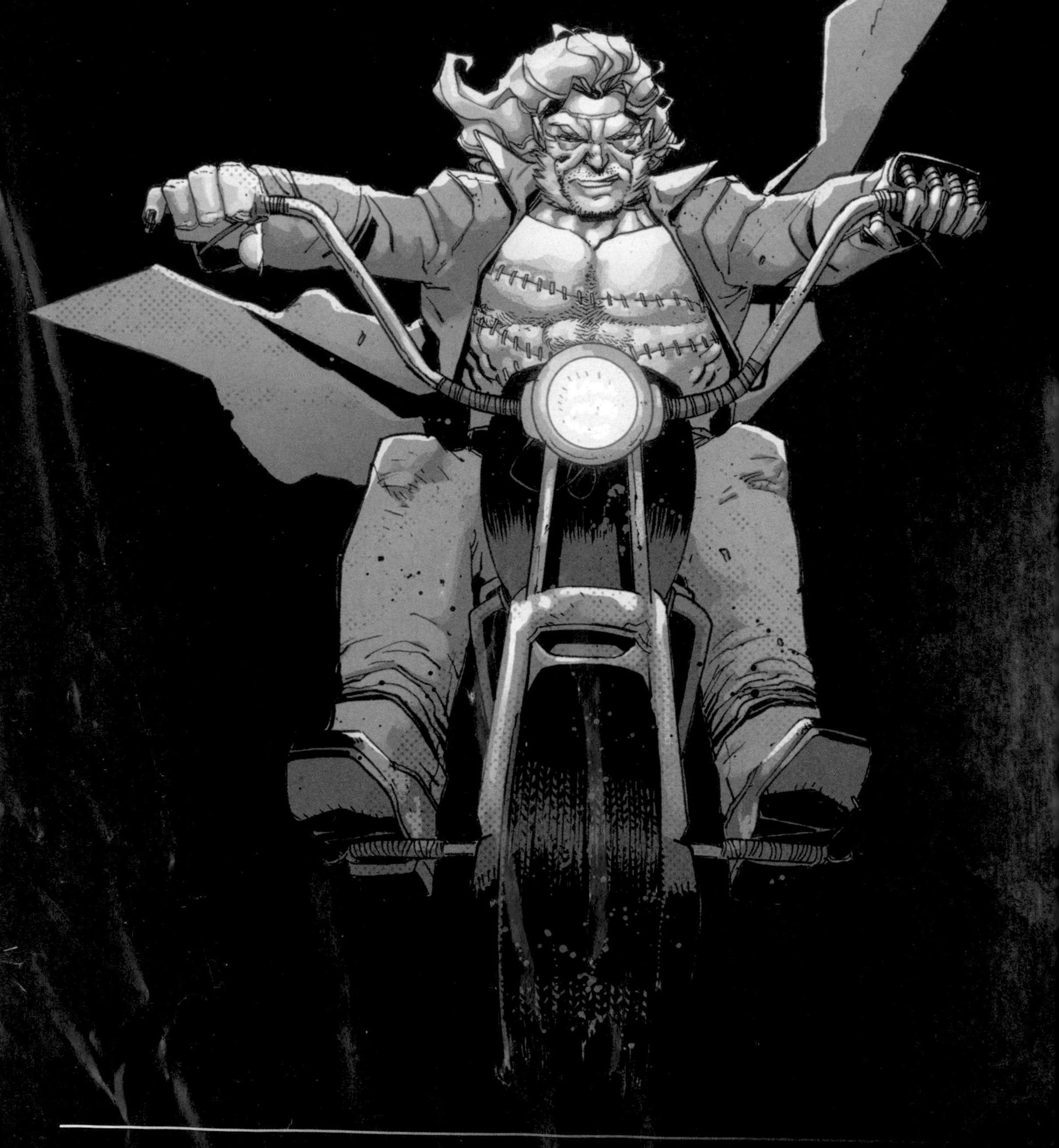

COLLECTION EDITOR **MARK D. BEAZLEY**
ASSISTANT EDITOR **CAITLIN O'CONNELL**
ASSOCIATE MANAGING EDITOR **KATERI WOODY**
SENIOR EDITOR, SPECIAL PROJECTS **JENNIFER GRÜNWALD**
VP PRODUCTION & SPECIAL PROJECTS **JEFF YOUNGQUIST**
BOOK DESIGNERS **STACIE ZUCKER, SALENA MAHINA, ADAM DEL RE** & **ANTHONY GAMBINO**

SVP PRINT, SALES & MARKETING **DAVID GABRIEL**
DIRECTOR, LICENSED PUBLISHING **SVEN LARSEN**
EDITOR IN CHIEF **C.B. CEBULSKI**
CHIEF CREATIVE OFFICER **JOE QUESADA**
PRESIDENT **DAN BUCKLEY**
EXECUTIVE PRODUCER **ALAN FINE**

DEAD MAN LOGAN VOL. 2: WELCOME BACK, LOGAN. Contains material originally published in magazine form as DEAD MAN LOGAN (2019) #7-12. First printing 2019. ISBN 978-1-302-91466-0. Published by MARVEL WORLDWIDE, INC., a subsidiary of MARVEL ENTERTAINMENT, LLC. OFFICE OF PUBLICATION: 135 West 50th Street, New York, NY 10020.

Printed in Canada. DAN BUCKLEY, President, Marvel Entertainment; JOHN NEE, Publisher; JOE QUESADA, Chief Creative Officer; TOM BREVOORT, SVP of Publishing; DAVID BOGART, Associate Publisher & SVP of Talent Affairs; DAVID GABRIEL, VP of Print & Digital Publishing; JEFF YOUNGQUIST, VP of Production & Special Projects; DAN CARR, Executive Director of Publishing Technology; ALEX MORALES, Director of Publishing Operations; DAN EDINGTON, Managing Editor; SUSAN CRESPI, Production Manager; STAN LEE, Chairman Emeritus. For information regarding advertising in Marvel Comics or on Marvel.com, please contact Vit DeBellis, Custom Solutions & Integrated Advertising Manager, at vdebellis@marvel.com. For Marvel subscription inquiries, please call 888-511-5480. **Manufactured between 10/25/2019 and 11/26/2019 by SOLISCO PRINTERS, SCOTT, QC, CANADA.**

10 9 8 7 6 5 4 3 2 1

DEAD MAN LOGAN

AFTER AN EXTENDED STAY IN THE PRIME UNIVERSE, LOGAN HAS BEEN SENT BACK TO HIS ORIGINAL TIMELINE...

WELCOME BACK, LOGAN

ED BRISSON
WRITER

MIKE HENDERSON
ARTIST

NOLAN WOODARD
COLOR ARTIST

VC's CORY PETIT
LETTERER

DECLAN SHALVEY
COVER ARTIST

CHRIS ROBINSON
EDITOR

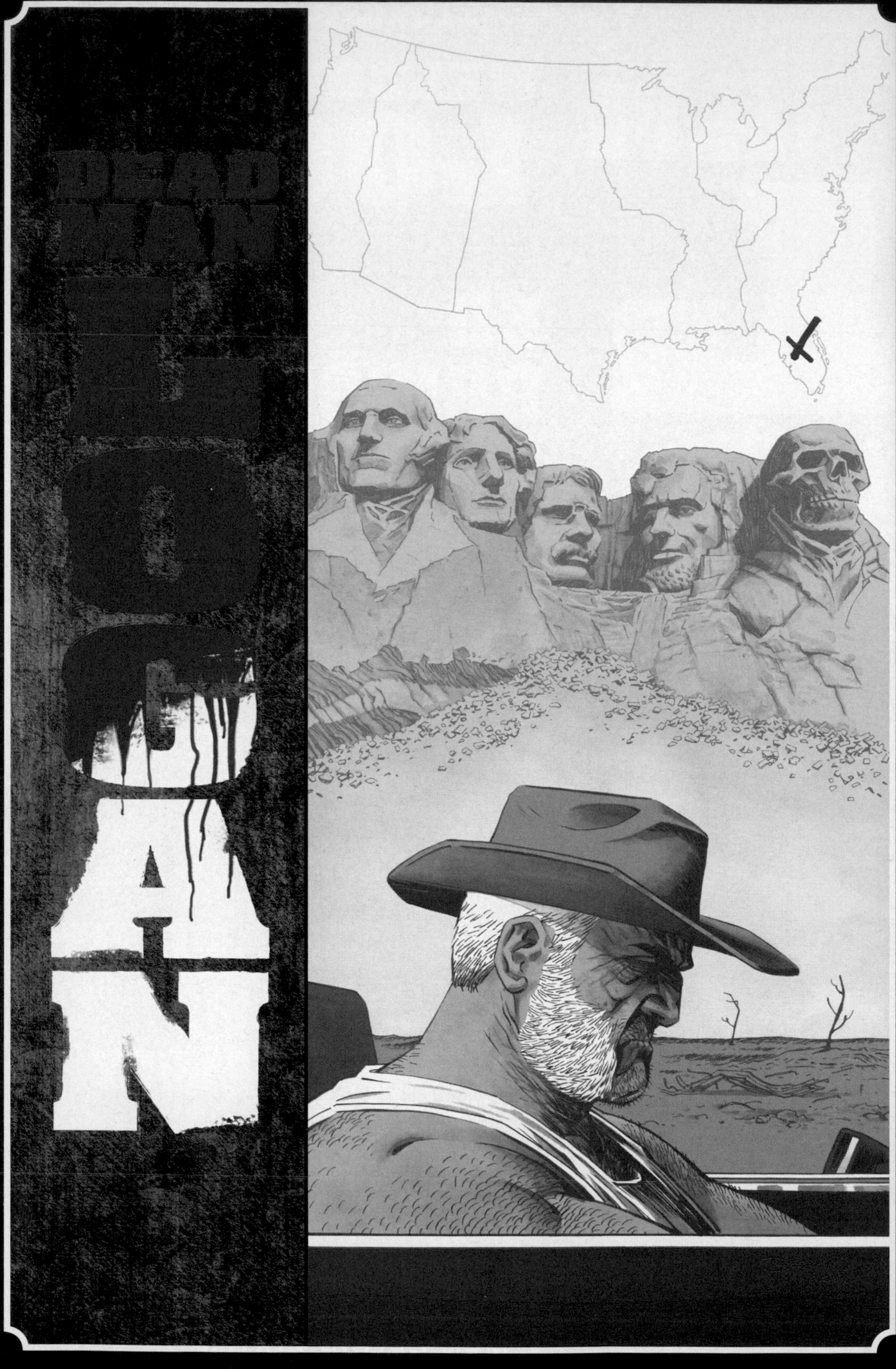
DEAD MAN
LOGAN

7

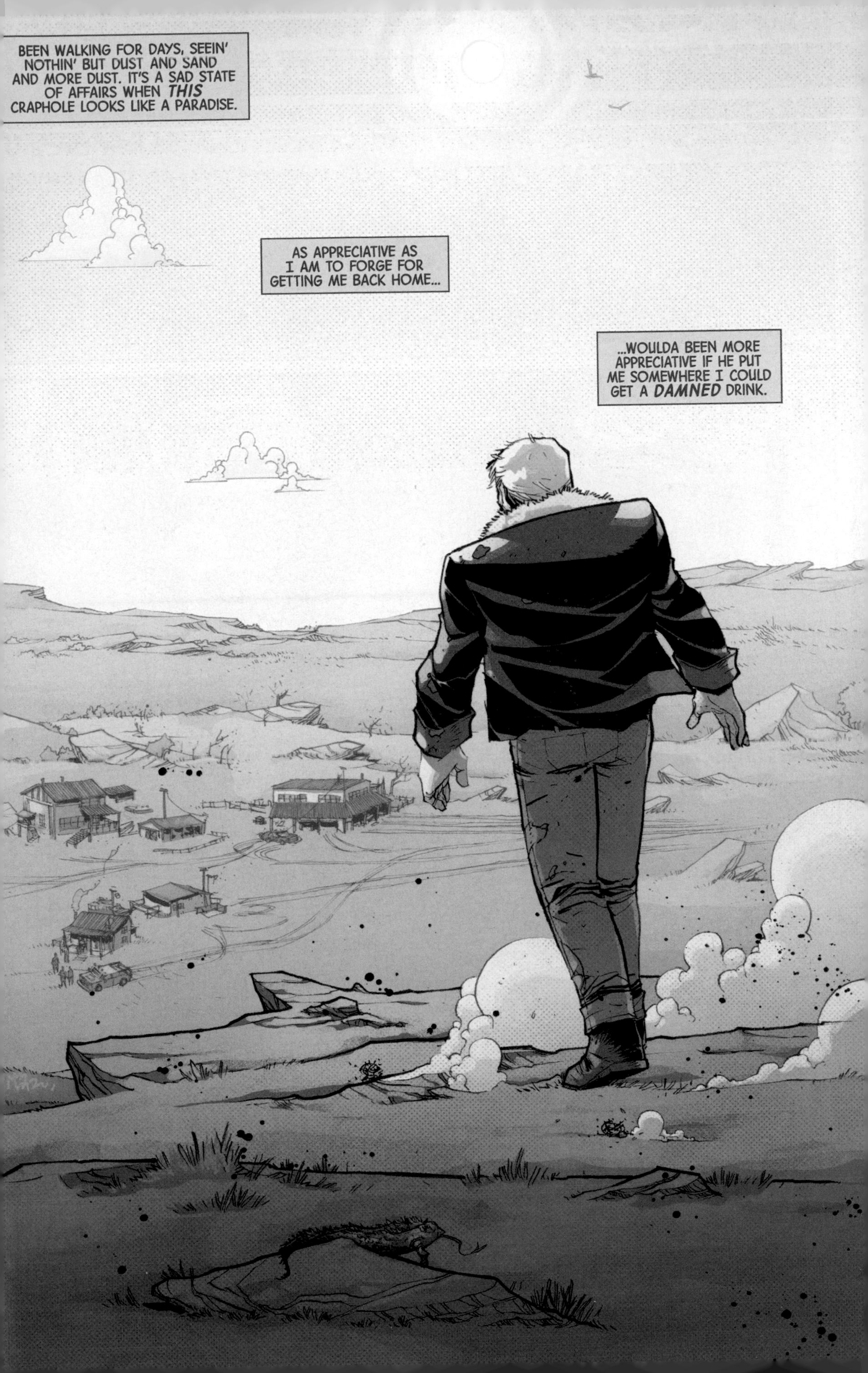
BEEN WALKING FOR DAYS, SEEIN' NOTHIN' BUT DUST AND SAND AND MORE DUST. IT'S A SAD STATE OF AFFAIRS WHEN THIS CRAPHOLE LOOKS LIKE A PARADISE.
AS APPRECIATIVE AS I AM TO FORGE FOR GETTING ME BACK HOME...
...WOULDA BEEN MORE APPRECIATIVE IF HE PUT ME SOMEWHERE I COULD GET A DAMNED DRINK.

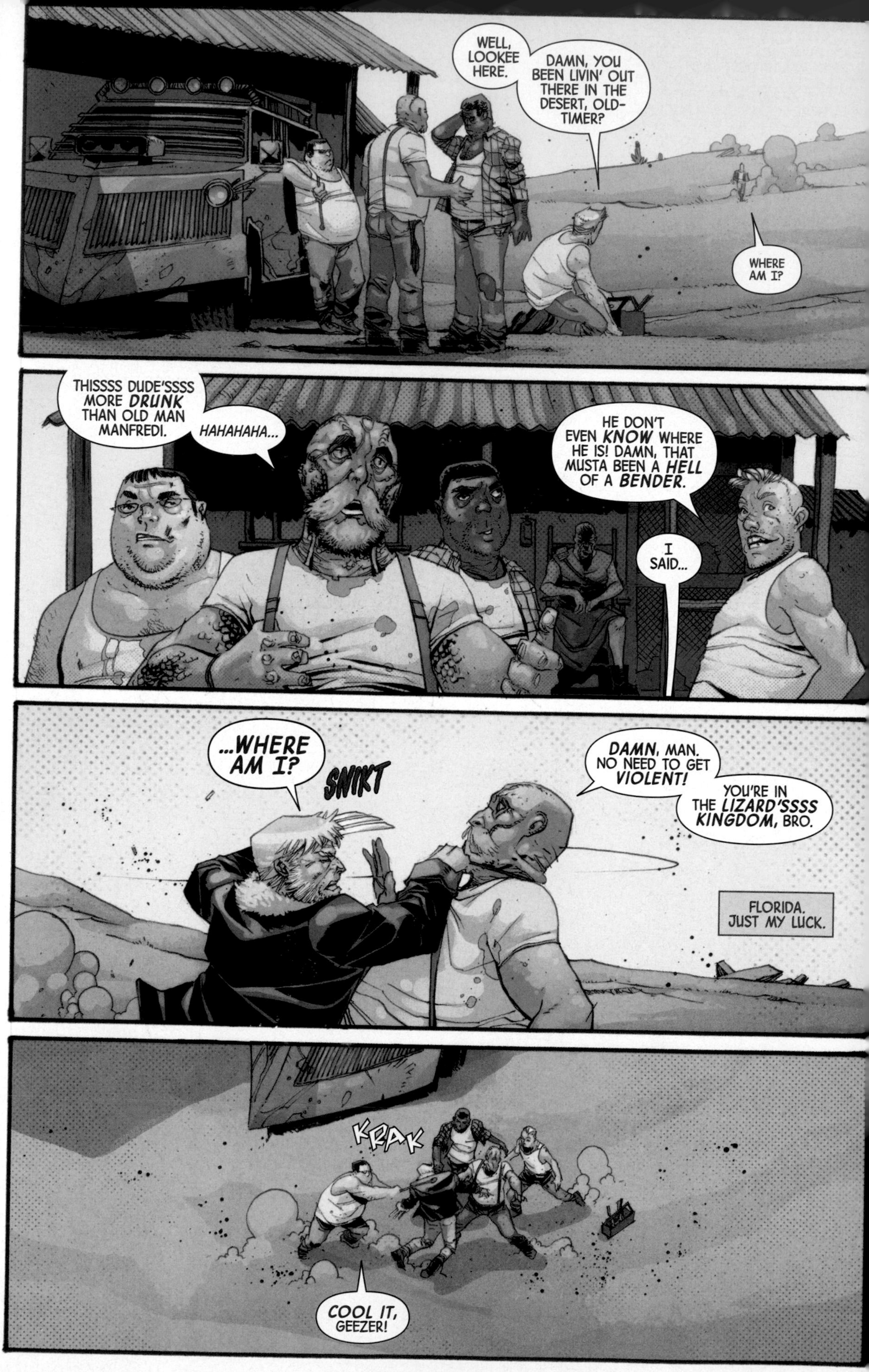
WELL, LOOKEE HERE.
DAMN, YOU BEEN LIVIN' OUT THERE IN THE DESERT, OLD-TIMER?
WHERE AM I?
THISSSS DUDE'SSSS MORE DRUNK THAN OLD MAN MANFREDI.
HAHAHAHA...
HE DON'T EVEN KNOW WHERE HE IS! DAMN, THAT MUSTA BEEN A HELL OF A BENDER.
I SAID...
...WHERE AM I?
SNIKT
DAMN, MAN. NO NEED TO GET VIOLENT!
YOU'RE IN THE LIZARD'SSSS KINGDOM, BRO.
FLORIDA. JUST MY LUCK.
KRAK
COOL IT, GEEZER!

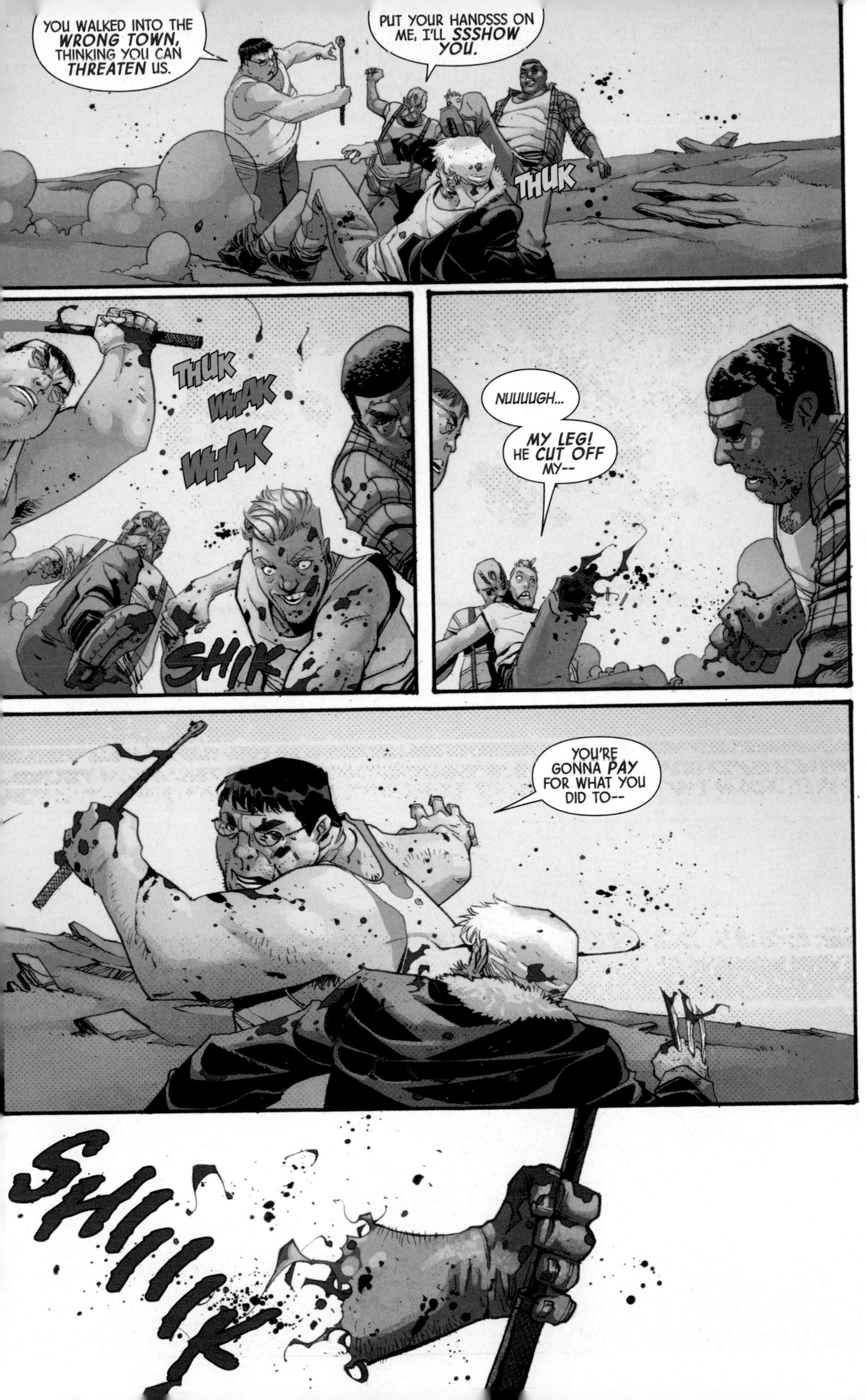

YOU WALKED INTO THE WRONG TOWN, THINKING YOU CAN THREATEN US.
PUT YOUR HANDSSS ON ME, I'LL SSSHOW YOU.
THUK
THUK
WHAK
WHAK
SHIK
NUUUUGH...
MY LEG! HE CUT OFF MY--
YOU'RE GONNA PAY FOR WHAT YOU DID TO--
SHIIIK

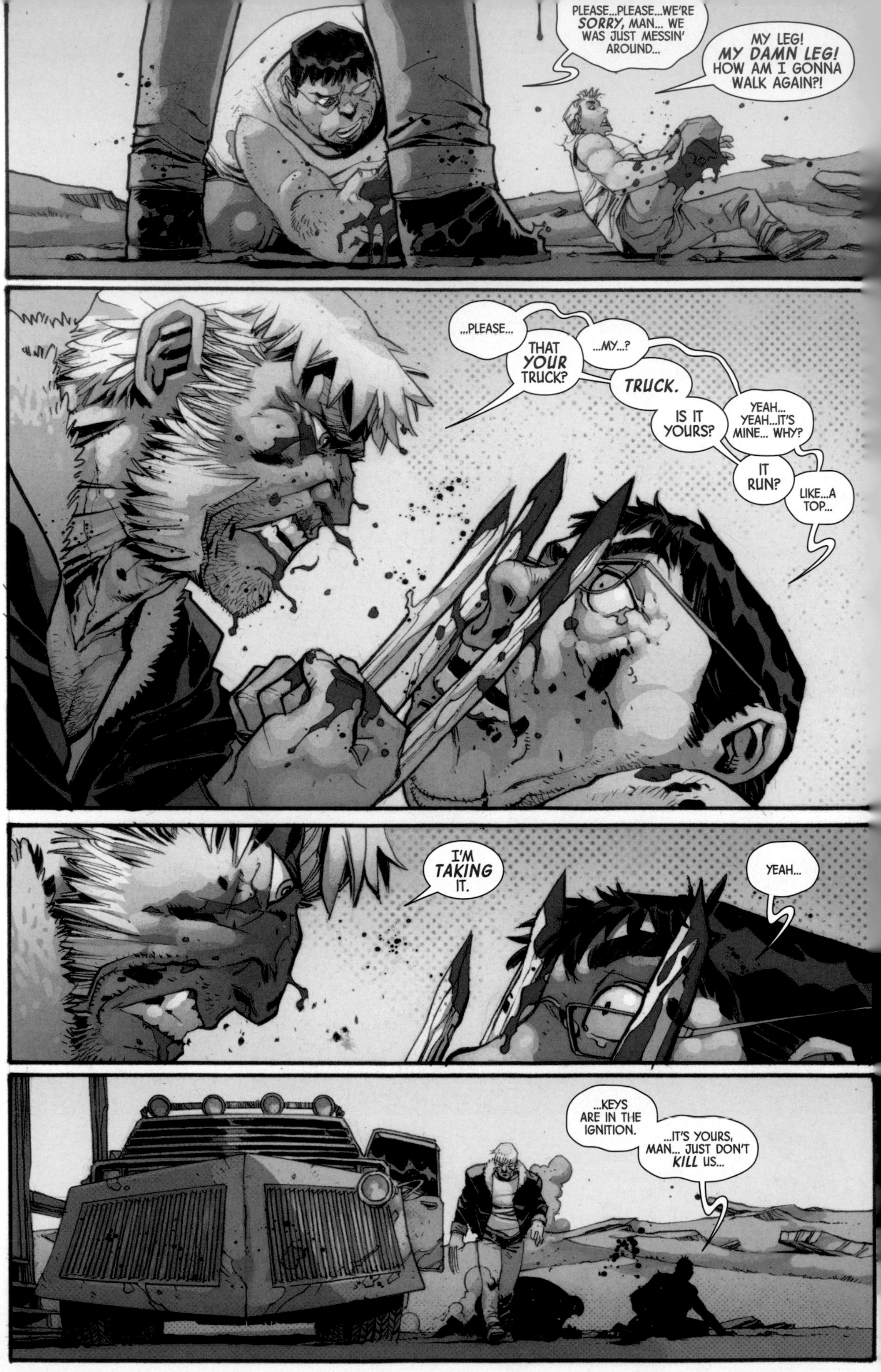
PLEASE...PLEASE...WE'RE SORRY, MAN... WE WAS JUST MESSIN' AROUND...
MY LEG! MY DAMN LEG! HOW AM I GONNA WALK AGAIN?!
THAT YOUR TRUCK?
...PLEASE...
...MY...?
TRUCK.
IS IT YOURS?
YEAH... YEAH...IT'S MINE... WHY?
IT RUN?
LIKE...A TOP...
I'M TAKING IT.
YEAH...
...KEYS ARE IN THE IGNITION.
...IT'S YOURS, MAN... JUST DON'T KILL US...

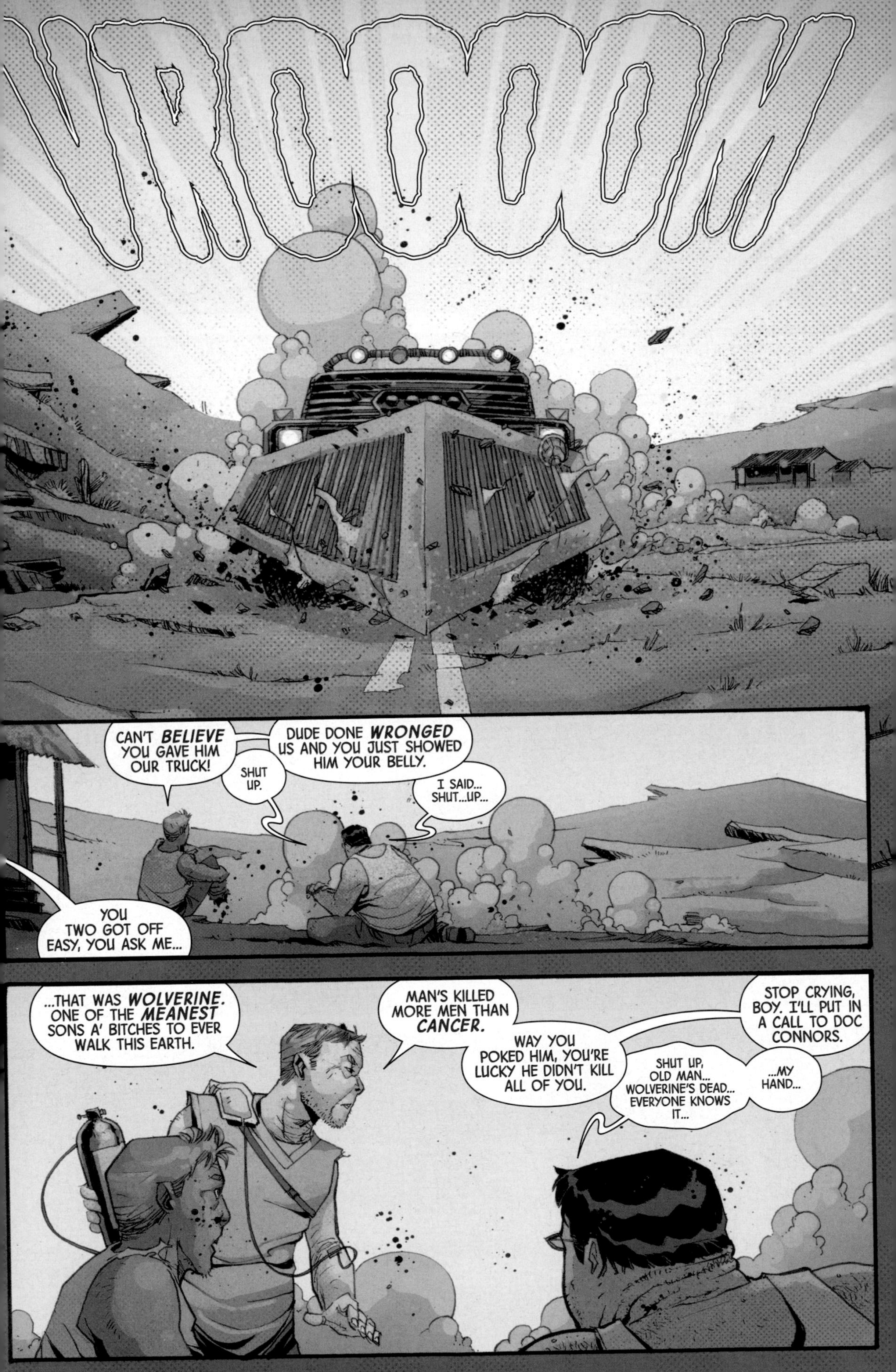
VROOOOM
CAN'T BELIEVE YOU GAVE HIM OUR TRUCK!
DUDE DONE WRONGED US AND YOU JUST SHOWED HIM YOUR BELLY.
SHUT UP.
I SAID... SHUT...UP...
YOU TWO GOT OFF EASY, YOU ASK ME...
...THAT WAS WOLVERINE. ONE OF THE MEANEST SONS A' BITCHES TO EVER WALK THIS EARTH.
MAN'S KILLED MORE MEN THAN CANCER.
WAY YOU POKED HIM, YOU'RE LUCKY HE DIDN'T KILL ALL OF YOU.
SHUT UP, OLD MAN... WOLVERINE'S DEAD... EVERYONE KNOWS IT...
STOP CRYING, BOY. I'LL PUT IN A CALL TO DOC CONNORS.
...MY HAND...

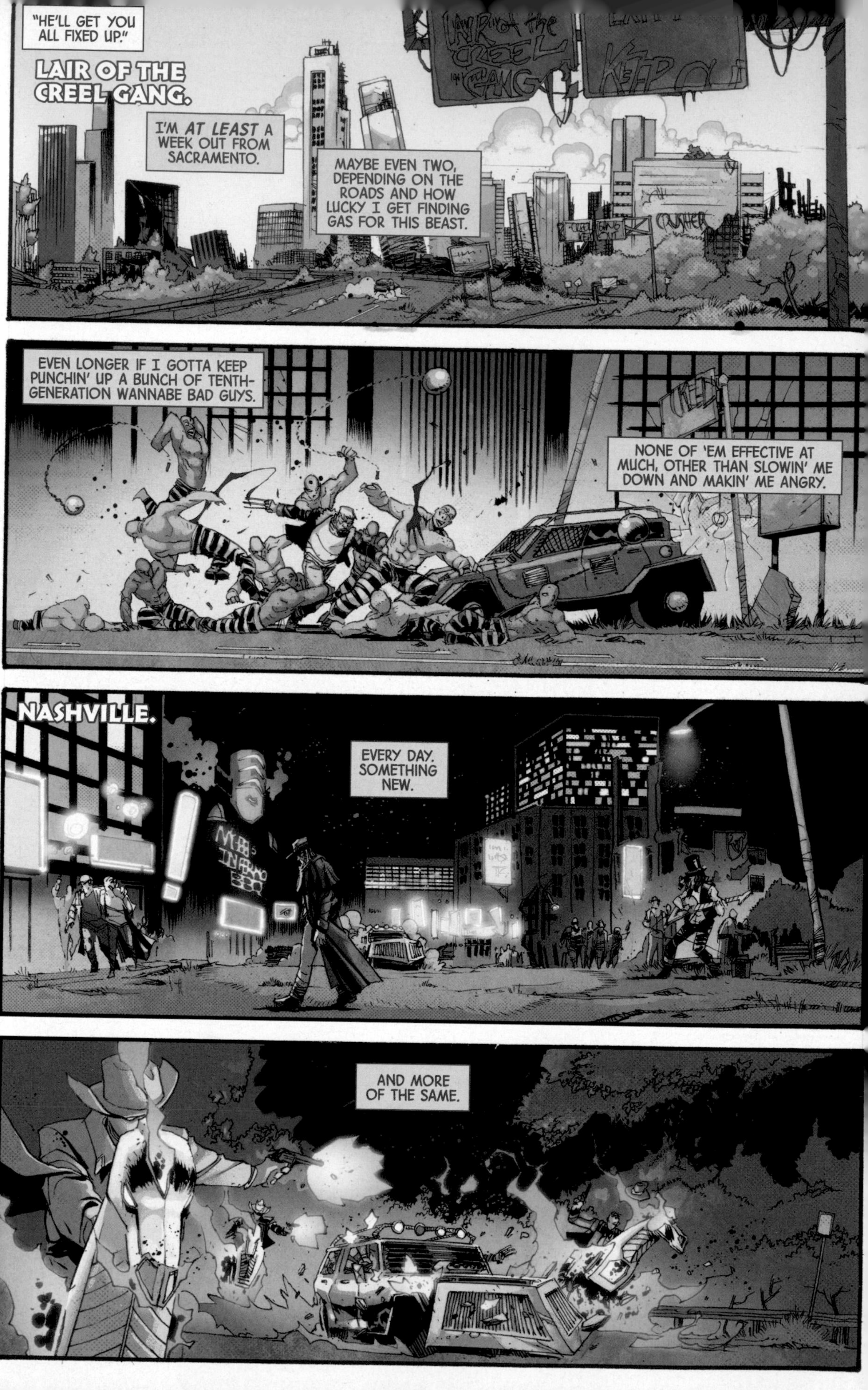
"HE'LL GET YOU ALL FIXED UP."
LAIR OF THE CREEL GANG.
I'M AT LEAST A WEEK OUT FROM SACRAMENTO.
MAYBE EVEN TWO, DEPENDING ON THE ROADS AND HOW LUCKY I GET FINDING GAS FOR THIS BEAST.
EVEN LONGER IF I GOTTA KEEP PUNCHIN' UP A BUNCH OF TENTH-GENERATION WANNABE BAD GUYS.
NONE OF 'EM EFFECTIVE AT MUCH, OTHER THAN SLOWIN' ME DOWN AND MAKIN' ME ANGRY.
NASHVILLE.
EVERY DAY. SOMETHING NEW.
AND MORE OF THE SAME.

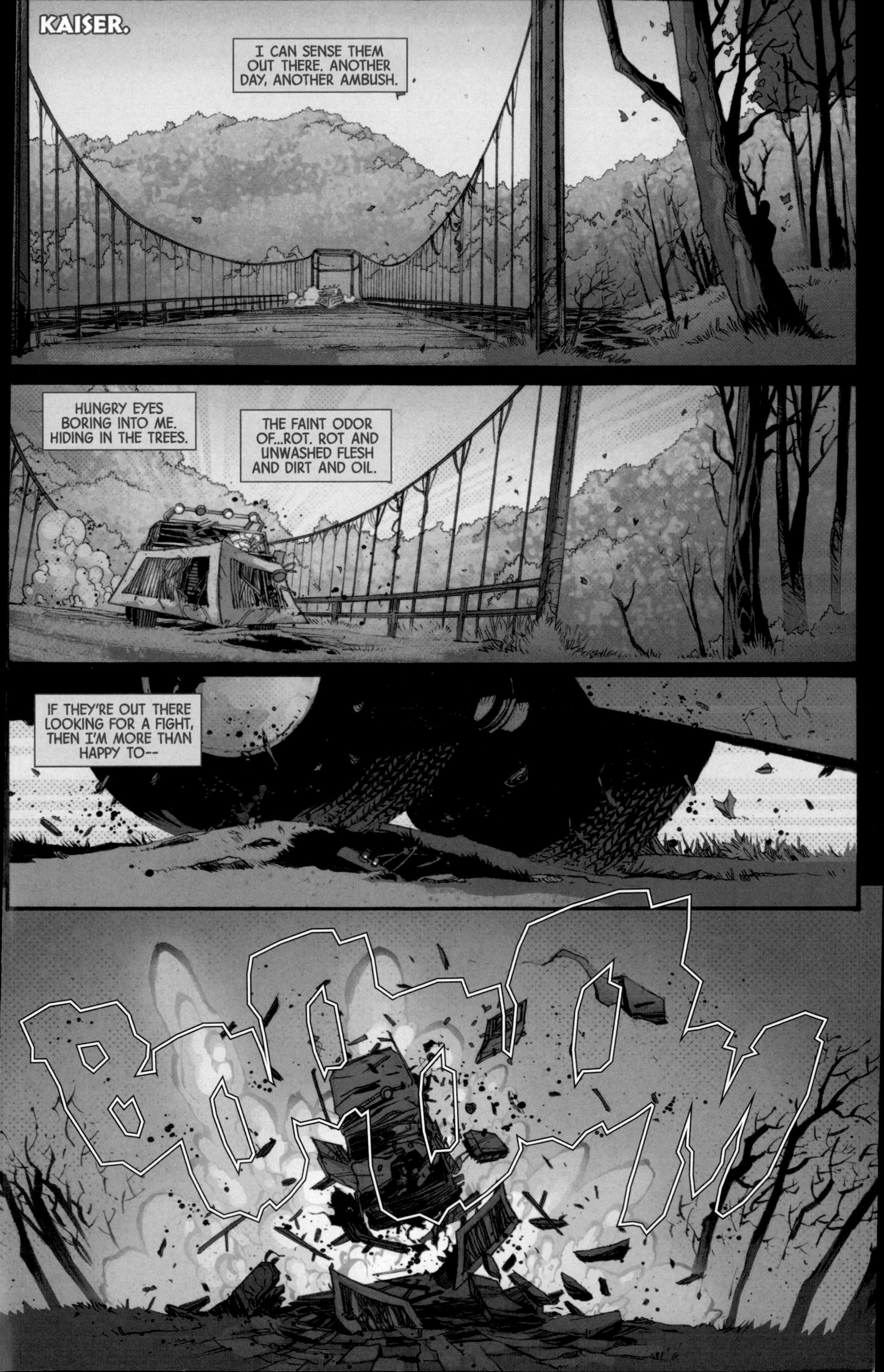
KAISER.
I CAN SENSE THEM OUT THERE. ANOTHER DAY, ANOTHER AMBUSH.
HUNGRY EYES BORING INTO ME. HIDING IN THE TREES.
THE FAINT ODOR OF...ROT. ROT AND UNWASHED FLESH AND DIRT AND OIL.
IF THEY'RE OUT THERE LOOKING FOR A FIGHT, THEN I'M MORE THAN HAPPY TO--
BOOOOOM

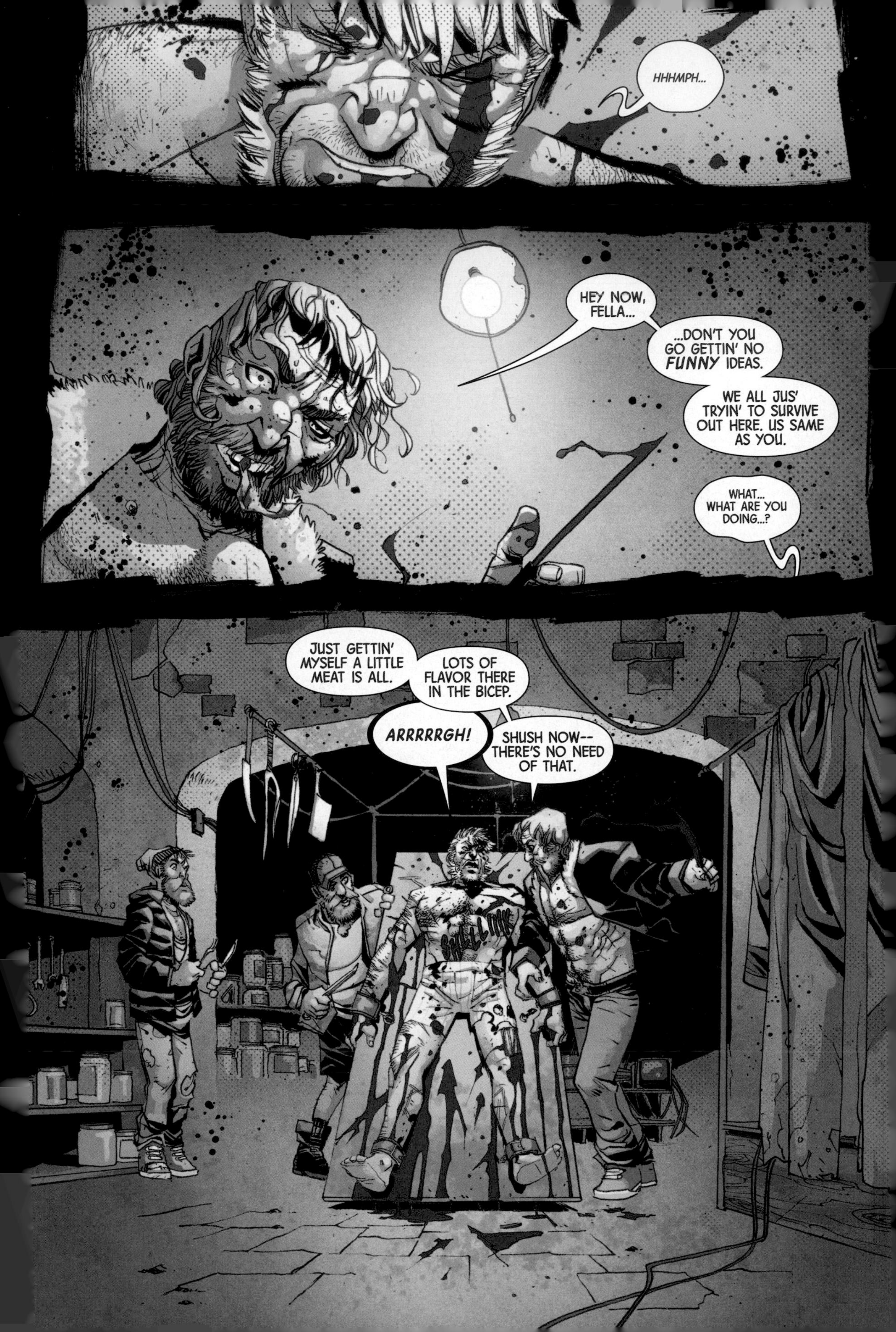
HHHMPH...
HEY NOW, FELLA...
...DON'T YOU GO GETTIN' NO FUNNY IDEAS.
WE ALL JUS' TRYIN' TO SURVIVE OUT HERE. US SAME AS YOU.
WHAT... WHAT ARE YOU DOING...?
JUST GETTIN' MYSELF A LITTLE MEAT IS ALL.
LOTS OF FLAVOR THERE IN THE BICEP.
ARRRRRGH!
SHUSH NOW-- THERE'S NO NEED OF THAT.

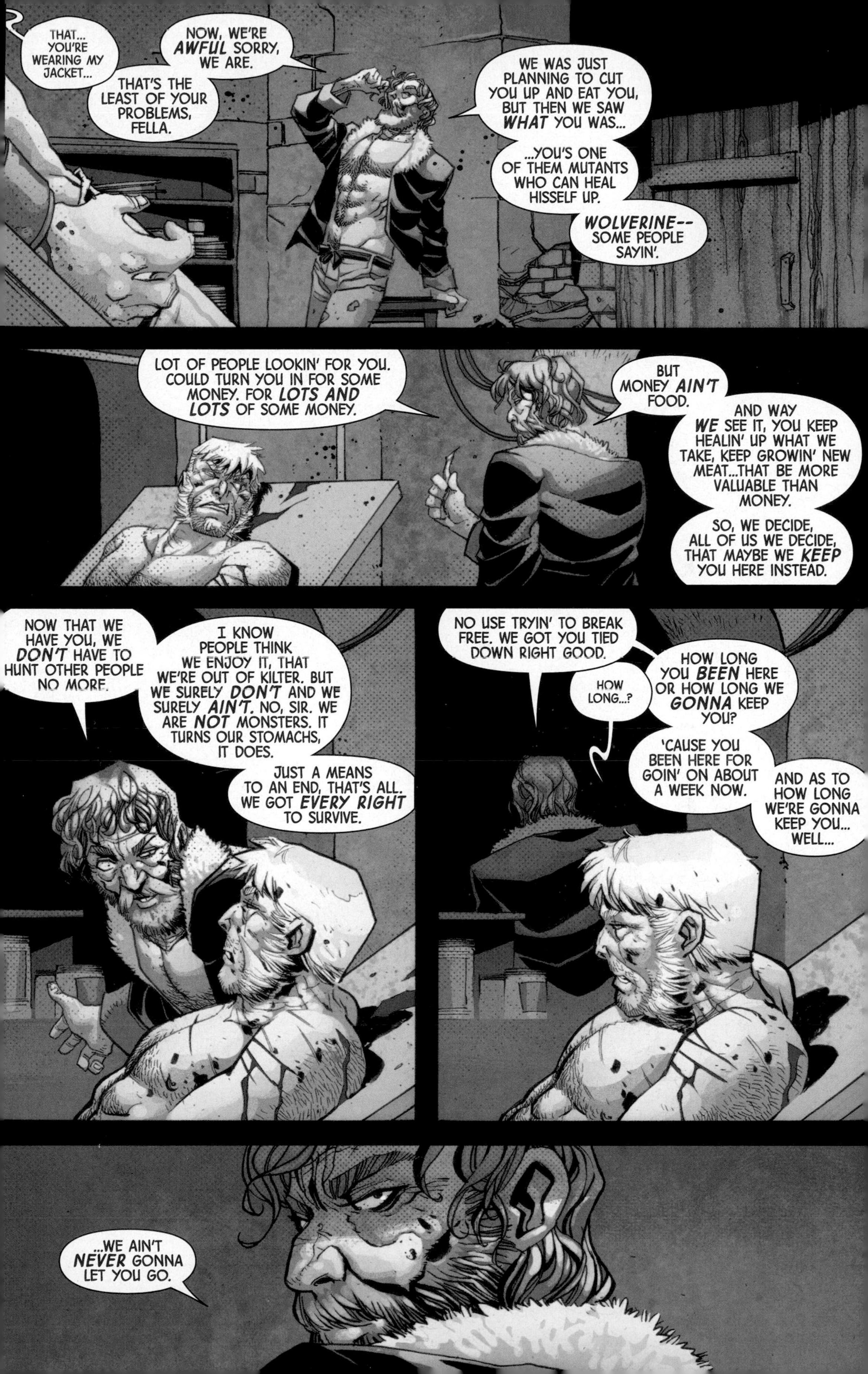

THAT... YOU'RE WEARING MY JACKET...
NOW, WE'RE AWFUL SORRY, WE ARE.
THAT'S THE LEAST OF YOUR PROBLEMS, FELLA.
WE WAS JUST PLANNING TO CUT YOU UP AND EAT YOU, BUT THEN WE SAW WHAT YOU WAS...
...YOU'S ONE OF THEM MUTANTS WHO CAN HEAL HISSELF UP.
WOLVERINE-- SOME PEOPLE SAYIN'.
LOT OF PEOPLE LOOKIN' FOR YOU. COULD TURN YOU IN FOR SOME MONEY. FOR LOTS AND LOTS OF SOME MONEY.
BUT MONEY AIN'T FOOD.
AND WAY WE SEE IT, YOU KEEP HEALIN' UP WHAT WE TAKE, KEEP GROWIN' NEW MEAT...THAT BE MORE VALUABLE THAN MONEY.
SO, WE DECIDE, ALL OF US WE DECIDE, THAT MAYBE WE KEEP YOU HERE INSTEAD.
NOW THAT WE HAVE YOU, WE DON'T HAVE TO HUNT OTHER PEOPLE NO MORE.
I KNOW PEOPLE THINK WE ENJOY IT, THAT WE'RE OUT OF KILTER. BUT WE SURELY DON'T AND WE SURELY AIN'T. NO, SIR. WE ARE NOT MONSTERS. IT TURNS OUR STOMACHS, IT DOES.
JUST A MEANS TO AN END, THAT'S ALL. WE GOT EVERY RIGHT TO SURVIVE.
NO USE TRYIN' TO BREAK FREE. WE GOT YOU TIED DOWN RIGHT GOOD.
HOW LONG...?
HOW LONG YOU BEEN HERE OR HOW LONG WE GONNA KEEP YOU?
'CAUSE YOU BEEN HERE FOR GOIN' ON ABOUT A WEEK NOW.
AND AS TO HOW LONG WE'RE GONNA KEEP YOU... WELL...
...WE AIN'T NEVER GONNA LET YOU GO.

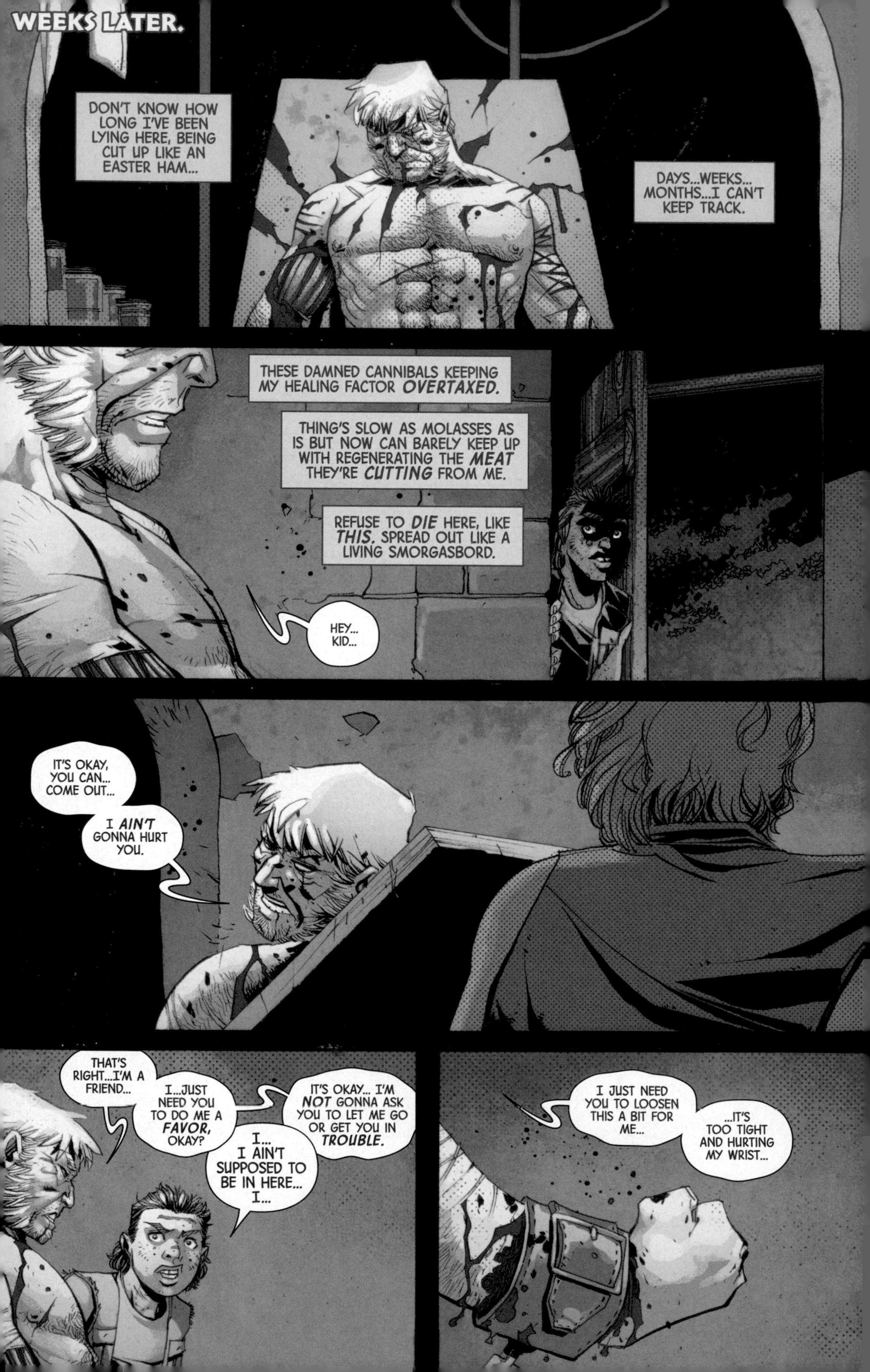
WEEKS LATER.
DON'T KNOW HOW LONG I'VE BEEN LYING HERE, BEING CUT UP LIKE AN EASTER HAM...
DAYS...WEEKS... MONTHS...I CAN'T KEEP TRACK.
THESE DAMNED CANNIBALS KEEPING MY HEALING FACTOR OVERTAXED.
THING'S SLOW AS MOLASSES AS IS BUT NOW CAN BARELY KEEP UP WITH REGENERATING THE MEAT THEY'RE CUTTING FROM ME.
REFUSE TO DIE HERE, LIKE THIS. SPREAD OUT LIKE A LIVING SMORGASBORD.
HEY... KID...
IT'S OKAY, YOU CAN... COME OUT...
I AIN'T GONNA HURT YOU.
THAT'S RIGHT...I'M A FRIEND...
I...JUST NEED YOU TO DO ME A FAVOR, OKAY?
I... I AIN'T SUPPOSED TO BE IN HERE... I...
IT'S OKAY... I'M NOT GONNA ASK YOU TO LET ME GO OR GET YOU IN TROUBLE.
I JUST NEED YOU TO LOOSEN THIS A BIT FOR ME...
...IT'S TOO TIGHT AND HURTING MY WRIST...

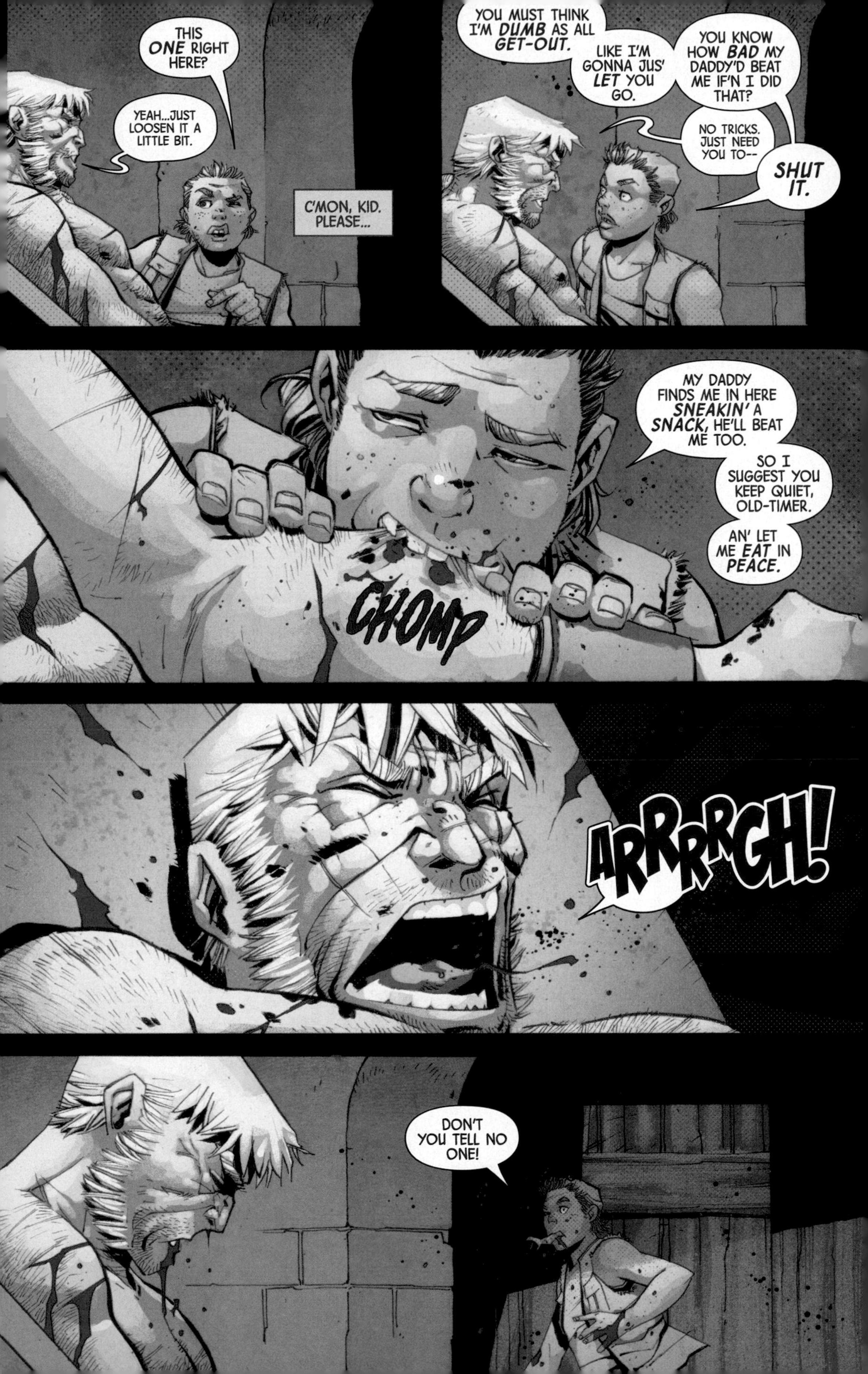
THIS ONE RIGHT HERE?
YEAH...JUST LOOSEN IT A LITTLE BIT.
C'MON, KID. PLEASE...
YOU MUST THINK I'M DUMB AS ALL GET-OUT.
LIKE I'M GONNA JUS' LET YOU GO.
YOU KNOW HOW BAD MY DADDY'D BEAT ME IF'N I DID THAT?
NO TRICKS. JUST NEED YOU TO--
SHUT IT.
MY DADDY FINDS ME IN HERE SNEAKIN' A SNACK, HE'LL BEAT ME TOO.
SO I SUGGEST YOU KEEP QUIET, OLD-TIMER.
AN' LET ME EAT IN PEACE.
CHOMP
ARRRRGH!
DON'T YOU TELL NO ONE!

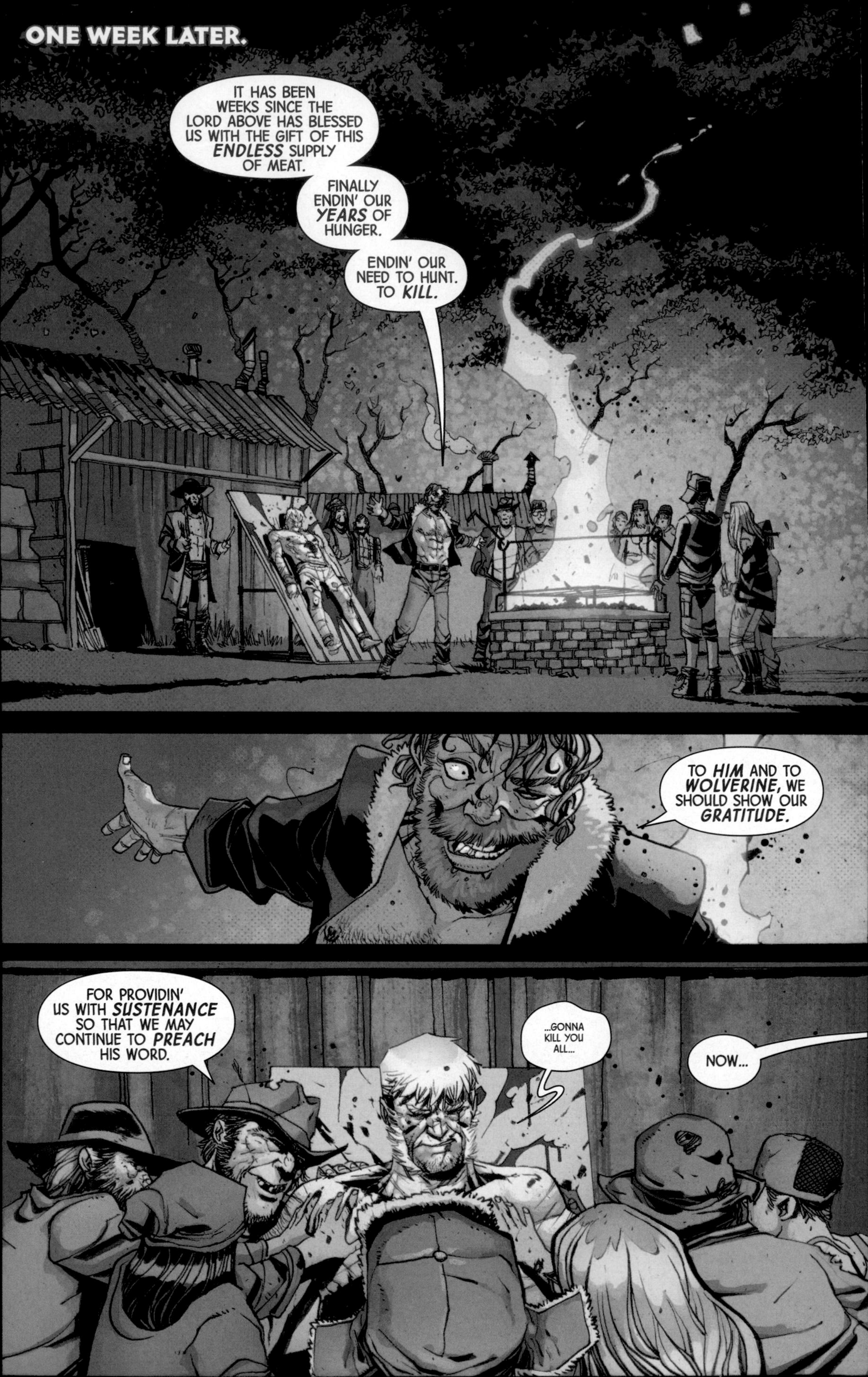
ONE WEEK LATER.
IT HAS BEEN WEEKS SINCE THE LORD ABOVE HAS BLESSED US WITH THE GIFT OF THIS ENDLESS SUPPLY OF MEAT.
FINALLY ENDIN' OUR YEARS OF HUNGER.
ENDIN' OUR NEED TO HUNT. TO KILL.
TO HIM AND TO WOLVERINE, WE SHOULD SHOW OUR GRATITUDE.
FOR PROVIDIN' US WITH SUSTENANCE SO THAT WE MAY CONTINUE TO PREACH HIS WORD.
...GONNA KILL YOU ALL...
NOW...

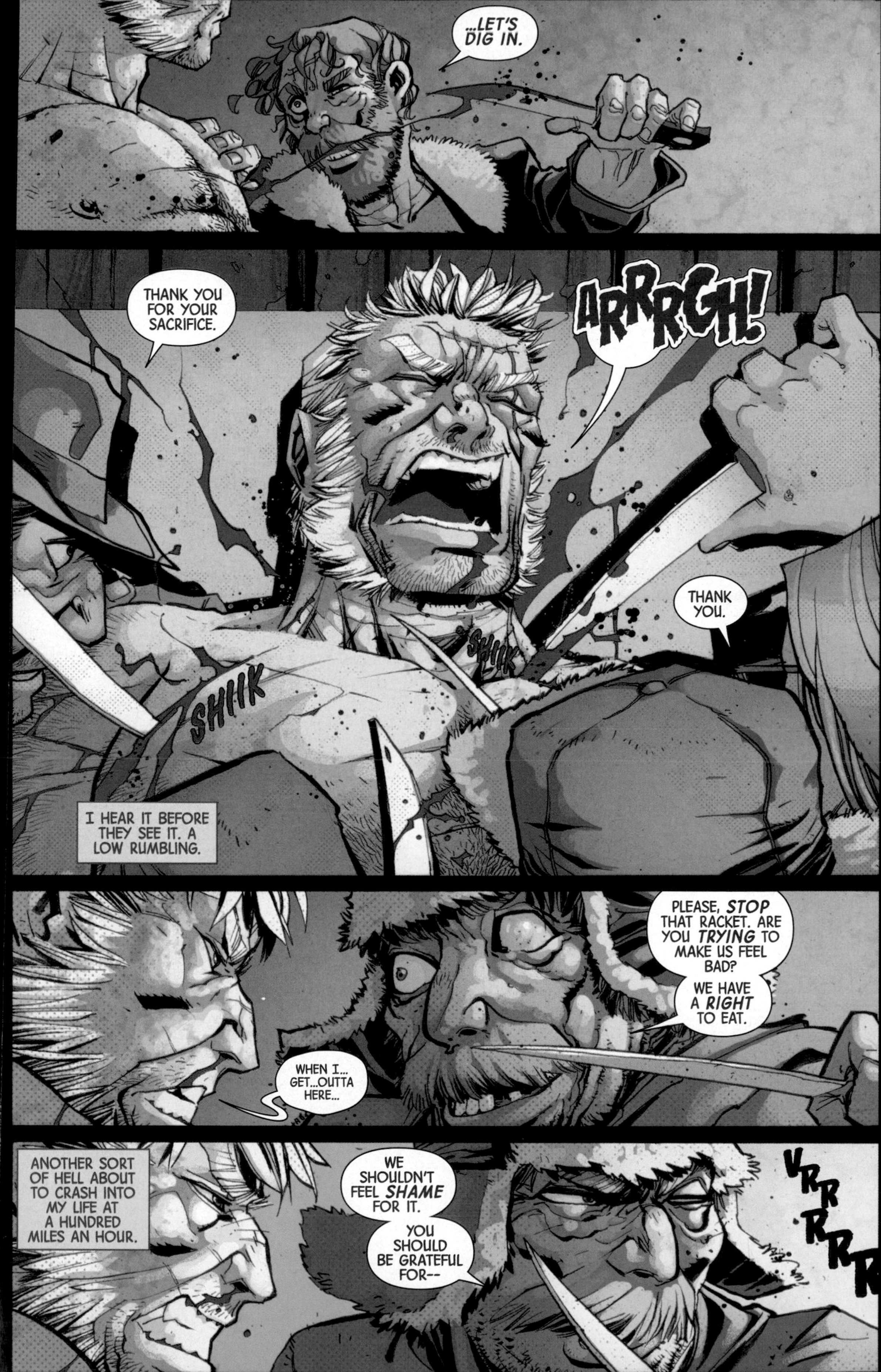
...LET'S DIG IN.
THANK YOU FOR YOUR SACRIFICE.
ARRRGH!
THANK YOU.
SHIIK
SHIIK
I HEAR IT BEFORE THEY SEE IT. A LOW RUMBLING.
PLEASE, STOP THAT RACKET. ARE YOU TRYING TO MAKE US FEEL BAD?
WE HAVE A RIGHT TO EAT.
WHEN I... GET...OUTTA HERE...
ANOTHER SORT OF HELL ABOUT TO CRASH INTO MY LIFE AT A HUNDRED MILES AN HOUR.
WE SHOULDN'T FEEL SHAME FOR IT.
YOU SHOULD BE GRATEFUL FOR--
VRRRRRR

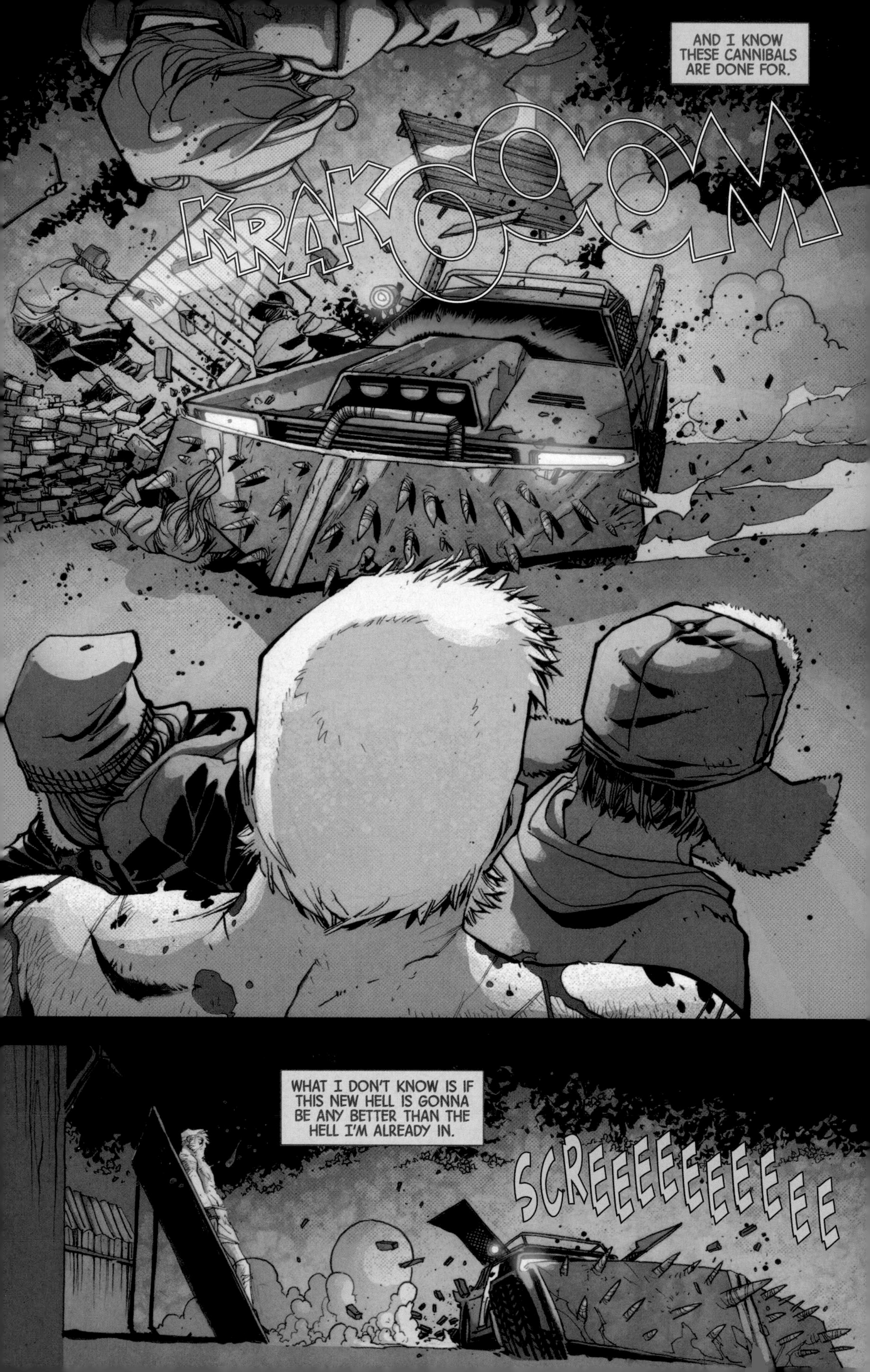
AND I KNOW THESE CANNIBALS ARE DONE FOR.
KRAKOOOOM
WHAT I DON'T KNOW IS IF THIS NEW HELL IS GONNA BE ANY BETTER THAN THE HELL I'M ALREADY IN.
SCREEEEEEEEEE

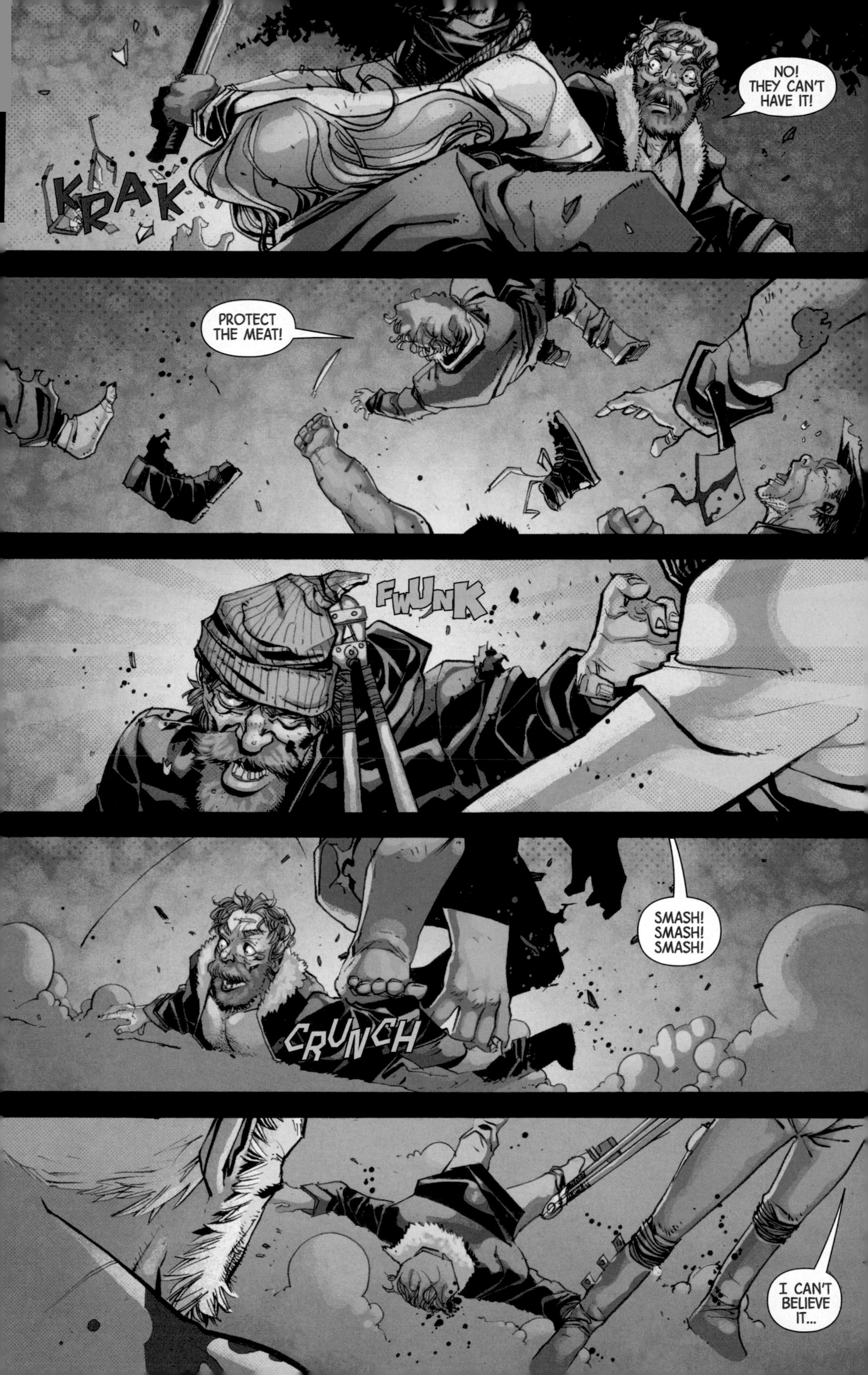
NO! THEY CAN'T HAVE IT!
KRAK
PROTECT THE MEAT!
FWUNK
SMASH! SMASH! SMASH!
CRUNCH
I CAN'T BELIEVE IT...

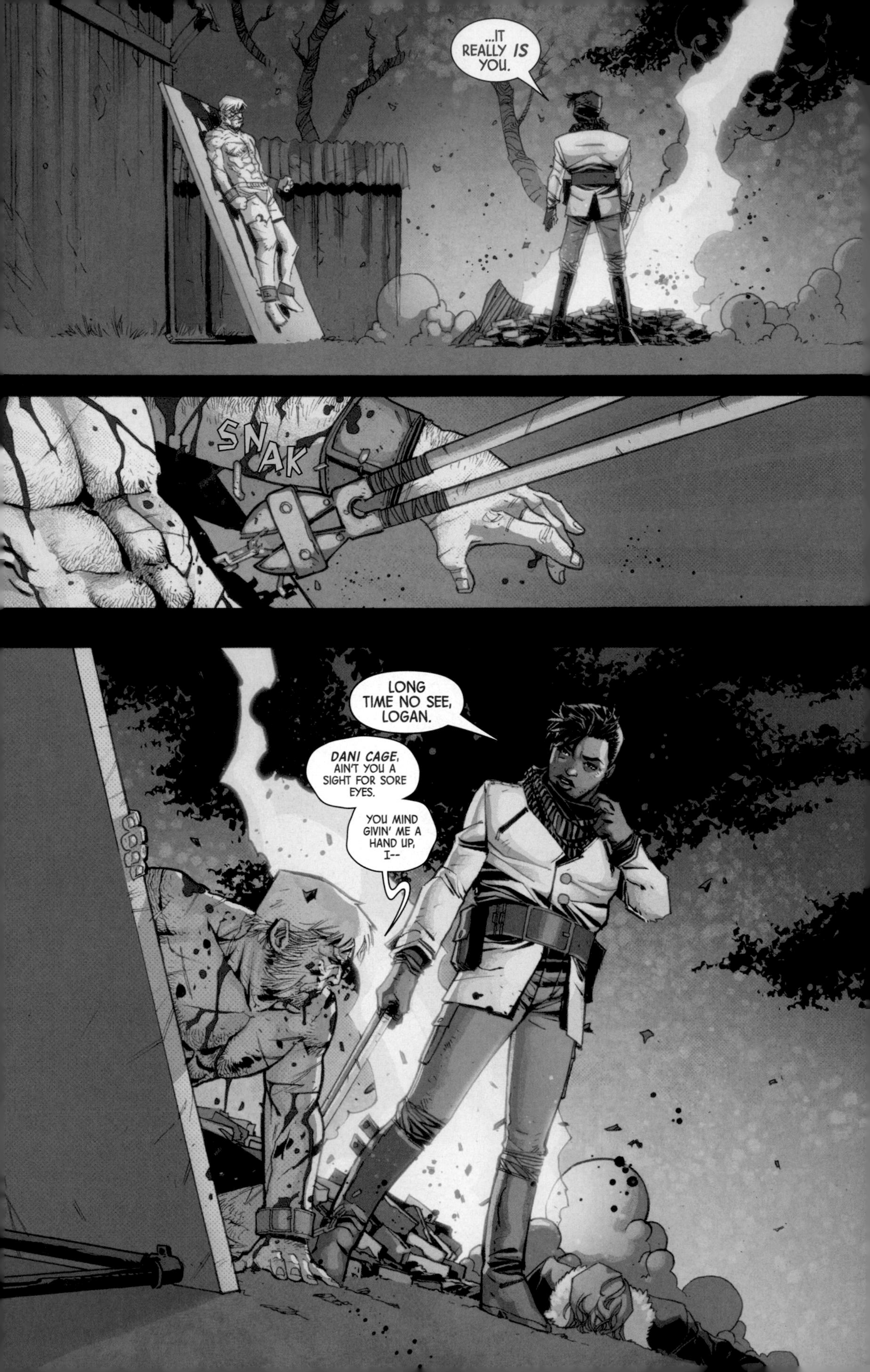

...IT REALLY *IS* YOU.
SNAK
LONG TIME NO SEE, LOGAN.
DANI CAGE, AIN'T YOU A SIGHT FOR SORE EYES.
YOU MIND GIVIN' ME A HAND UP, I--

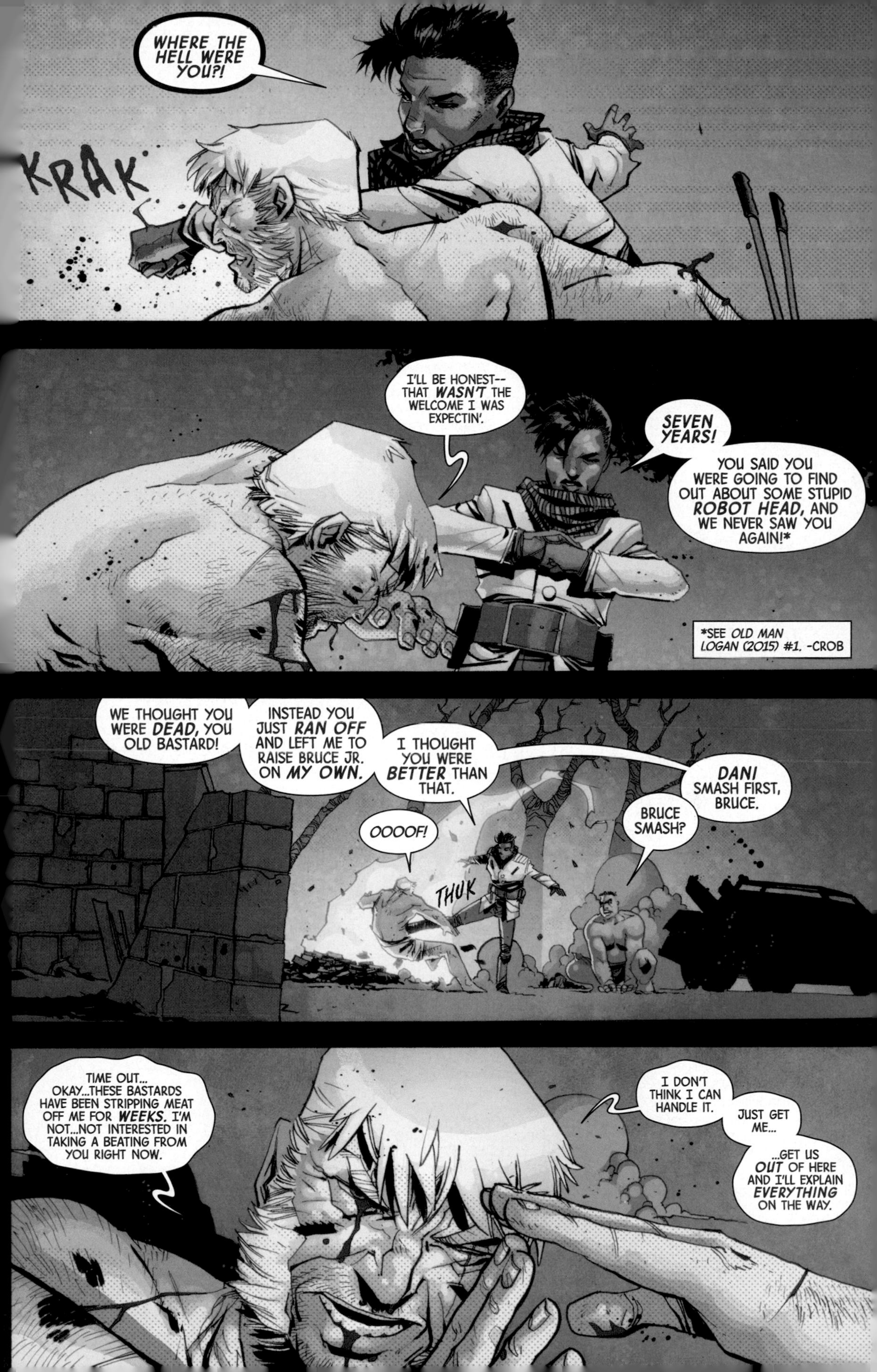

WHERE THE HELL WERE YOU?!
KRAK
I'LL BE HONEST-- THAT WASN'T THE WELCOME I WAS EXPECTIN'.
SEVEN YEARS!
YOU SAID YOU WERE GOING TO FIND OUT ABOUT SOME STUPID ROBOT HEAD, AND WE NEVER SAW YOU AGAIN!*
*SEE OLD MAN LOGAN (2015) #1. -CROB
WE THOUGHT YOU WERE DEAD, YOU OLD BASTARD!
INSTEAD YOU JUST RAN OFF AND LEFT ME TO RAISE BRUCE JR. ON MY OWN.
I THOUGHT YOU WERE BETTER THAN THAT.
DANI SMASH FIRST, BRUCE.
BRUCE SMASH?
OOOOF!
THUK
TIME OUT... OKAY...THESE BASTARDS HAVE BEEN STRIPPING MEAT OFF ME FOR WEEKS. I'M NOT...NOT INTERESTED IN TAKING A BEATING FROM YOU RIGHT NOW.
I DON'T THINK I CAN HANDLE IT.
JUST GET ME...
...GET US OUT OF HERE AND I'LL EXPLAIN EVERYTHING ON THE WAY.

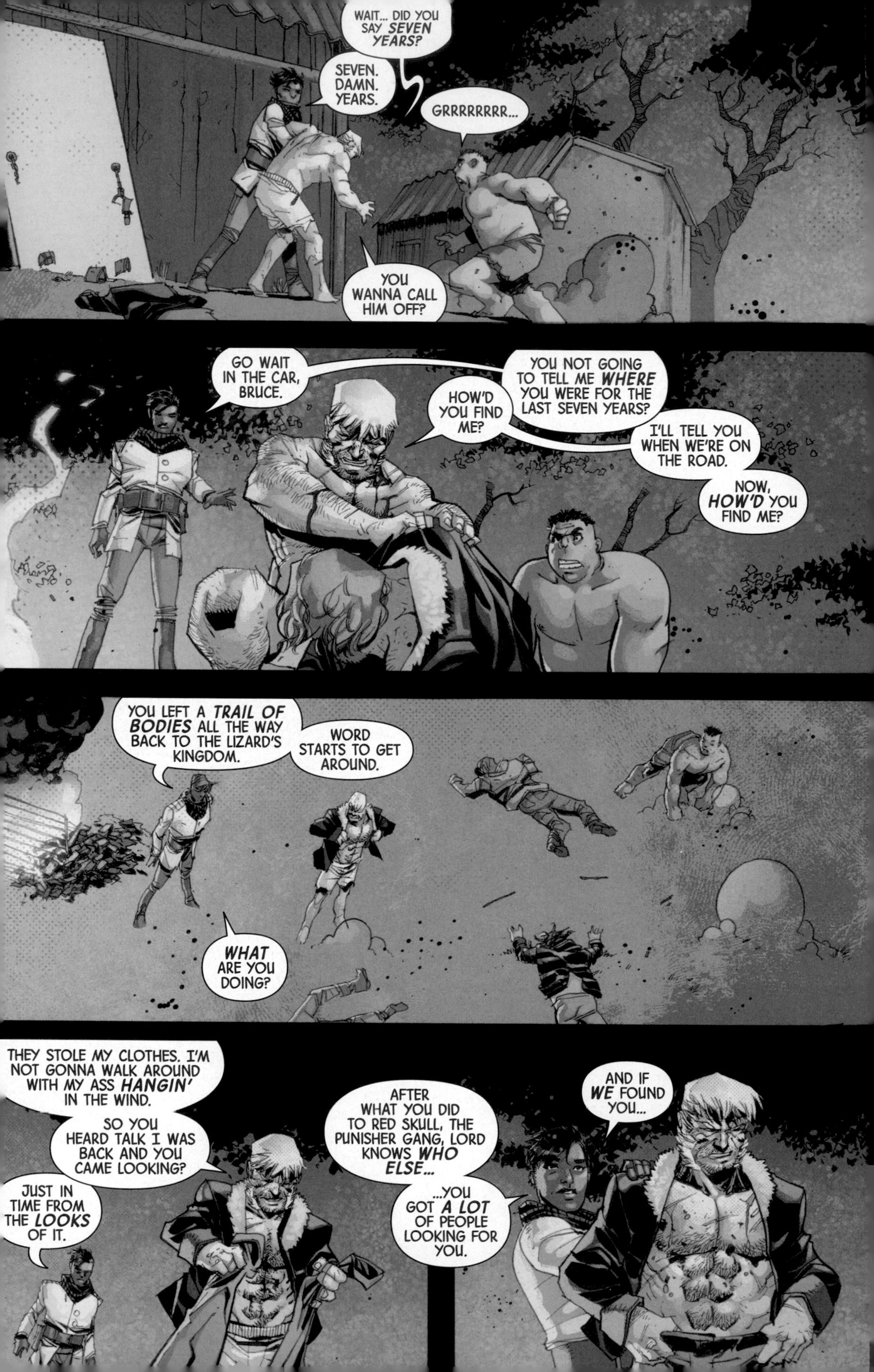
WAIT... DID YOU SAY SEVEN YEARS?
SEVEN. DAMN. YEARS.
GRRRRRRRR...
YOU WANNA CALL HIM OFF?
GO WAIT IN THE CAR, BRUCE.
YOU NOT GOING TO TELL ME WHERE YOU WERE FOR THE LAST SEVEN YEARS?
HOW'D YOU FIND ME?
I'LL TELL YOU WHEN WE'RE ON THE ROAD.
NOW, HOW'D YOU FIND ME?
YOU LEFT A TRAIL OF BODIES ALL THE WAY BACK TO THE LIZARD'S KINGDOM.
WORD STARTS TO GET AROUND.
WHAT ARE YOU DOING?
THEY STOLE MY CLOTHES. I'M NOT GONNA WALK AROUND WITH MY ASS HANGIN' IN THE WIND.
SO YOU HEARD TALK I WAS BACK AND YOU CAME LOOKING?
JUST IN TIME FROM THE LOOKS OF IT.
AFTER WHAT YOU DID TO RED SKULL, THE PUNISHER GANG, LORD KNOWS WHO ELSE...
...YOU GOT A LOT OF PEOPLE LOOKING FOR YOU.
AND IF WE FOUND YOU...

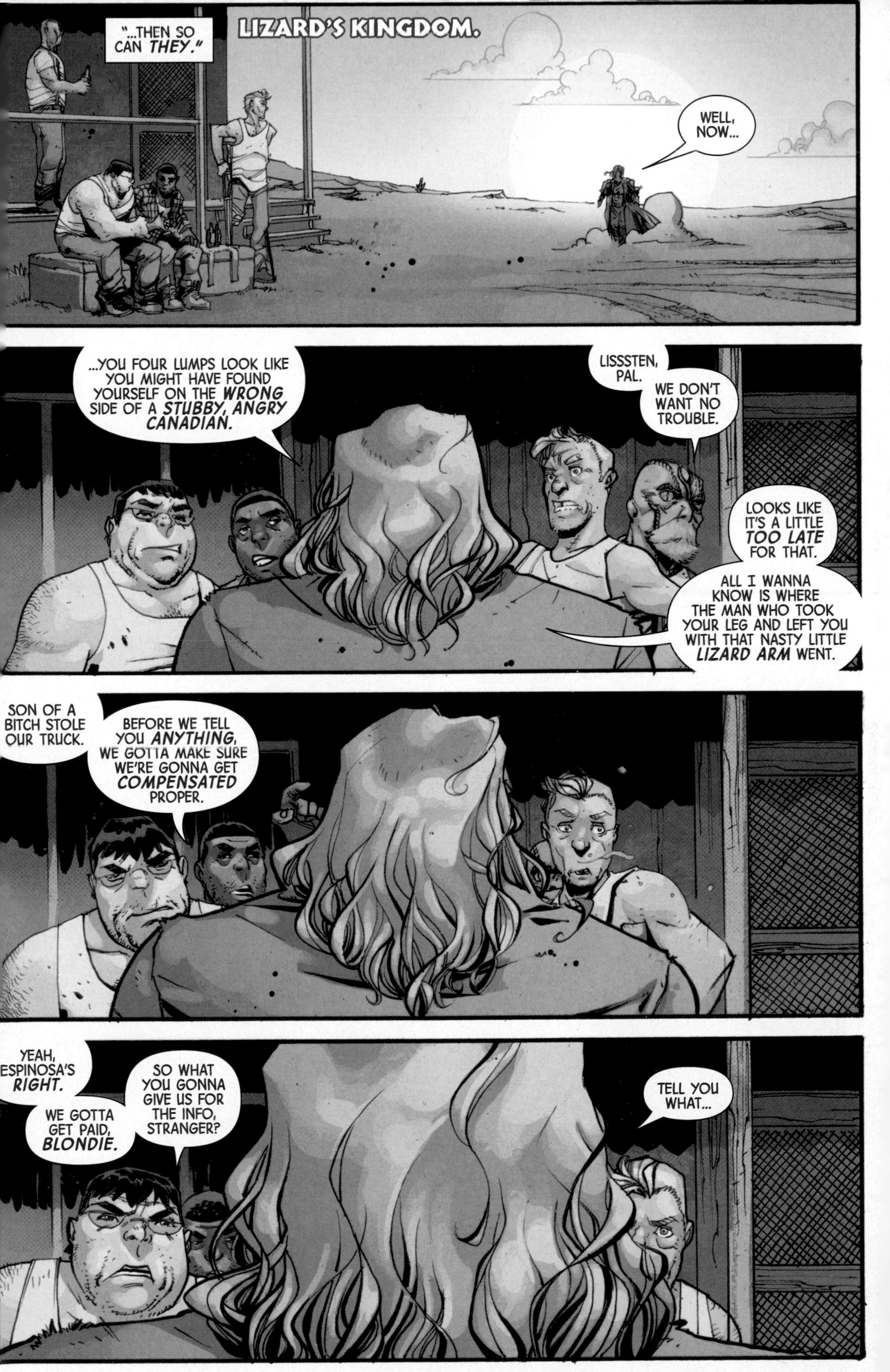
"...THEN SO CAN THEY."
LIZARD'S KINGDOM.
WELL, NOW...
...YOU FOUR LUMPS LOOK LIKE YOU MIGHT HAVE FOUND YOURSELF ON THE WRONG SIDE OF A STUBBY, ANGRY CANADIAN.
LISSSTEN, PAL.
WE DON'T WANT NO TROUBLE.
LOOKS LIKE IT'S A LITTLE TOO LATE FOR THAT.
ALL I WANNA KNOW IS WHERE THE MAN WHO TOOK YOUR LEG AND LEFT YOU WITH THAT NASTY LITTLE LIZARD ARM WENT.
SON OF A BITCH STOLE OUR TRUCK.
BEFORE WE TELL YOU ANYTHING, WE GOTTA MAKE SURE WE'RE GONNA GET COMPENSATED PROPER.
YEAH, ESPINOSA'S RIGHT.
WE GOTTA GET PAID, BLONDIE.
SO WHAT YOU GONNA GIVE US FOR THE INFO, STRANGER?
TELL YOU WHAT...

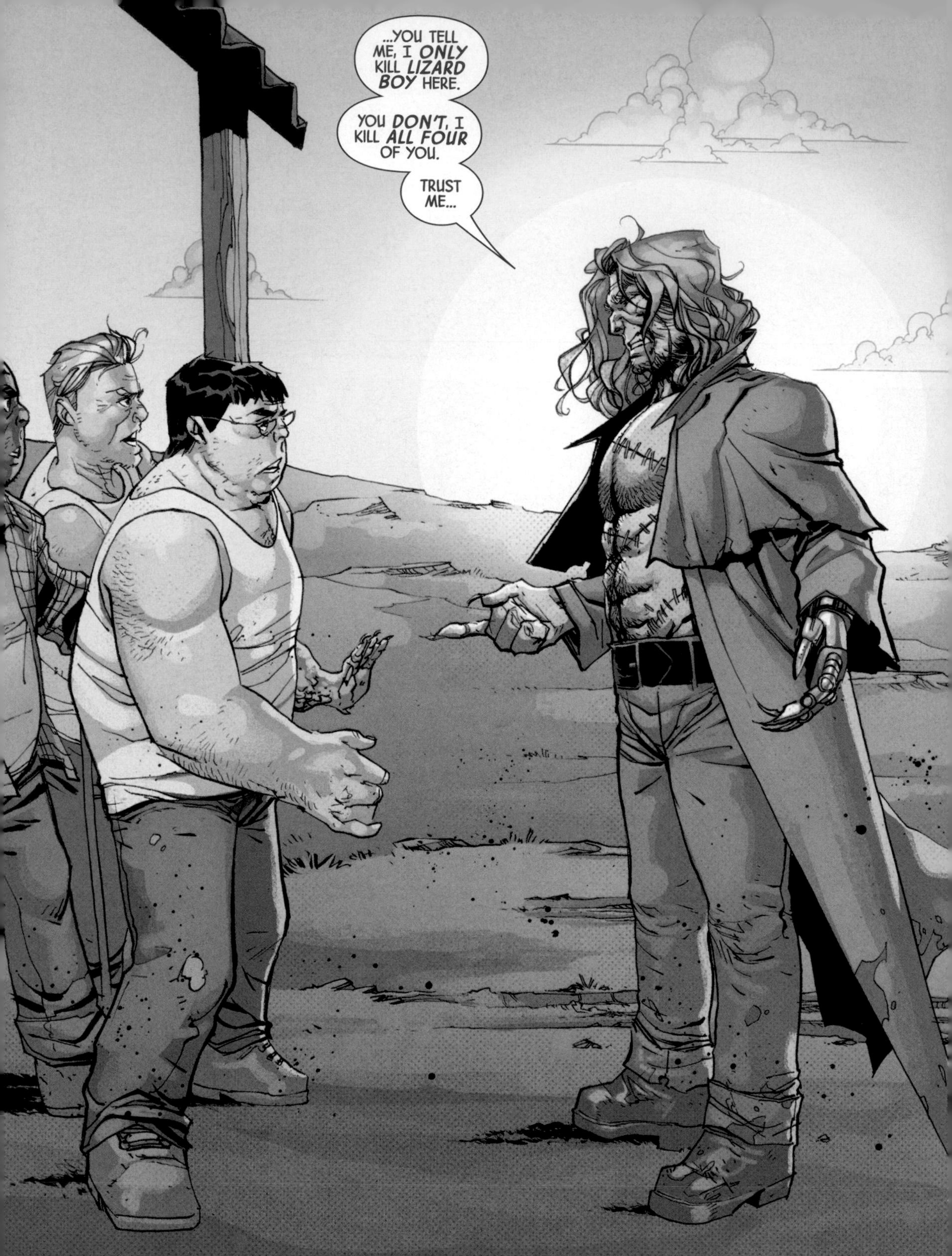
...YOU TELL ME, I ONLY KILL LIZARD BOY HERE.
YOU DON'T, I KILL ALL FOUR OF YOU.
TRUST ME...
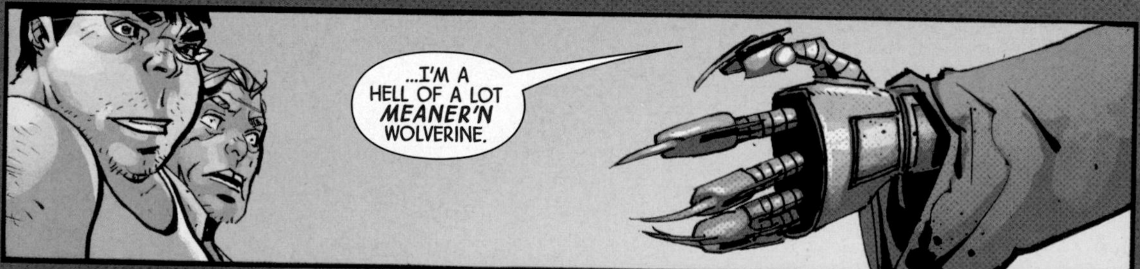
...I'M A HELL OF A LOT MEANER'N WOLVERINE.

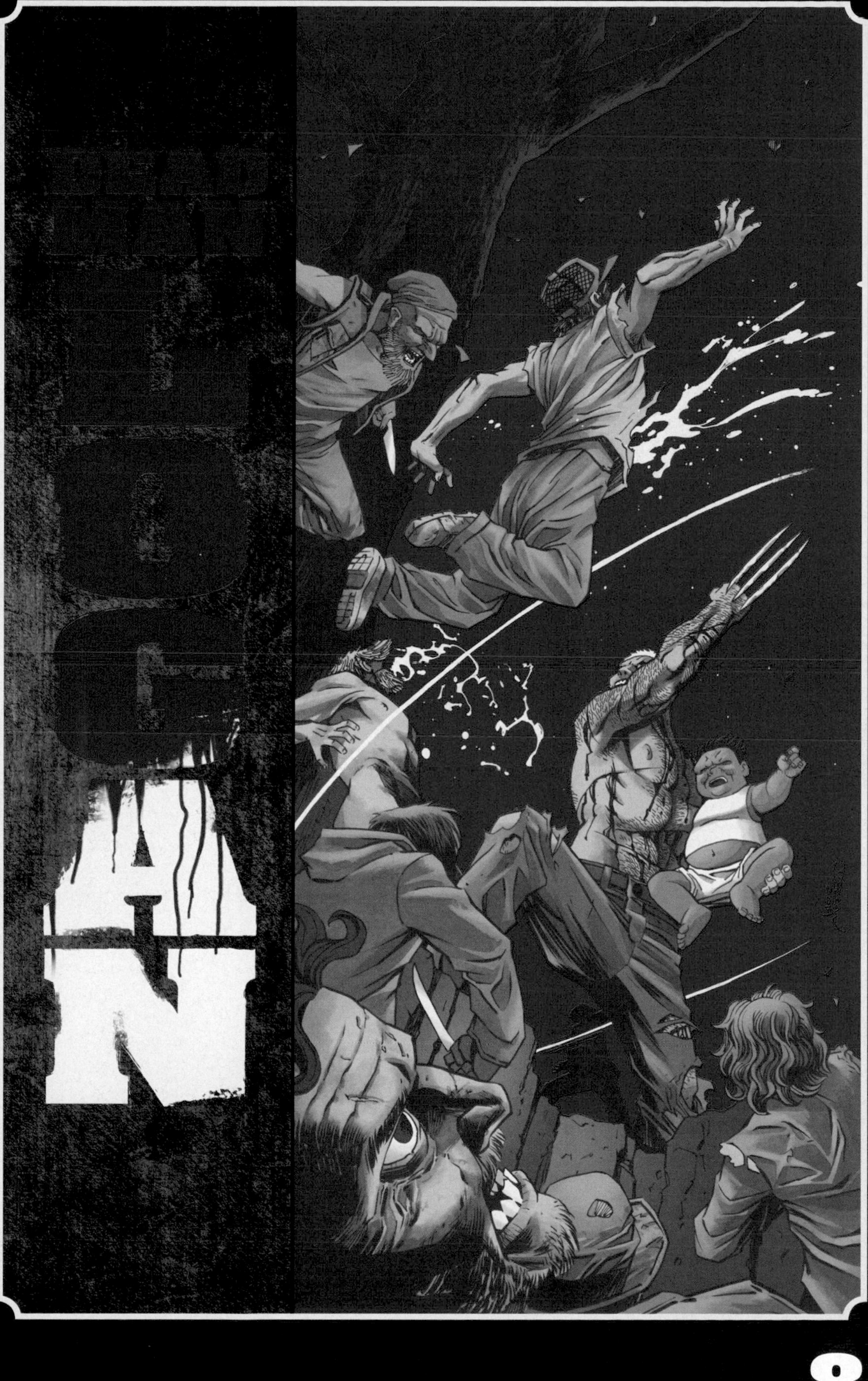

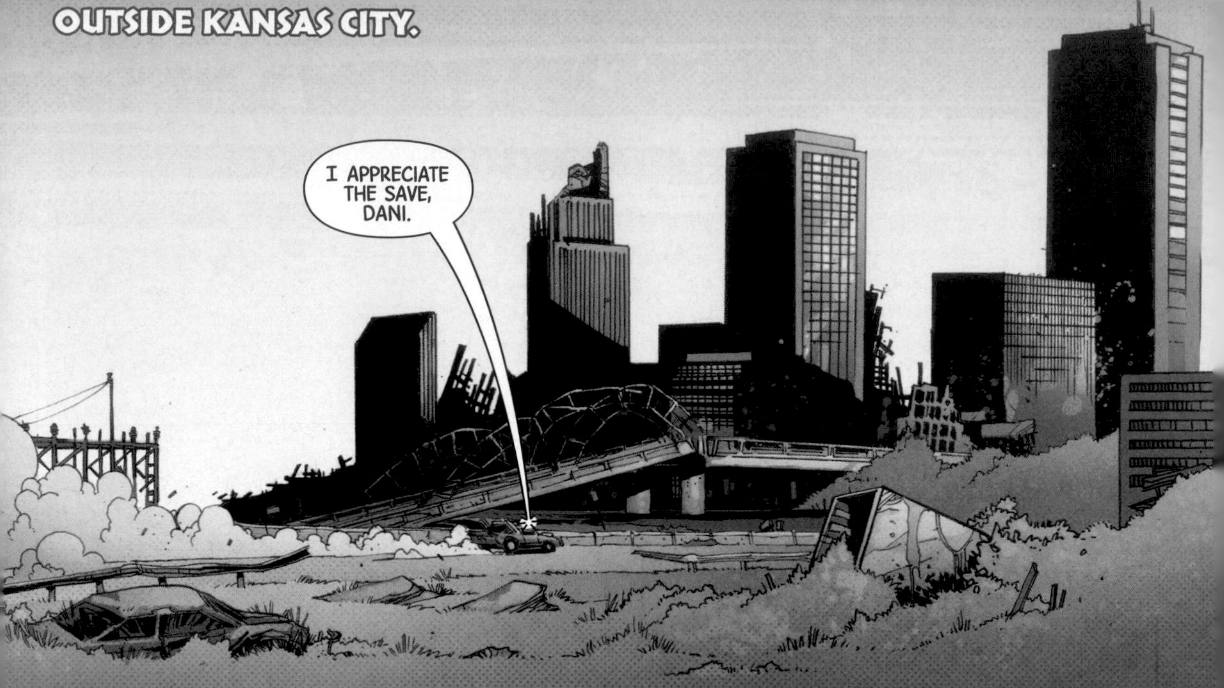
OUTSIDE KANSAS CITY.
I APPRECIATE THE SAVE, DANI.

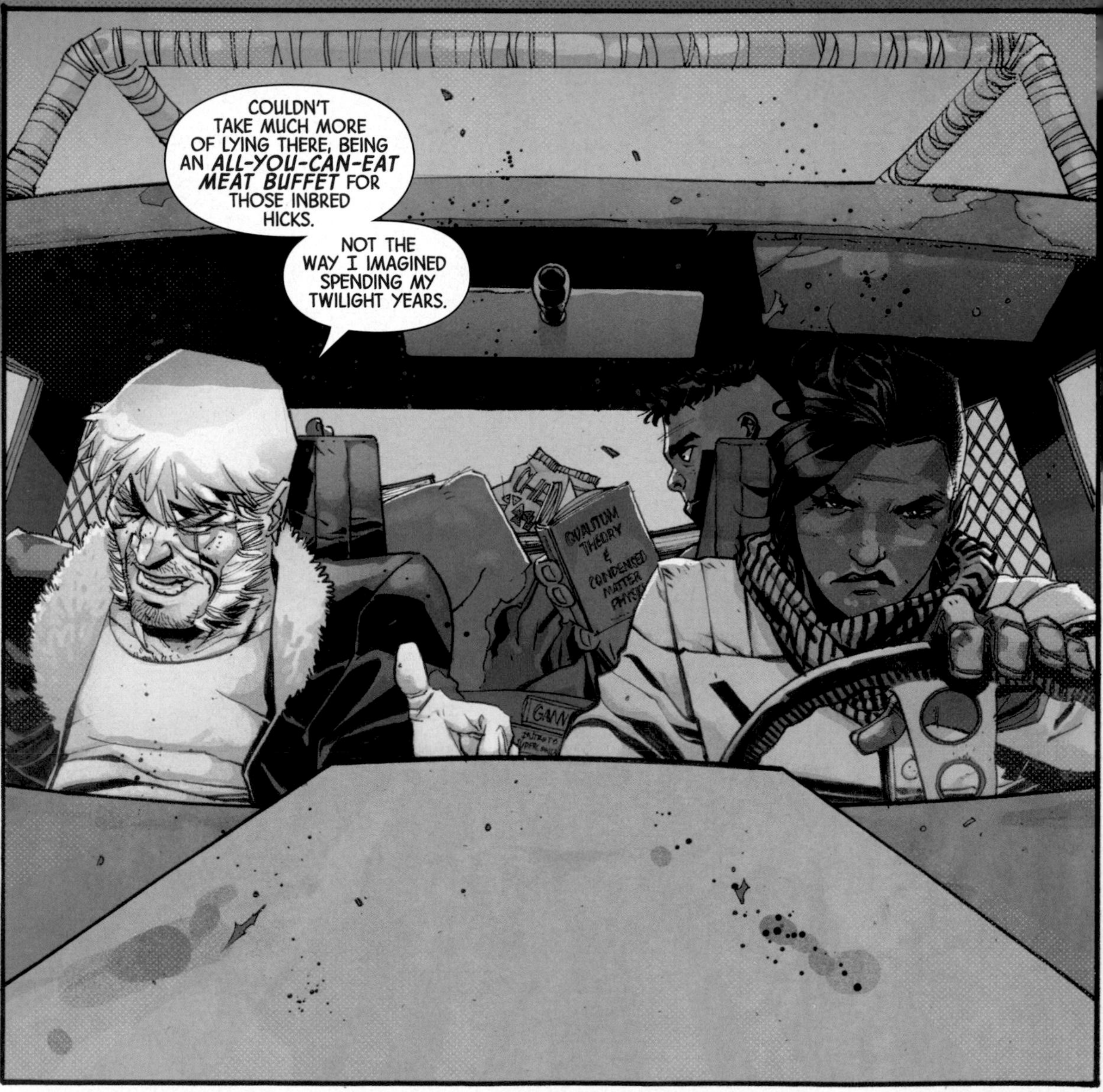
COULDN'T TAKE MUCH MORE OF LYING THERE, BEING AN ALL-YOU-CAN-EAT MEAT BUFFET FOR THOSE INBRED HICKS.
NOT THE WAY I IMAGINED SPENDING MY TWILIGHT YEARS.
QUANTUM THEORY & CONDENSED MATTER PHYSICS

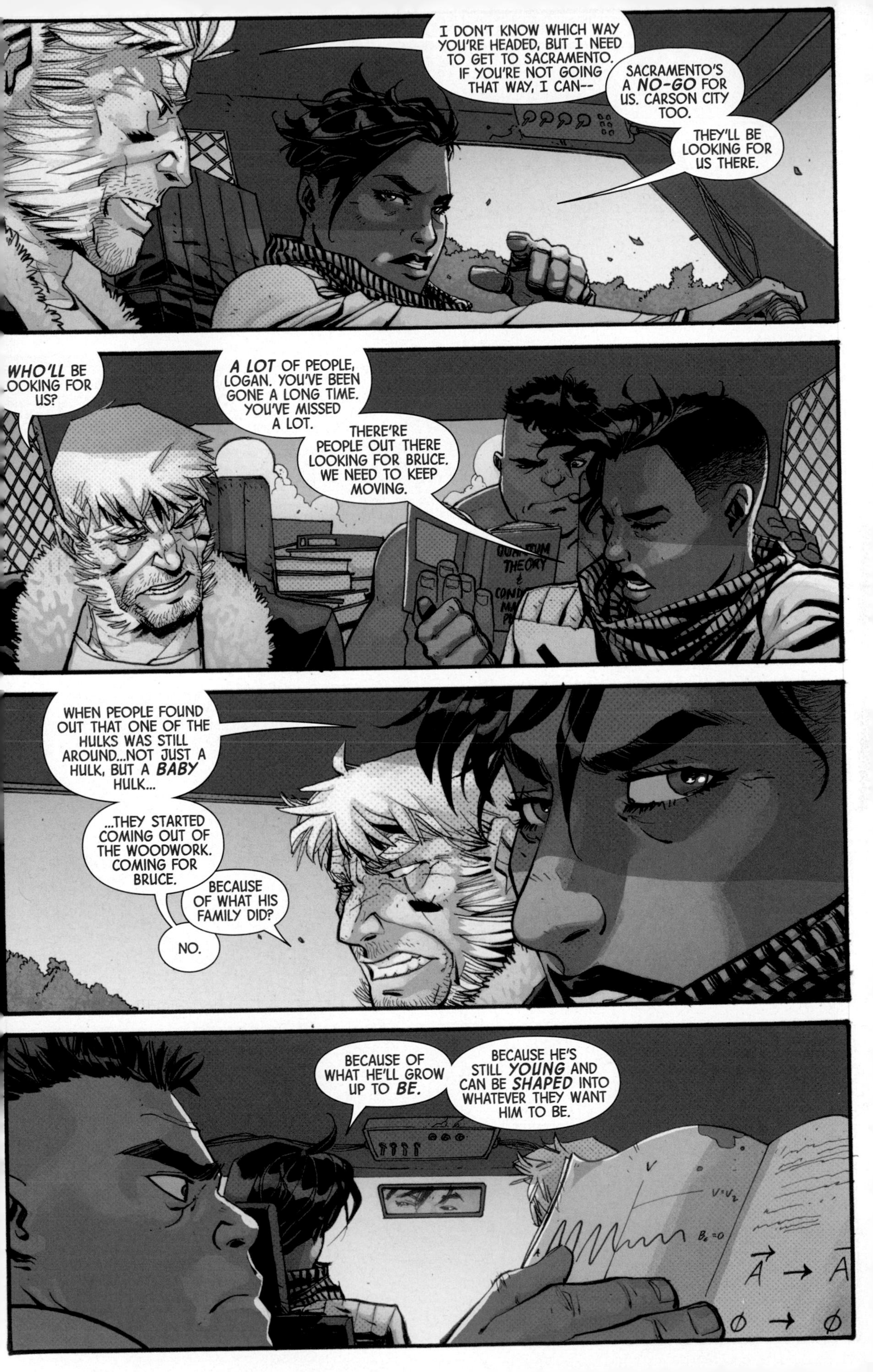
I DON'T KNOW WHICH WAY YOU'RE HEADED, BUT I NEED TO GET TO SACRAMENTO. IF YOU'RE NOT GOING THAT WAY, I CAN--
SACRAMENTO'S A NO-GO FOR US. CARSON CITY TOO.
THEY'LL BE LOOKING FOR US THERE.
WHO'LL BE LOOKING FOR US?
A LOT OF PEOPLE, LOGAN. YOU'VE BEEN GONE A LONG TIME. YOU'VE MISSED A LOT.
THERE'RE PEOPLE OUT THERE LOOKING FOR BRUCE. WE NEED TO KEEP MOVING.
WHEN PEOPLE FOUND OUT THAT ONE OF THE HULKS WAS STILL AROUND...NOT JUST A HULK, BUT A BABY HULK...
...THEY STARTED COMING OUT OF THE WOODWORK. COMING FOR BRUCE.
BECAUSE OF WHAT HIS FAMILY DID?
NO.
BECAUSE OF WHAT HE'LL GROW UP TO BE.
BECAUSE HE'S STILL YOUNG AND CAN BE SHAPED INTO WHATEVER THEY WANT HIM TO BE.

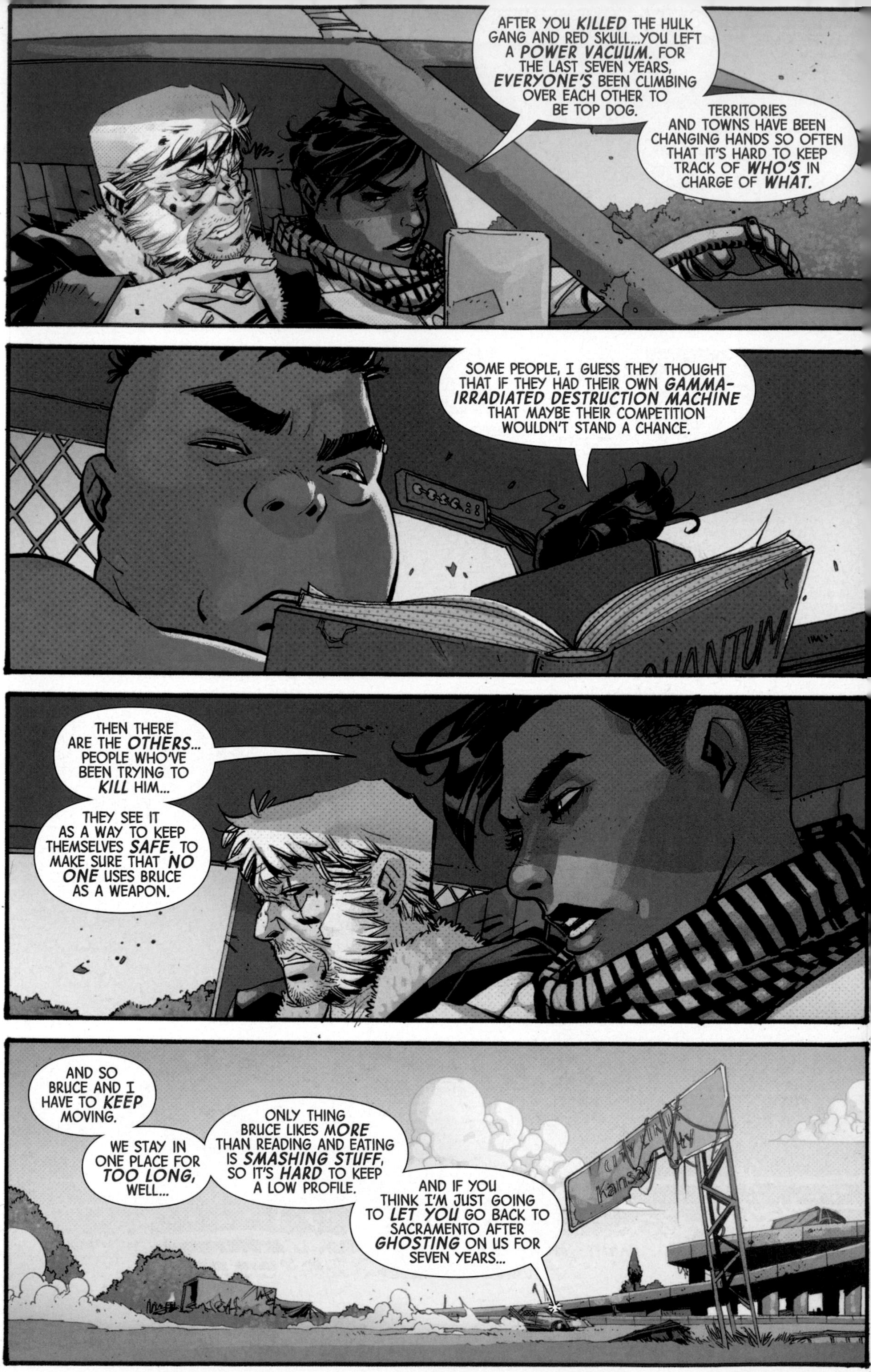
AFTER YOU KILLED THE HULK GANG AND RED SKULL... YOU LEFT A POWER VACUUM. FOR THE LAST SEVEN YEARS, EVERYONE'S BEEN CLIMBING OVER EACH OTHER TO BE TOP DOG.
TERRITORIES AND TOWNS HAVE BEEN CHANGING HANDS SO OFTEN THAT IT'S HARD TO KEEP TRACK OF WHO'S IN CHARGE OF WHAT.
SOME PEOPLE, I GUESS THEY THOUGHT THAT IF THEY HAD THEIR OWN GAMMA-IRRADIATED DESTRUCTION MACHINE THAT MAYBE THEIR COMPETITION WOULDN'T STAND A CHANCE.
THEN THERE ARE THE OTHERS... PEOPLE WHO'VE BEEN TRYING TO KILL HIM...
THEY SEE IT AS A WAY TO KEEP THEMSELVES SAFE. TO MAKE SURE THAT NO ONE USES BRUCE AS A WEAPON.
AND SO BRUCE AND I HAVE TO KEEP MOVING.
WE STAY IN ONE PLACE FOR TOO LONG, WELL...
ONLY THING BRUCE LIKES MORE THAN READING AND EATING IS SMASHING STUFF, SO IT'S HARD TO KEEP A LOW PROFILE.
AND IF YOU THINK I'M JUST GOING TO LET YOU GO BACK TO SACRAMENTO AFTER GHOSTING ON US FOR SEVEN YEARS...

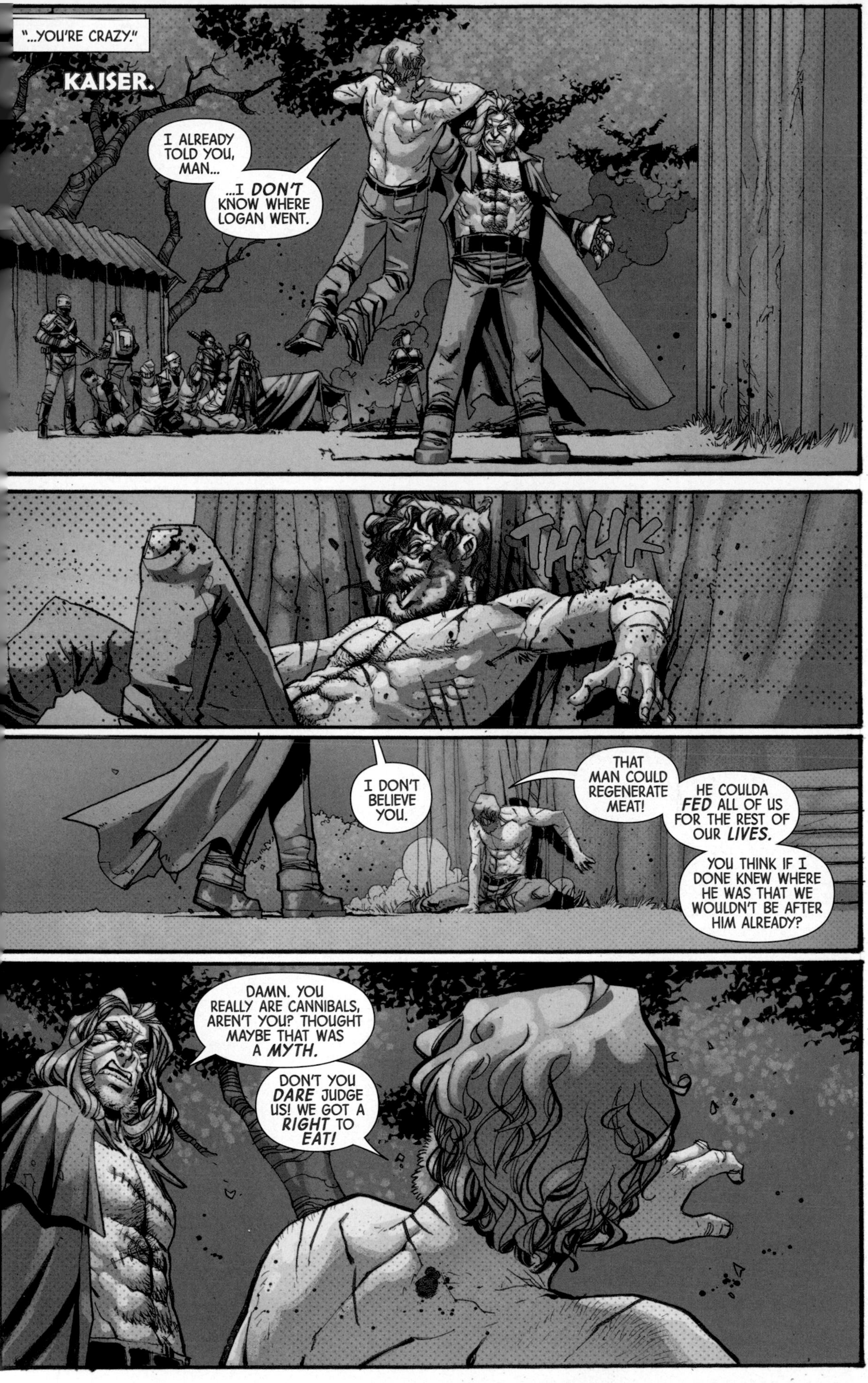
"...YOU'RE CRAZY."
KAISER.
I ALREADY TOLD YOU, MAN...
...I DON'T KNOW WHERE LOGAN WENT.
THUK
I DON'T BELIEVE YOU.
THAT MAN COULD REGENERATE MEAT!
HE COULDA FED ALL OF US FOR THE REST OF OUR LIVES.
YOU THINK IF I DONE KNEW WHERE HE WAS THAT WE WOULDN'T BE AFTER HIM ALREADY?
DAMN. YOU REALLY ARE CANNIBALS, AREN'T YOU? THOUGHT MAYBE THAT WAS A MYTH.
DON'T YOU DARE JUDGE US! WE GOT A RIGHT TO EAT!

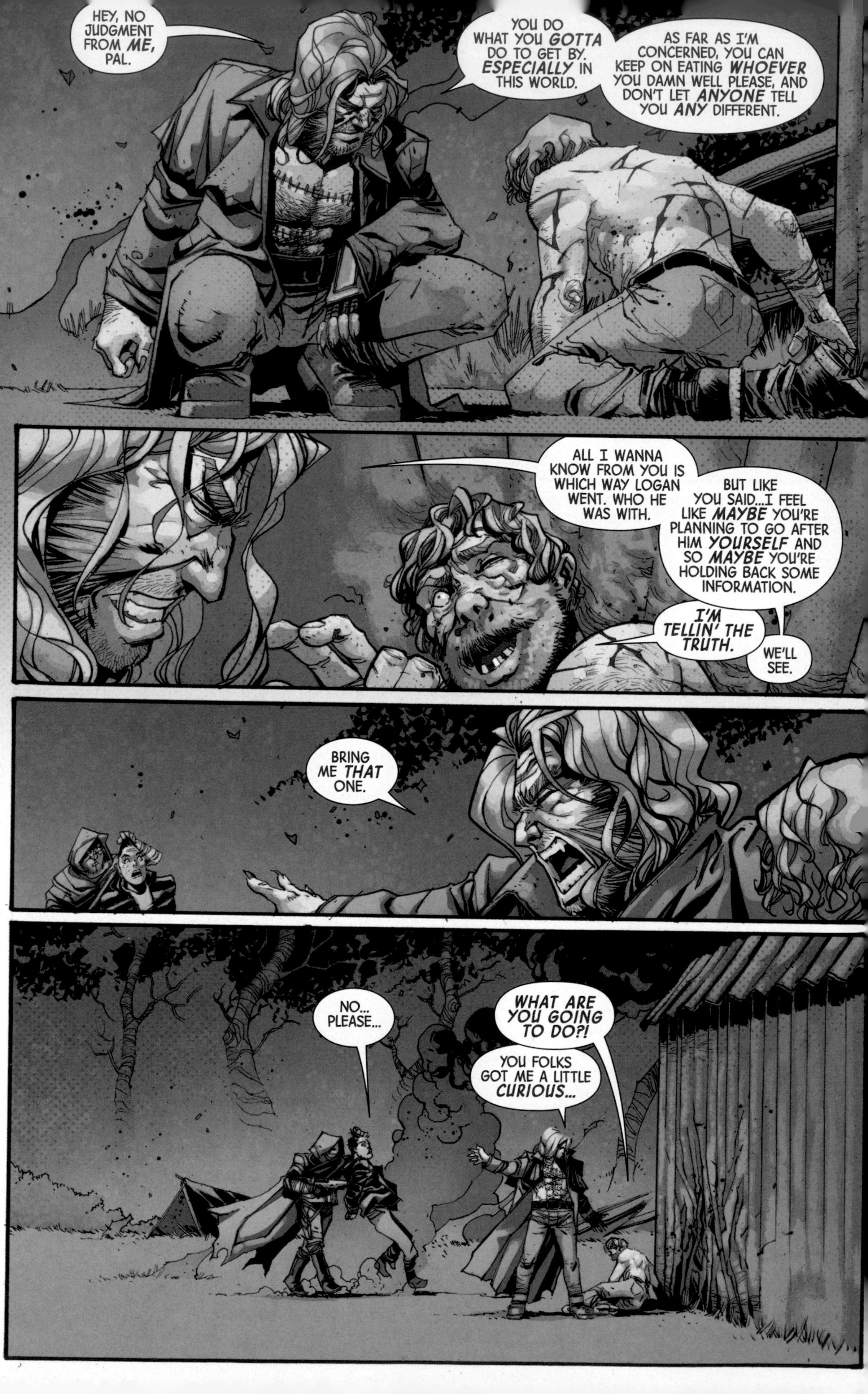
HEY, NO JUDGMENT FROM ME, PAL.
YOU DO WHAT YOU GOTTA DO TO GET BY. ESPECIALLY IN THIS WORLD.
AS FAR AS I'M CONCERNED, YOU CAN KEEP ON EATING WHOEVER YOU DAMN WELL PLEASE, AND DON'T LET ANYONE TELL YOU ANY DIFFERENT.
ALL I WANNA KNOW FROM YOU IS WHICH WAY LOGAN WENT. WHO HE WAS WITH.
BUT LIKE YOU SAID...I FEEL LIKE MAYBE YOU'RE PLANNING TO GO AFTER HIM YOURSELF AND SO MAYBE YOU'RE HOLDING BACK SOME INFORMATION.
I'M TELLIN' THE TRUTH.
WE'LL SEE.
BRING ME THAT ONE.
NO... PLEASE...
WHAT ARE YOU GOING TO DO?!
YOU FOLKS GOT ME A LITTLE CURIOUS...

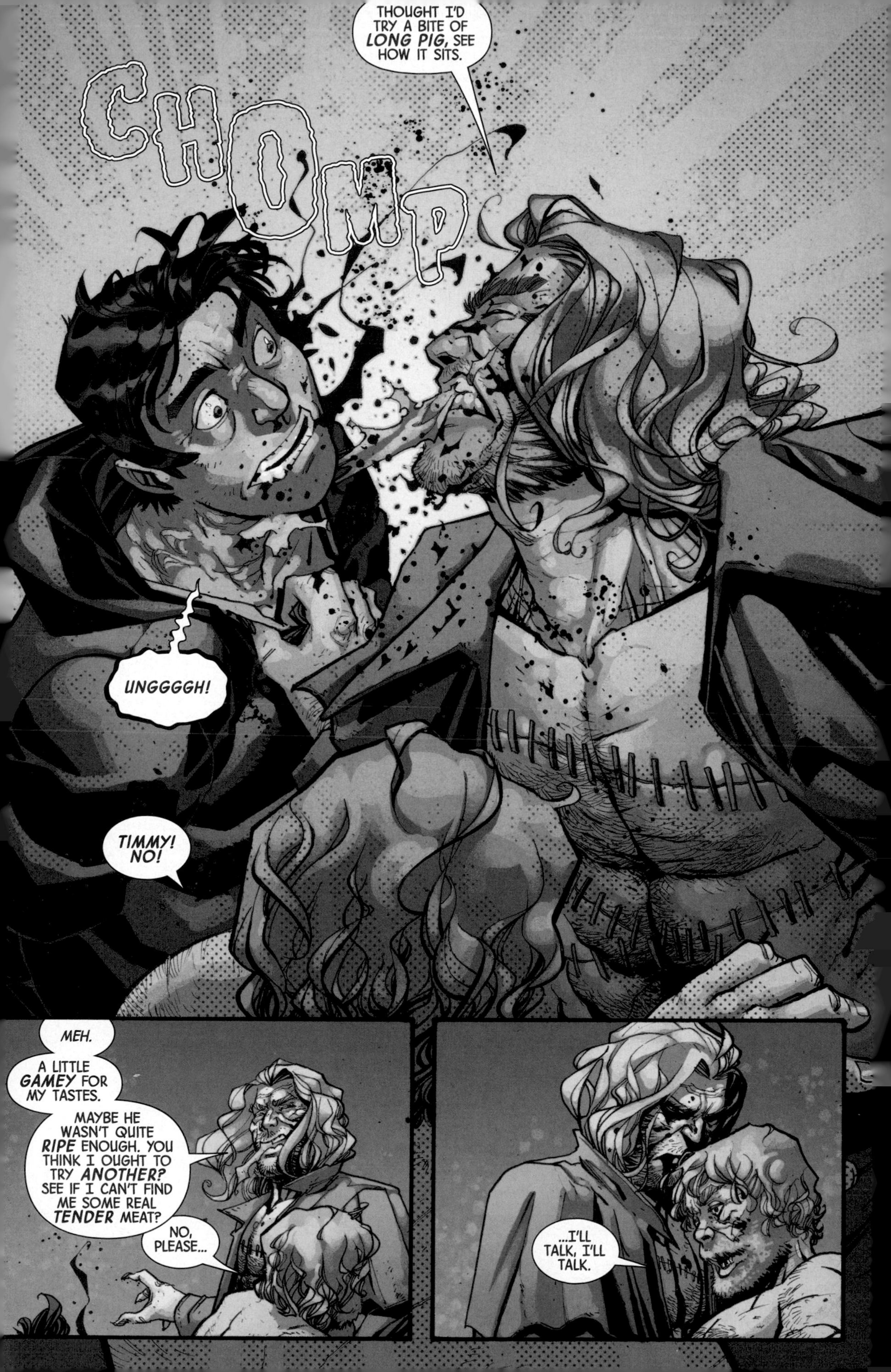
CHOMP
THOUGHT I'D TRY A BITE OF LONG PIG, SEE HOW IT SITS.
UNGGGGH!
TIMMY! NO!
MEH.
A LITTLE GAMEY FOR MY TASTES.
MAYBE HE WASN'T QUITE RIPE ENOUGH. YOU THINK I OUGHT TO TRY ANOTHER? SEE IF I CAN'T FIND ME SOME REAL TENDER MEAT?
NO, PLEASE...
...I'LL TALK, I'LL TALK.

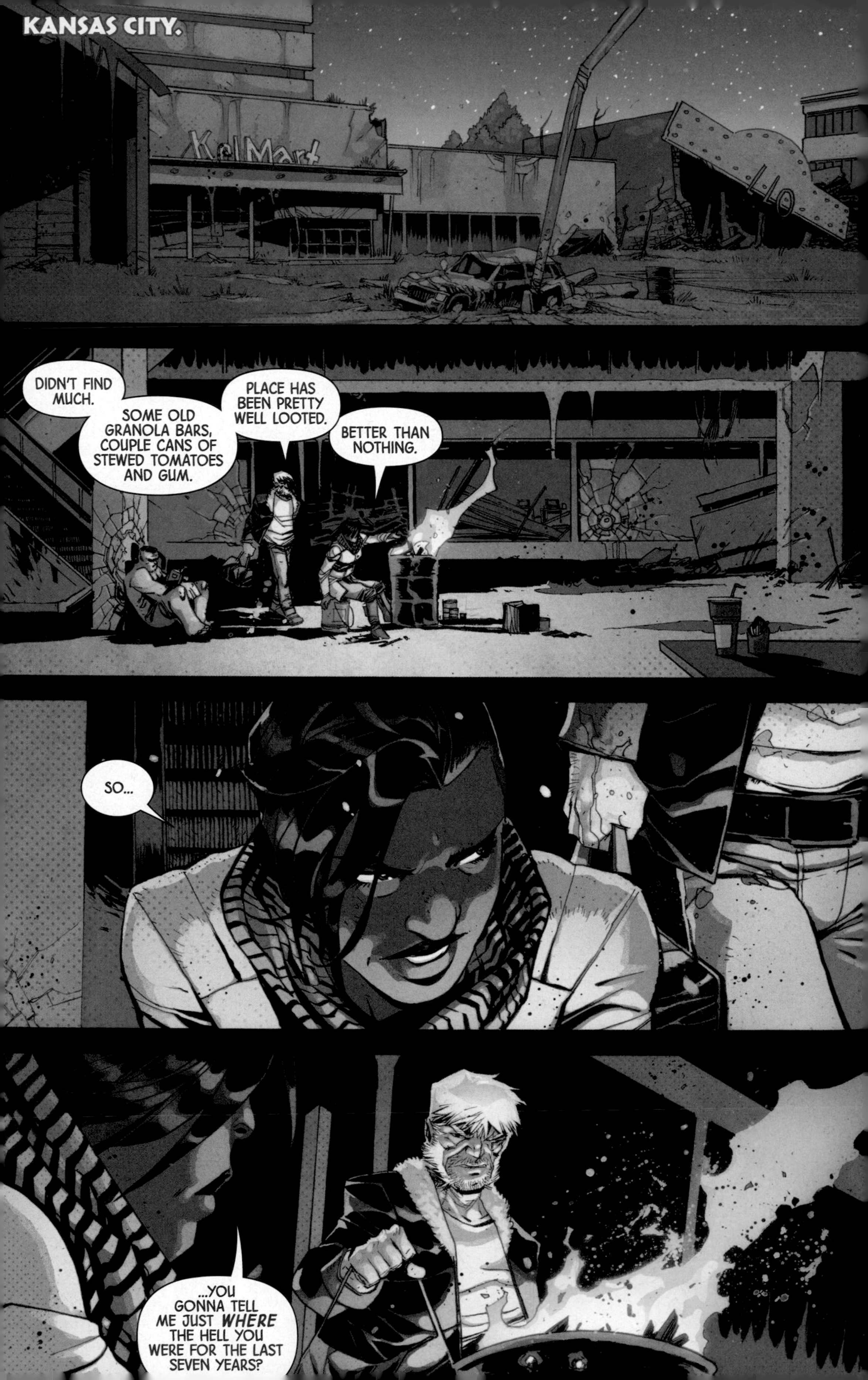
KANSAS CITY.
KelMart
DIDN'T FIND MUCH.
SOME OLD GRANOLA BARS, COUPLE CANS OF STEWED TOMATOES AND GUM.
PLACE HAS BEEN PRETTY WELL LOOTED.
BETTER THAN NOTHING.
SO...
...YOU GONNA TELL ME JUST WHERE THE HELL YOU WERE FOR THE LAST SEVEN YEARS?

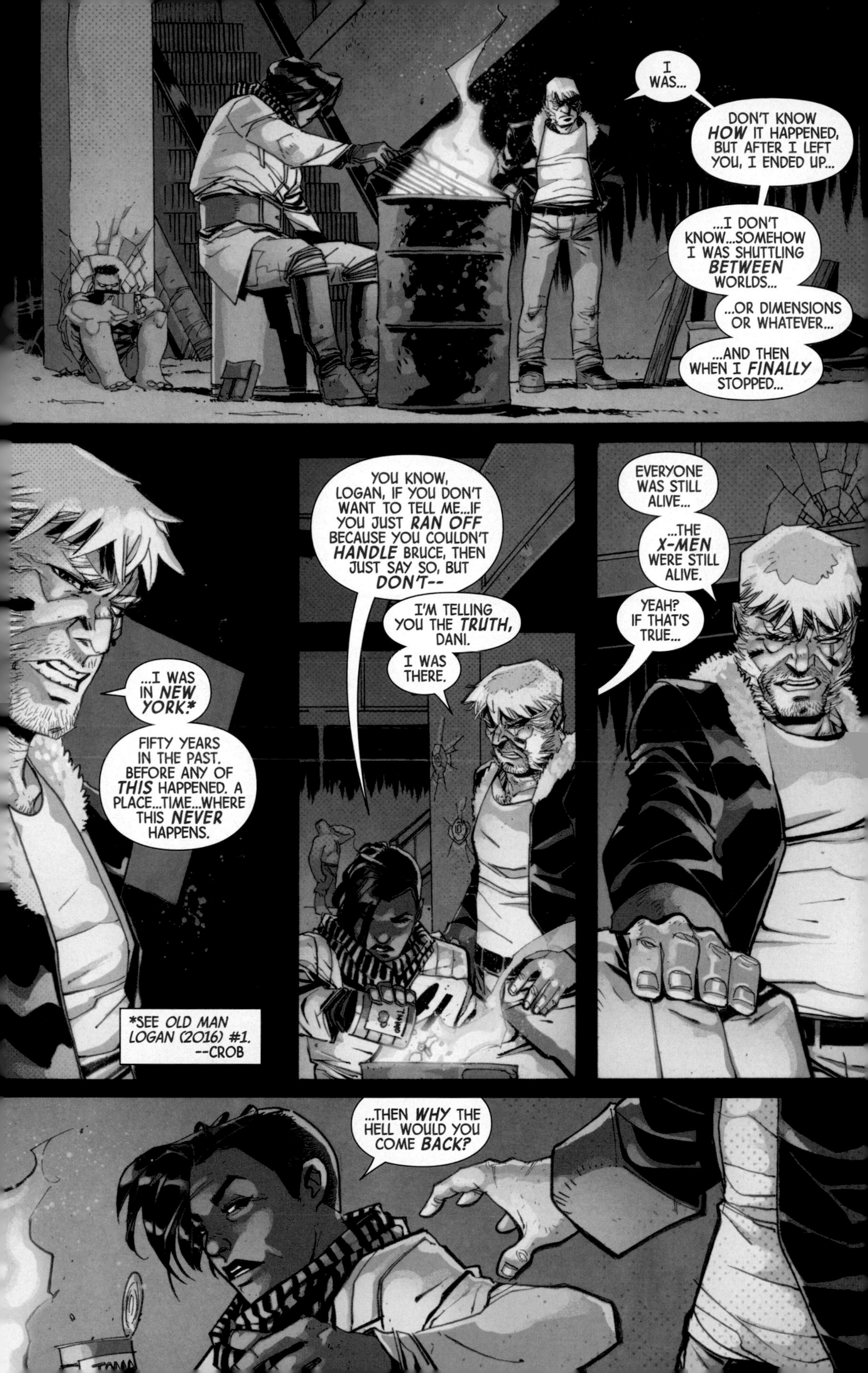
I WAS...
DON'T KNOW HOW IT HAPPENED, BUT AFTER I LEFT YOU, I ENDED UP...
...I DON'T KNOW...SOMEHOW I WAS SHUTTLING BETWEEN WORLDS...
...OR DIMENSIONS OR WHATEVER...
...AND THEN WHEN I FINALLY STOPPED...
...I WAS IN NEW YORK.*
FIFTY YEARS IN THE PAST. BEFORE ANY OF THIS HAPPENED. A PLACE...TIME...WHERE THIS NEVER HAPPENS.
*SEE OLD MAN LOGAN (2016) #1. --CROB
YOU KNOW, LOGAN, IF YOU DON'T WANT TO TELL ME...IF YOU JUST RAN OFF BECAUSE YOU COULDN'T HANDLE BRUCE, THEN JUST SAY SO, BUT DON'T--
I'M TELLING YOU THE TRUTH, DANI.
I WAS THERE.
EVERYONE WAS STILL ALIVE...
...THE X-MEN WERE STILL ALIVE.
YEAH? IF THAT'S TRUE...
...THEN WHY THE HELL WOULD YOU COME BACK?

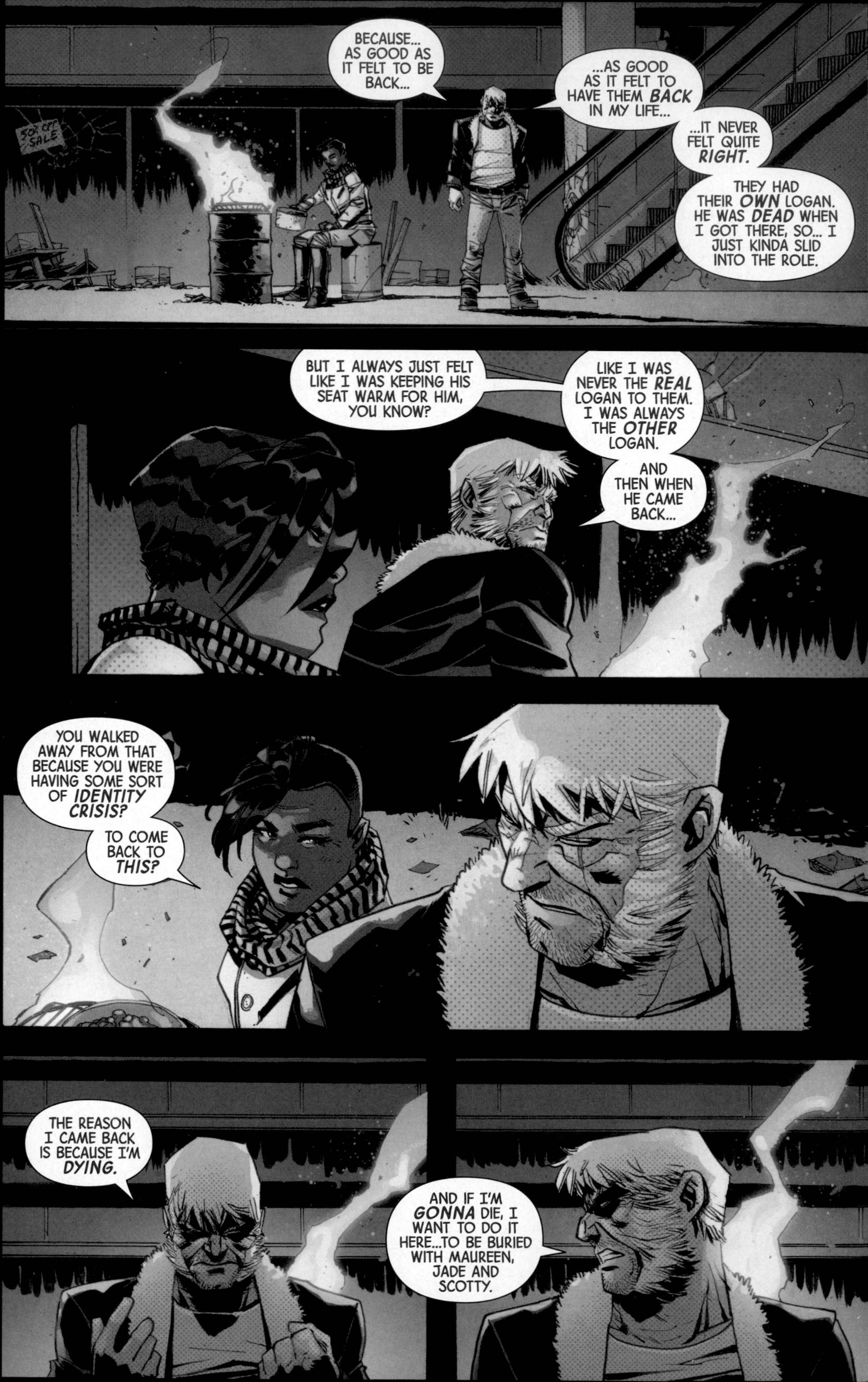

50% OFF SALE
BECAUSE... AS GOOD AS IT FELT TO BE BACK...
...AS GOOD AS IT FELT TO HAVE THEM BACK IN MY LIFE...
...IT NEVER FELT QUITE RIGHT.
THEY HAD THEIR OWN LOGAN. HE WAS DEAD WHEN I GOT THERE, SO... I JUST KINDA SLID INTO THE ROLE.
BUT I ALWAYS JUST FELT LIKE I WAS KEEPING HIS SEAT WARM FOR HIM, YOU KNOW?
LIKE I WAS NEVER THE REAL LOGAN TO THEM. I WAS ALWAYS THE OTHER LOGAN.
AND THEN WHEN HE CAME BACK...
YOU WALKED AWAY FROM THAT BECAUSE YOU WERE HAVING SOME SORT OF IDENTITY CRISIS?
TO COME BACK TO THIS?
THE REASON I CAME BACK IS BECAUSE I'M DYING.
AND IF I'M GONNA DIE, I WANT TO DO IT HERE...TO BE BURIED WITH MAUREEN, JADE AND SCOTTY.

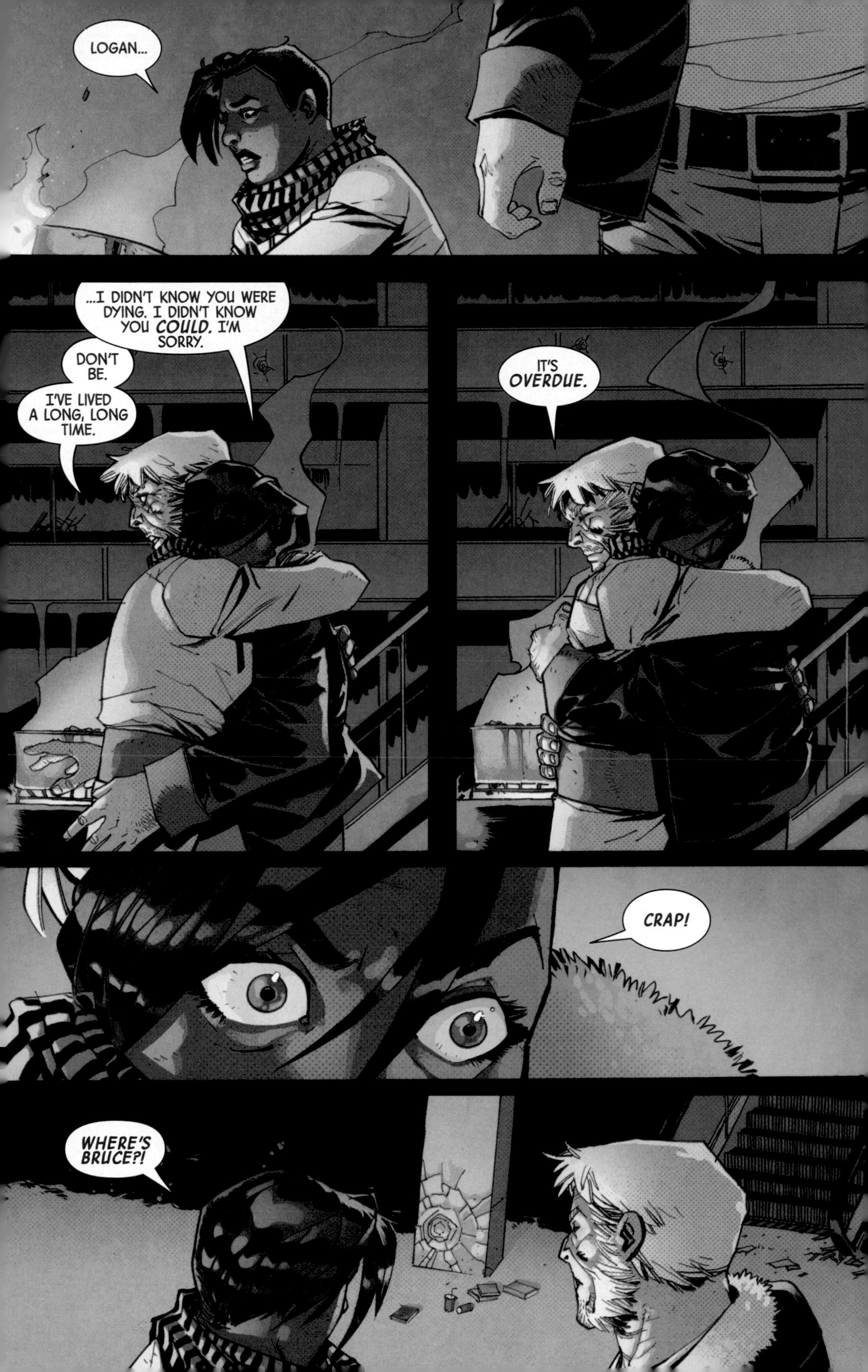
LOGAN...
...I DIDN'T KNOW YOU WERE DYING. I DIDN'T KNOW YOU COULD. I'M SORRY.
DON'T BE.
I'VE LIVED A LONG, LONG TIME.
IT'S OVERDUE.
CRAP!
WHERE'S BRUCE?!

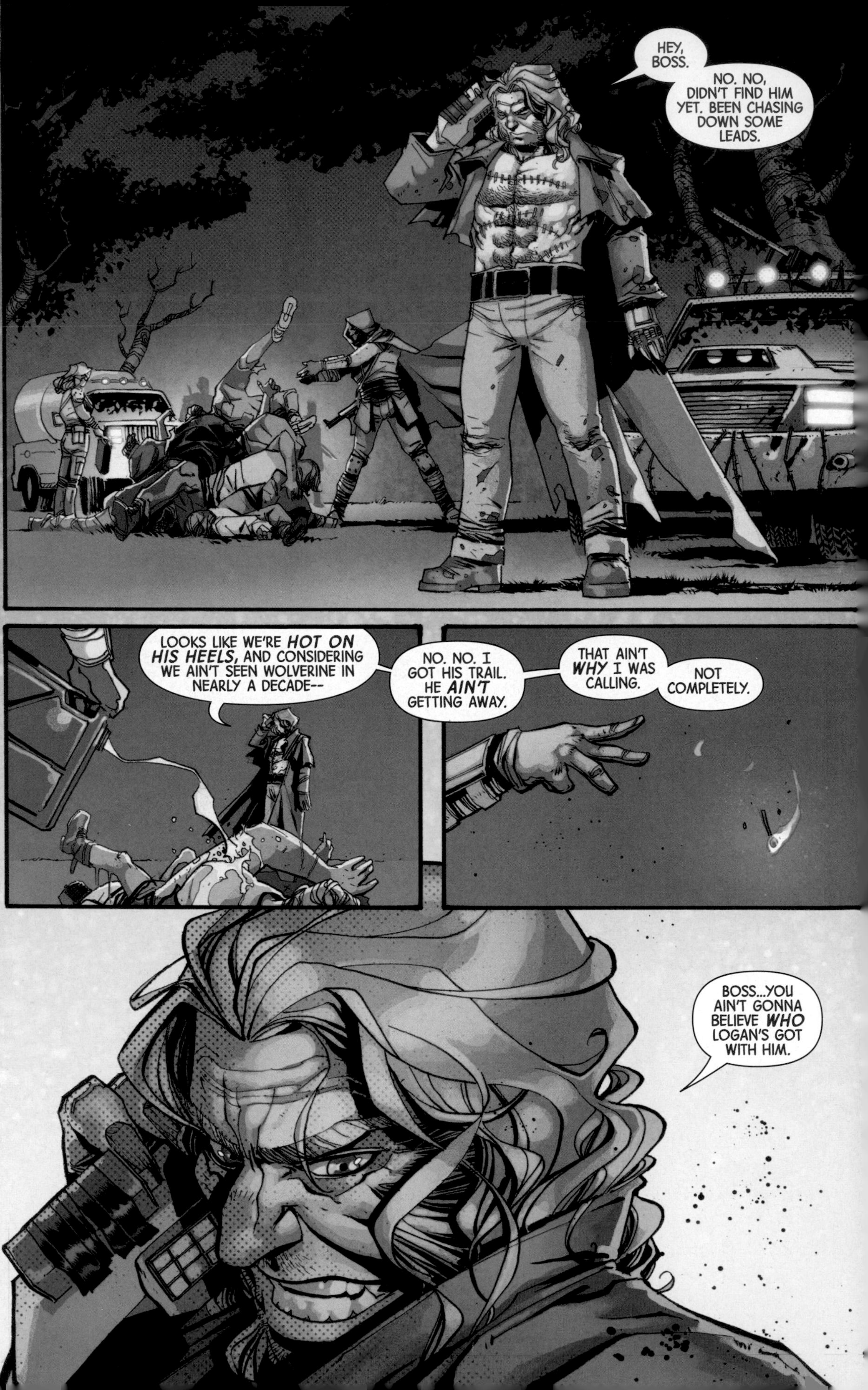
HEY, BOSS.
NO. NO, DIDN'T FIND HIM YET. BEEN CHASING DOWN SOME LEADS.
LOOKS LIKE WE'RE *HOT ON HIS HEELS,* AND CONSIDERING WE AIN'T SEEN WOLVERINE IN NEARLY A DECADE--
NO. NO. I GOT HIS TRAIL. HE *AIN'T* GETTING AWAY.
THAT AIN'T *WHY* I WAS CALLING.
NOT COMPLETELY.
BOSS...YOU AIN'T GONNA BELIEVE *WHO* LOGAN'S GOT WITH HIM.

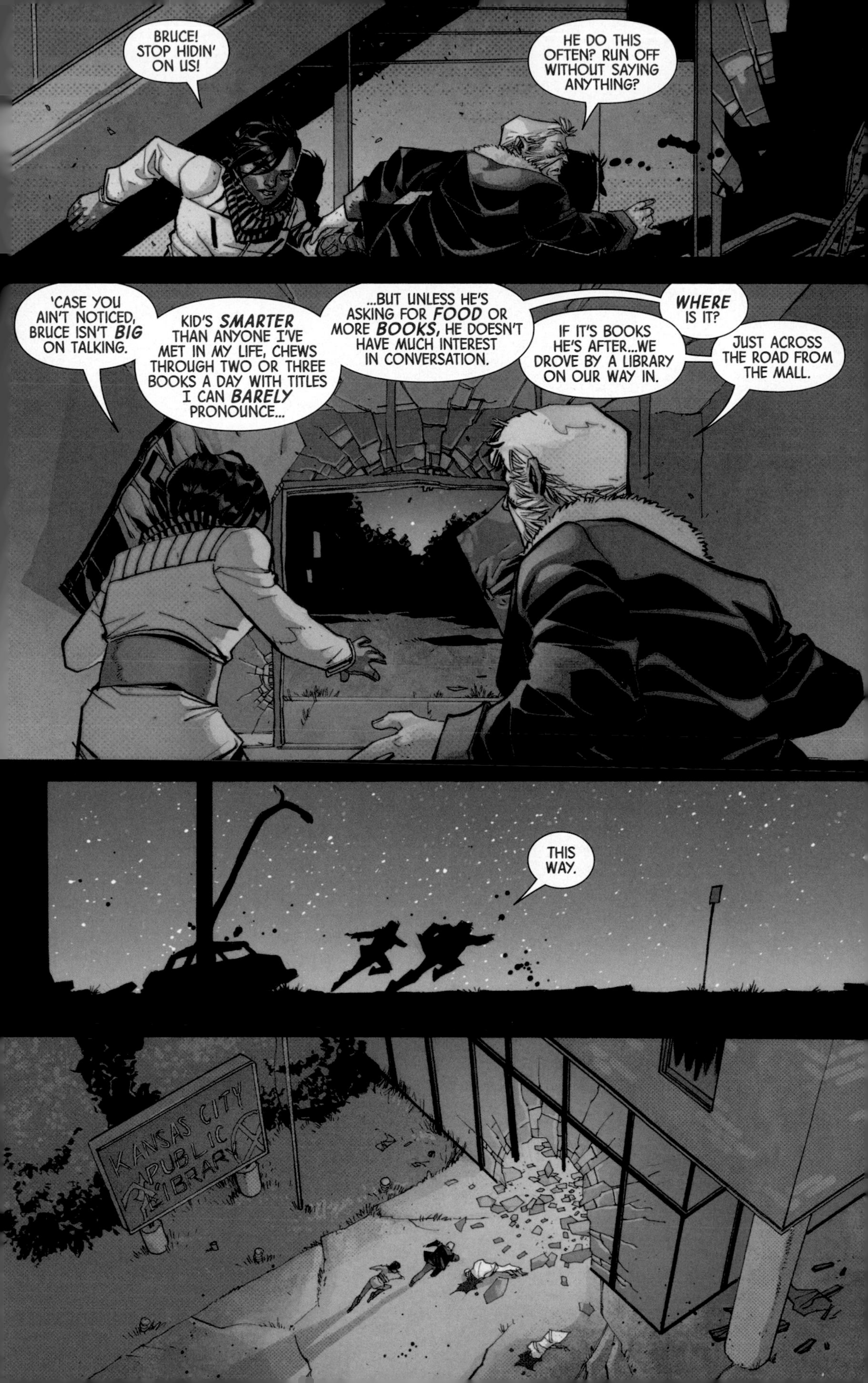

BRUCE! STOP HIDIN' ON US!
HE DO THIS OFTEN? RUN OFF WITHOUT SAYING ANYTHING?
'CASE YOU AIN'T NOTICED, BRUCE ISN'T *BIG* ON TALKING.
KID'S *SMARTER* THAN ANYONE I'VE MET IN MY LIFE, CHEWS THROUGH TWO OR THREE BOOKS A DAY WITH TITLES I CAN *BARELY* PRONOUNCE...
...BUT UNLESS HE'S ASKING FOR *FOOD* OR MORE *BOOKS*, HE DOESN'T HAVE MUCH INTEREST IN CONVERSATION.
IF IT'S BOOKS HE'S AFTER...WE DROVE BY A LIBRARY ON OUR WAY IN.
WHERE IS IT?
JUST ACROSS THE ROAD FROM THE MALL.
THIS WAY.
KANSAS CITY PUBLIC LIBRARY

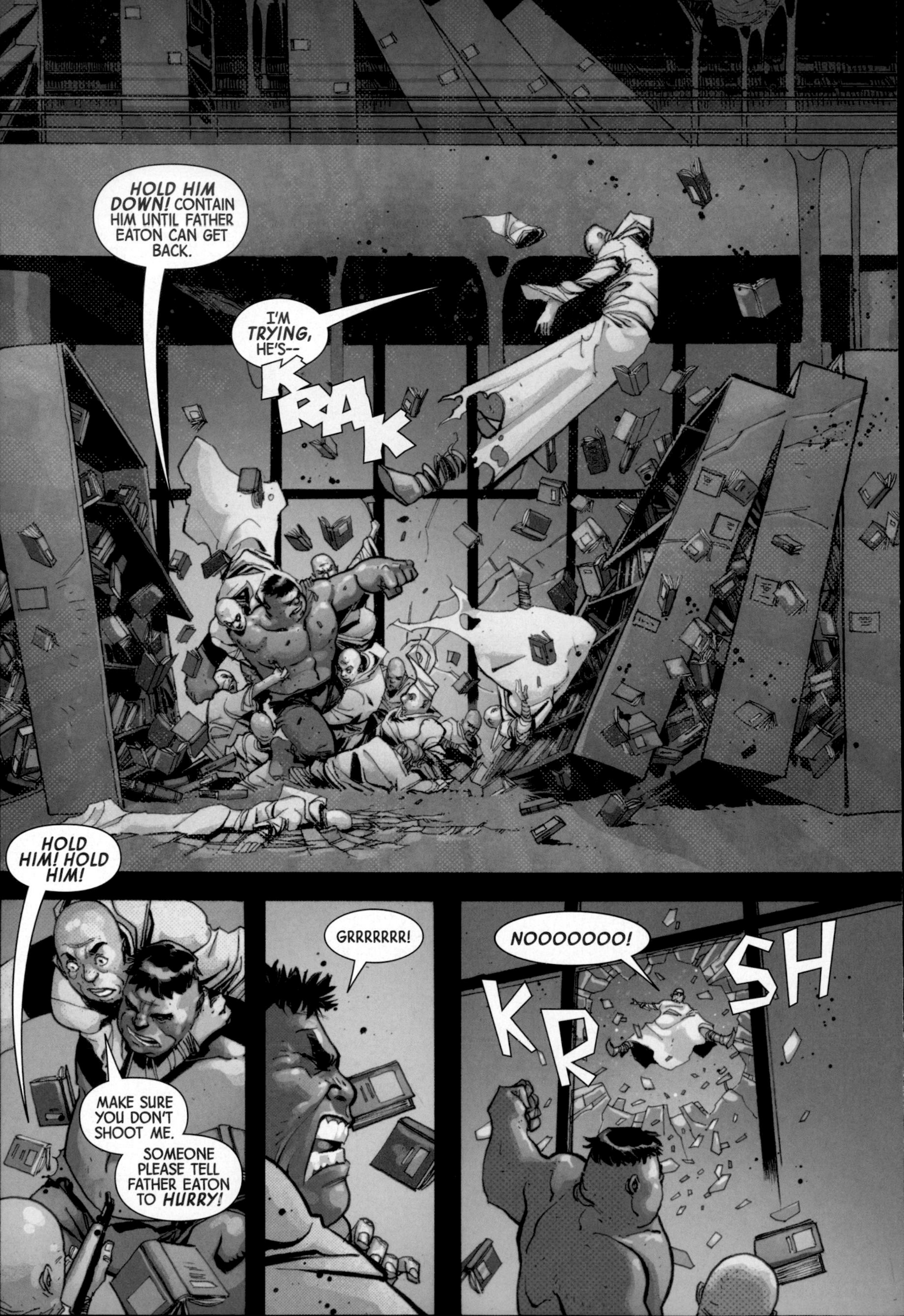
HOLD HIM DOWN! CONTAIN HIM UNTIL FATHER EATON CAN GET BACK.
I'M TRYING, HE'S--
KRAK
HOLD HIM! HOLD HIM!
MAKE SURE YOU DON'T SHOOT ME.
SOMEONE PLEASE TELL FATHER EATON TO HURRY!
GRRRRRRR!
NOOOOOOO!
KRSH

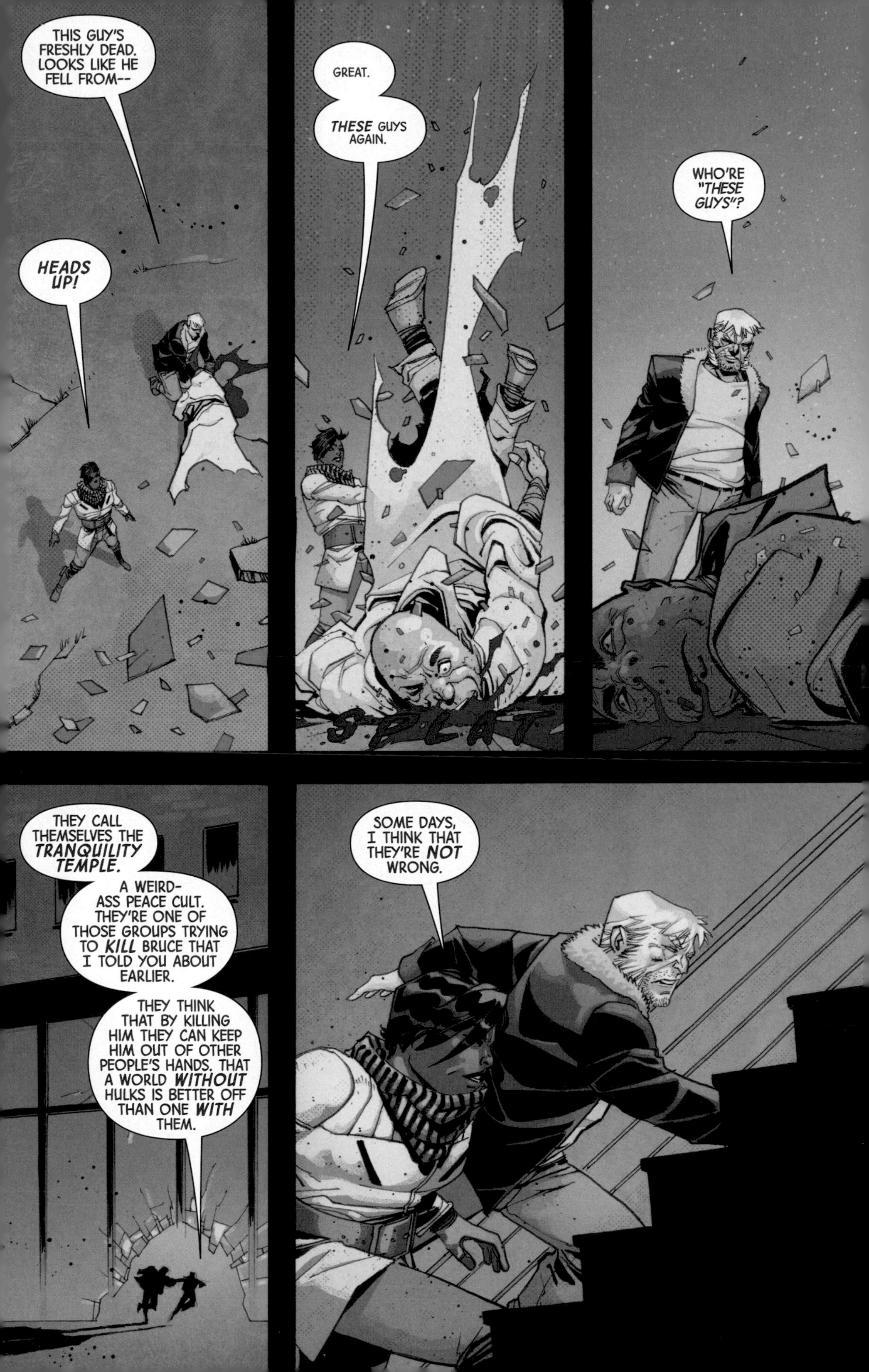
THIS GUY'S FRESHLY DEAD. LOOKS LIKE HE FELL FROM--
HEADS UP!
GREAT.
THESE GUYS AGAIN.
SPLAT
WHO'RE "THESE GUYS"?
THEY CALL THEMSELVES THE TRANQUILITY TEMPLE.
A WEIRD-ASS PEACE CULT. THEY'RE ONE OF THOSE GROUPS TRYING TO KILL BRUCE THAT I TOLD YOU ABOUT EARLIER.
THEY THINK THAT BY KILLING HIM THEY CAN KEEP HIM OUT OF OTHER PEOPLE'S HANDS. THAT A WORLD WITHOUT HULKS IS BETTER OFF THAN ONE WITH THEM.
SOME DAYS, I THINK THAT THEY'RE NOT WRONG.

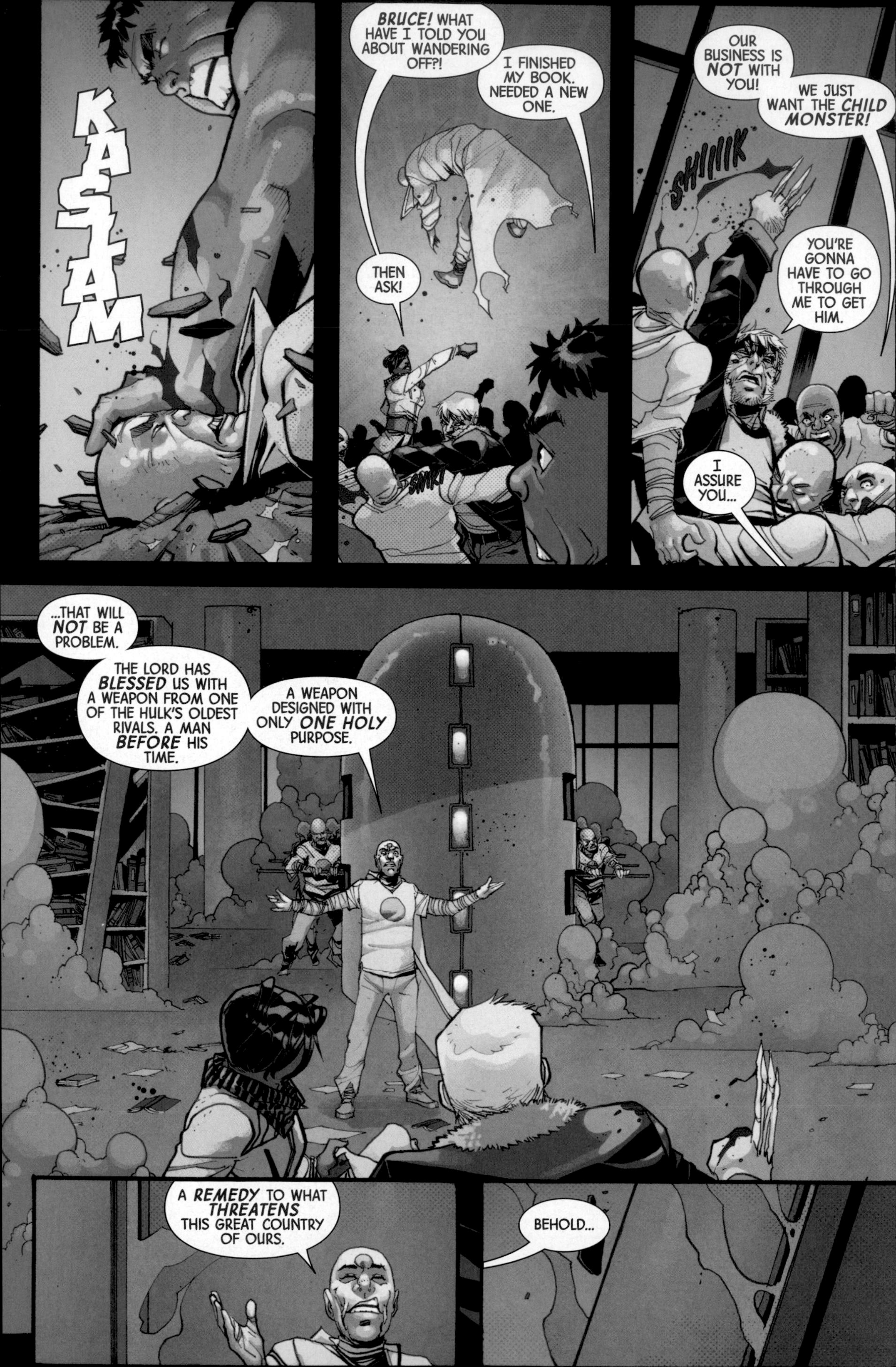
KASLAM
BRUCE! WHAT HAVE I TOLD YOU ABOUT WANDERING OFF?!
I FINISHED MY BOOK. NEEDED A NEW ONE.
THEN ASK!
SNIKT
OUR BUSINESS IS NOT WITH YOU!
WE JUST WANT THE CHILD MONSTER!
SHIIIIK
YOU'RE GONNA HAVE TO GO THROUGH ME TO GET HIM.
I ASSURE YOU...
...THAT WILL NOT BE A PROBLEM.
THE LORD HAS BLESSED US WITH A WEAPON FROM ONE OF THE HULK'S OLDEST RIVALS. A MAN BEFORE HIS TIME.
A WEAPON DESIGNED WITH ONLY ONE HOLY PURPOSE.
A REMEDY TO WHAT THREATENS THIS GREAT COUNTRY OF OURS.
BEHOLD...

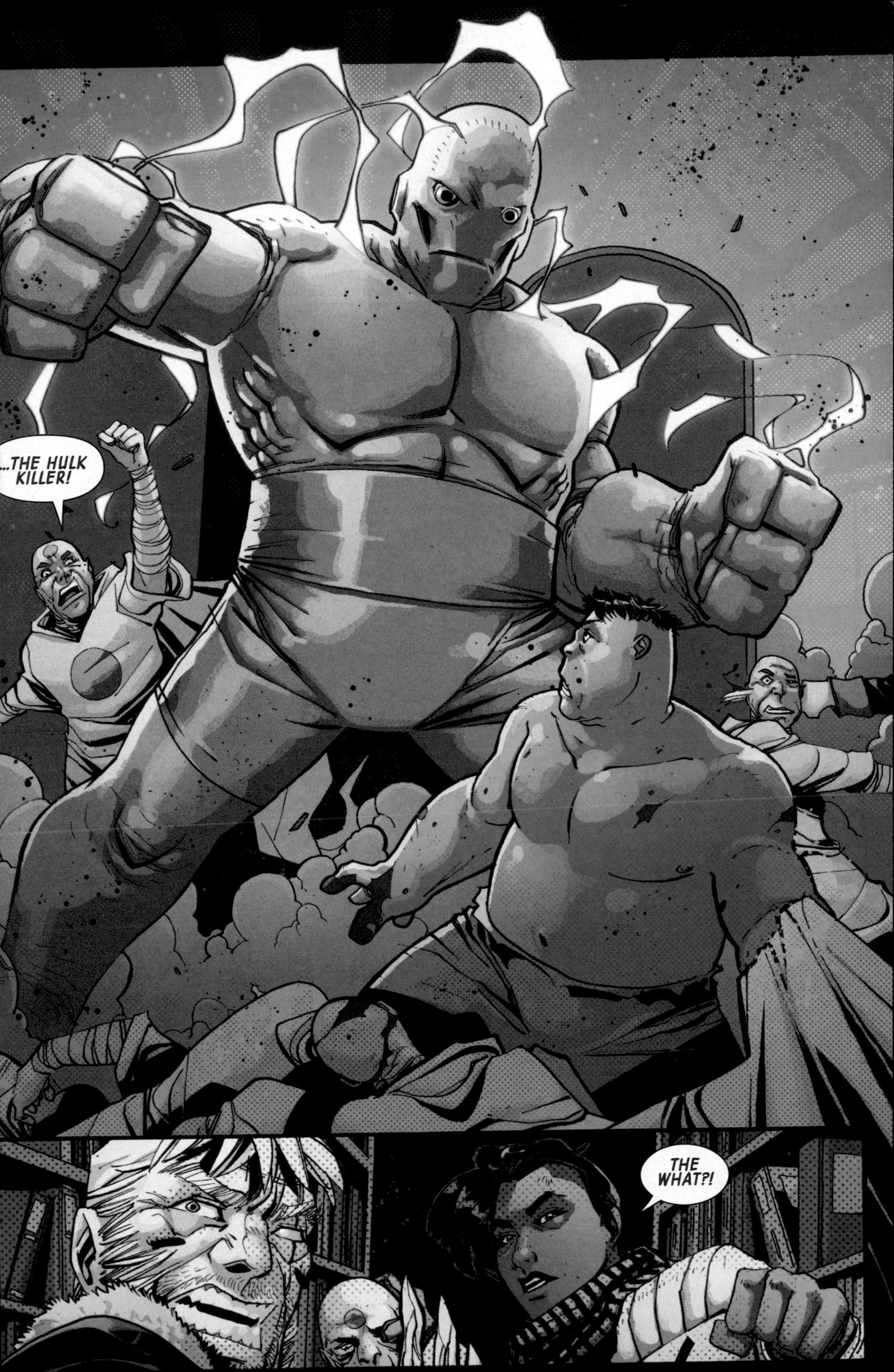
...THE HULK KILLER!
THE WHAT?!

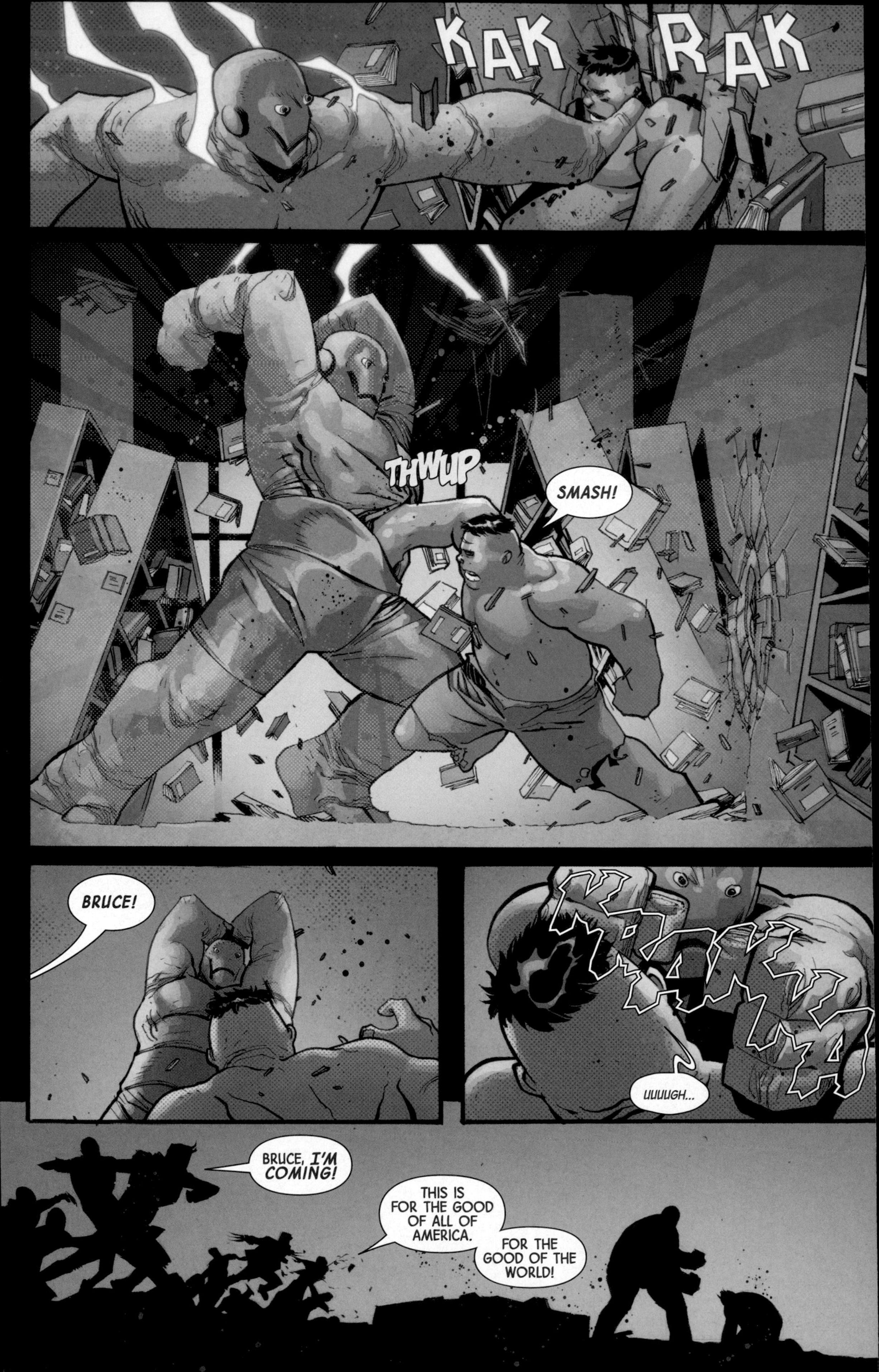
KAK RAK
THWUP
SMASH!
BRUCE!
UUUUGH...
BRUCE, I'M COMING!
THIS IS FOR THE GOOD OF ALL OF AMERICA.
FOR THE GOOD OF THE WORLD!

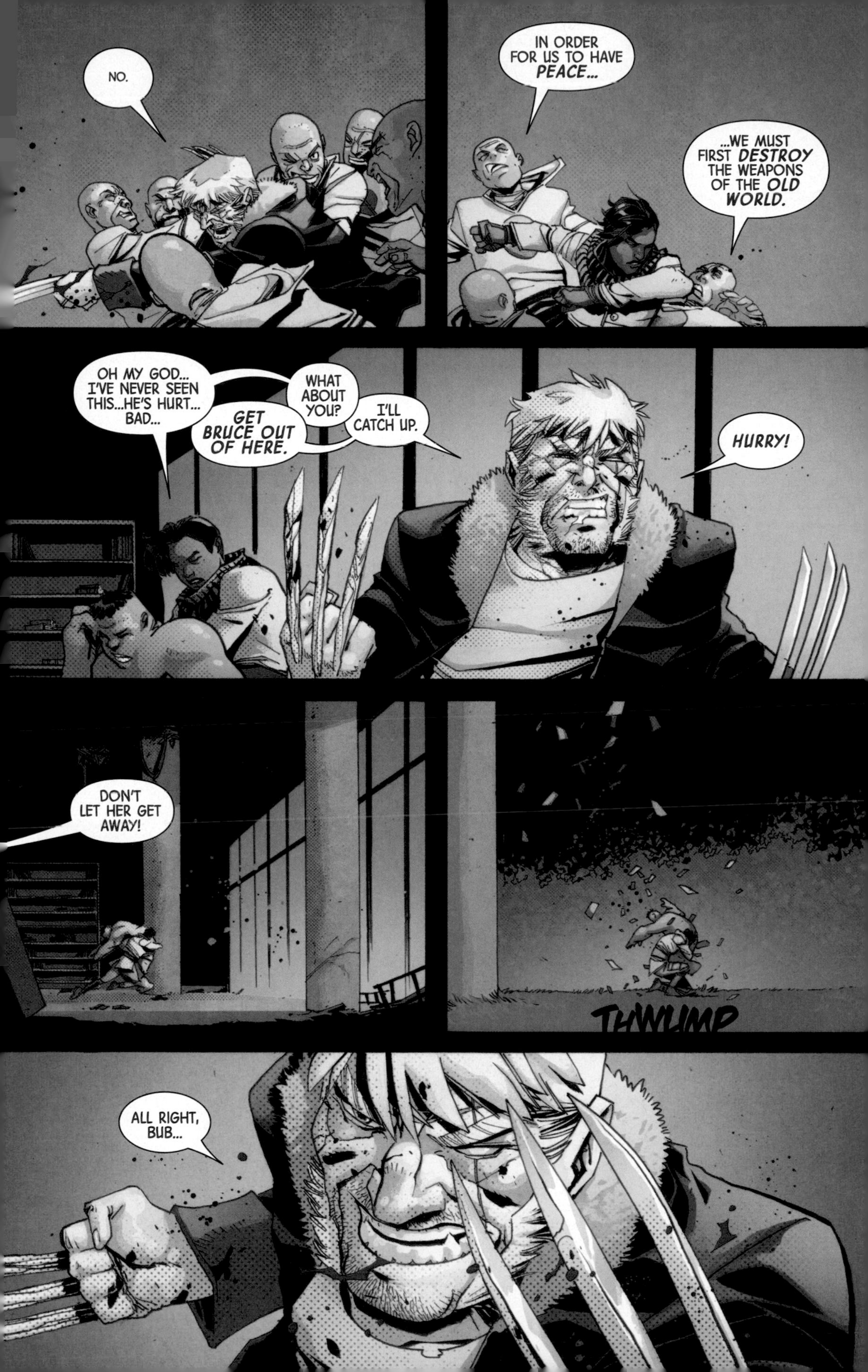
NO.
IN ORDER FOR US TO HAVE PEACE...
...WE MUST FIRST DESTROY THE WEAPONS OF THE OLD WORLD.
OH MY GOD... I'VE NEVER SEEN THIS...HE'S HURT... BAD...
GET BRUCE OUT OF HERE.
WHAT ABOUT YOU?
I'LL CATCH UP.
HURRY!
DON'T LET HER GET AWAY!
THWUMP
ALL RIGHT, BUB...

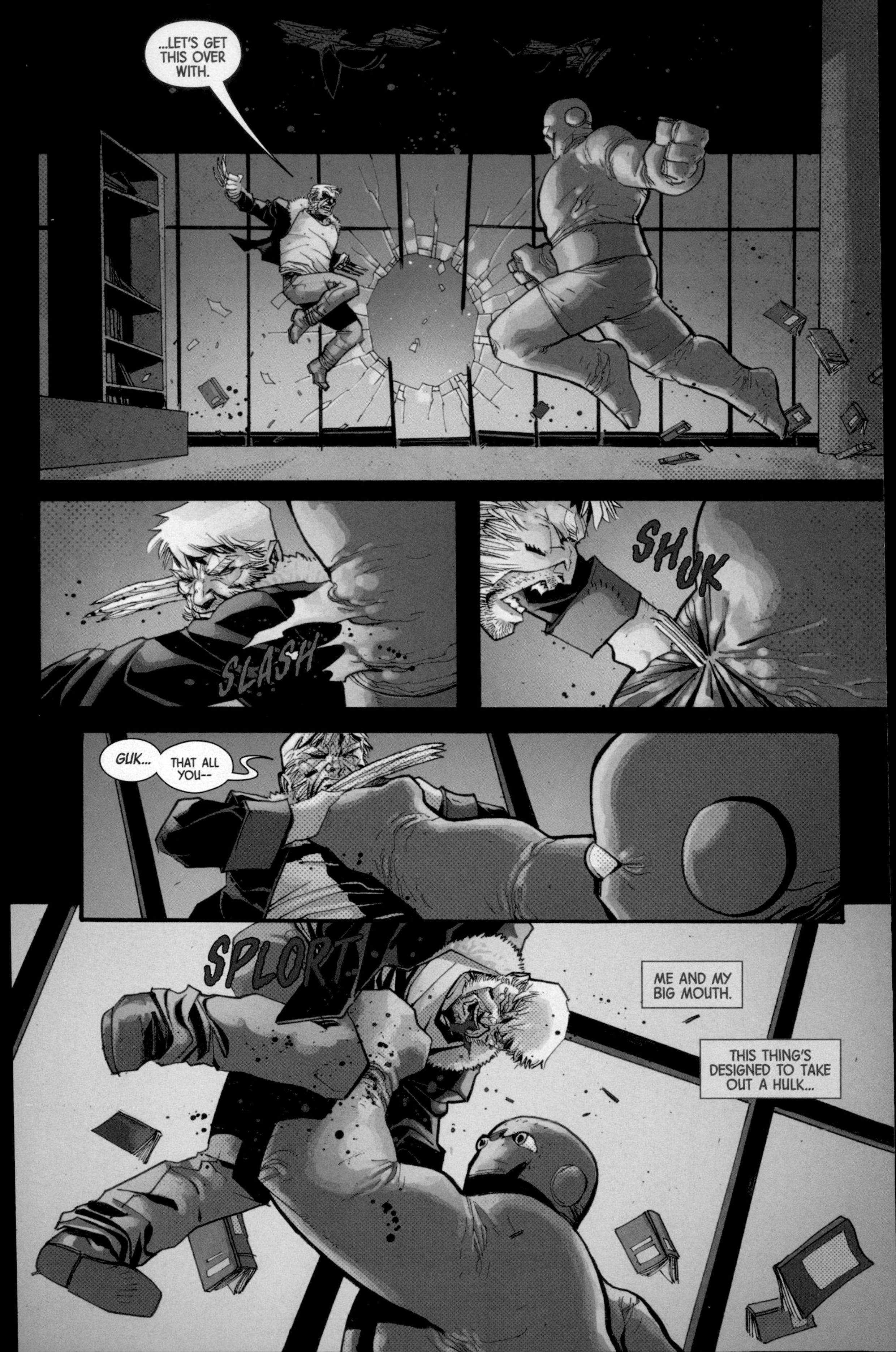
...LET'S GET THIS OVER WITH.
SLASH
SHUK
GUK...
THAT ALL YOU--
SPLORT
ME AND MY BIG MOUTH.
THIS THING'S DESIGNED TO TAKE OUT A HULK...

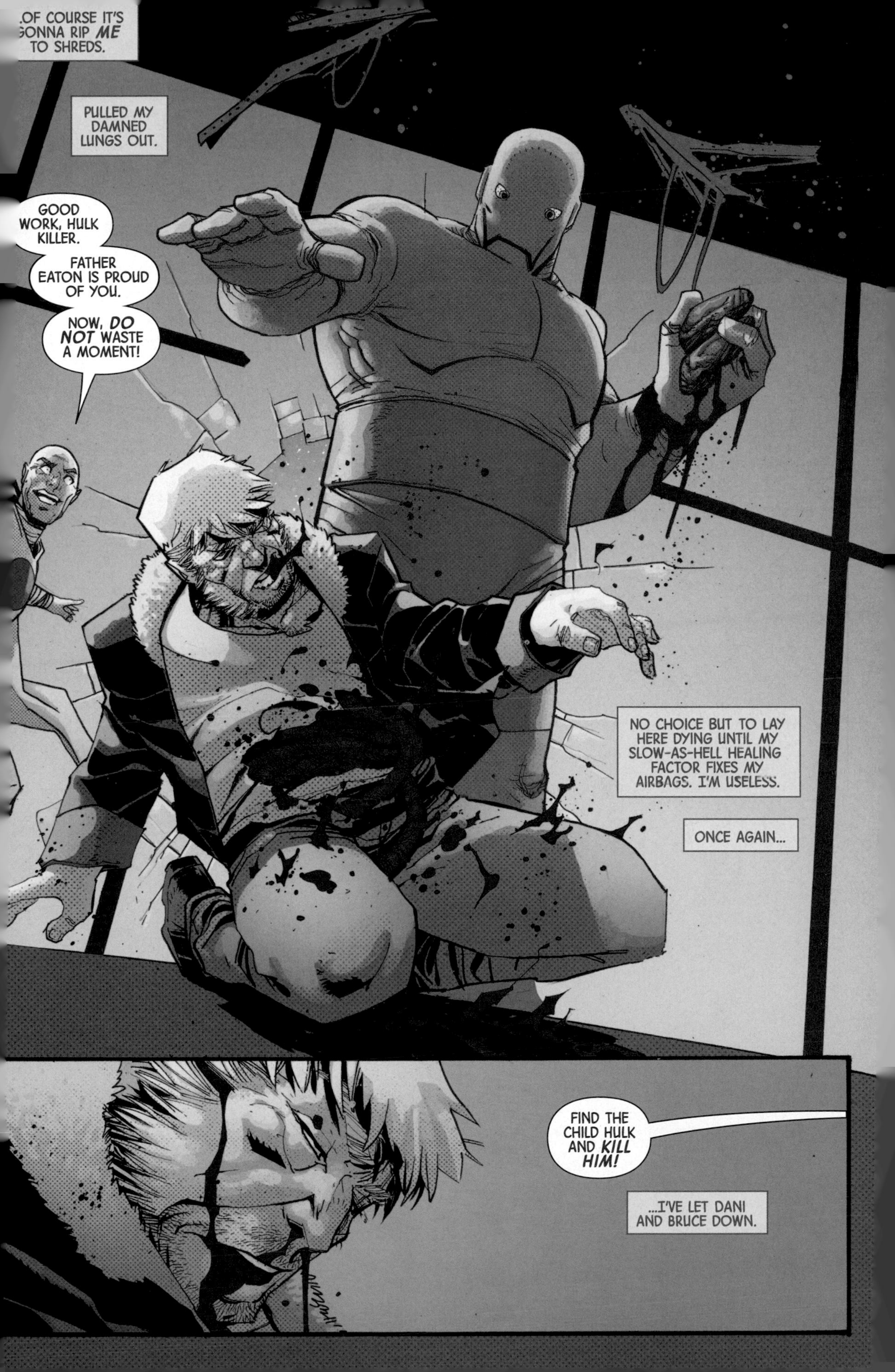
...OF COURSE IT'S GONNA RIP ME TO SHREDS.
PULLED MY DAMNED LUNGS OUT.
GOOD WORK, HULK KILLER.
FATHER EATON IS PROUD OF YOU.
NOW, DO NOT WASTE A MOMENT!
NO CHOICE BUT TO LAY HERE DYING UNTIL MY SLOW-AS-HELL HEALING FACTOR FIXES MY AIRBAGS. I'M USELESS.
ONCE AGAIN...
FIND THE CHILD HULK AND KILL HIM!
...I'VE LET DANI AND BRUCE DOWN.

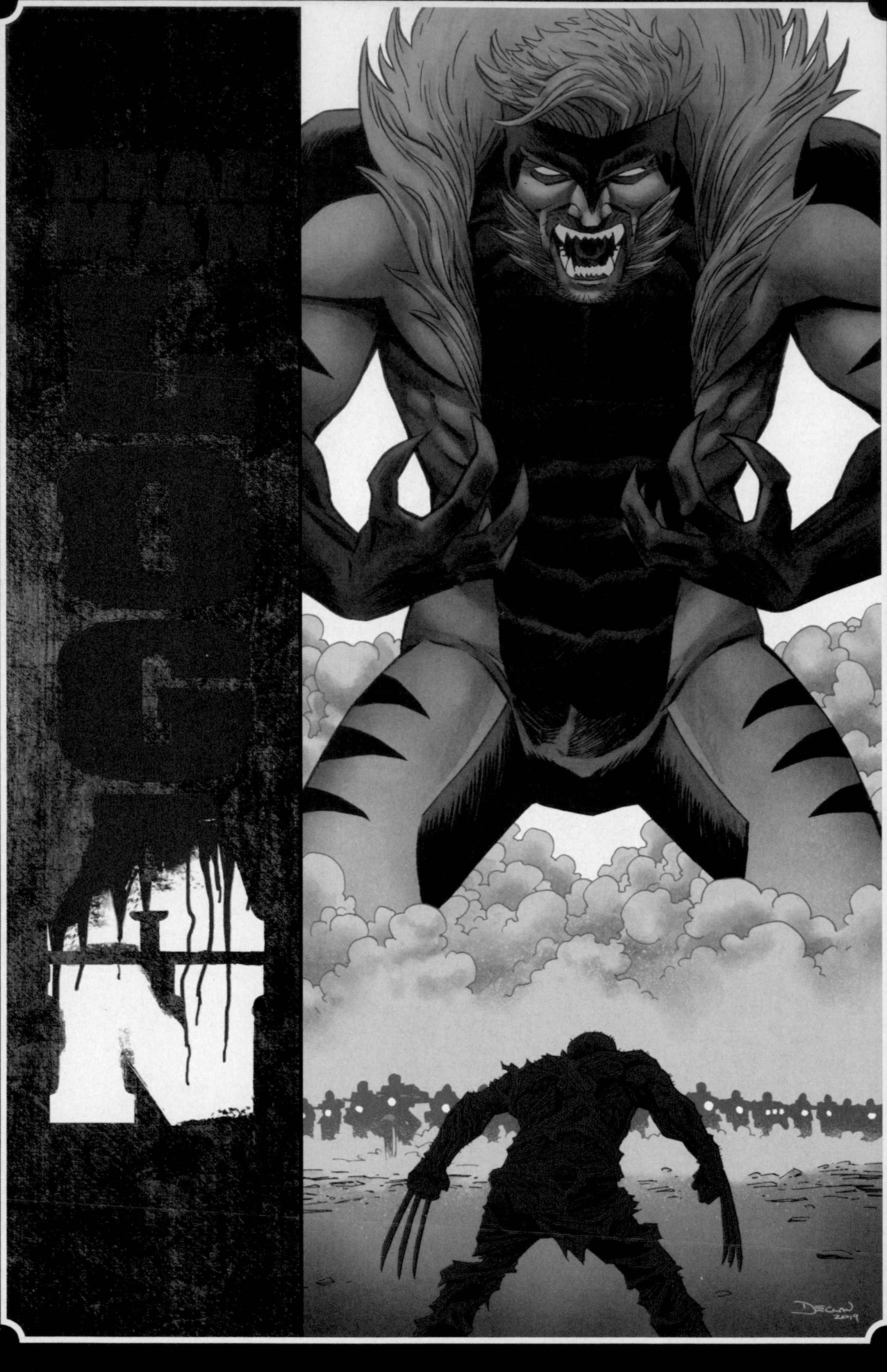

9

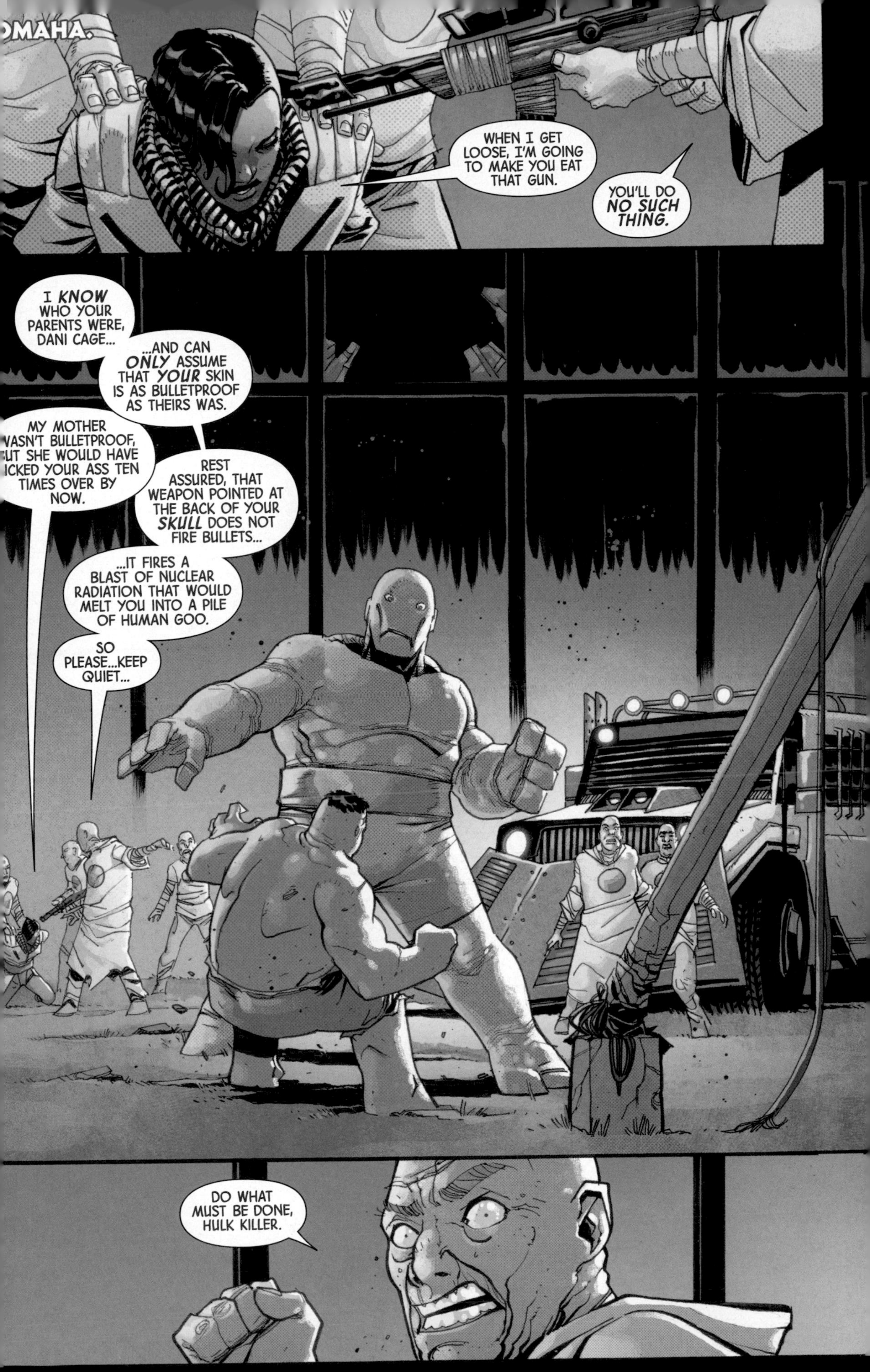
OMAHA.
WHEN I GET LOOSE, I'M GOING TO MAKE YOU EAT THAT GUN.
YOU'LL DO NO SUCH THING.
I KNOW WHO YOUR PARENTS WERE, DANI CAGE...
...AND CAN ONLY ASSUME THAT YOUR SKIN IS AS BULLETPROOF AS THEIRS WAS.
MY MOTHER WASN'T BULLETPROOF, BUT SHE WOULD HAVE KICKED YOUR ASS TEN TIMES OVER BY NOW.
REST ASSURED, THAT WEAPON POINTED AT THE BACK OF YOUR SKULL DOES NOT FIRE BULLETS...
...IT FIRES A BLAST OF NUCLEAR RADIATION THAT WOULD MELT YOU INTO A PILE OF HUMAN GOO.
SO PLEASE...KEEP QUIET...
DO WHAT MUST BE DONE, HULK KILLER.

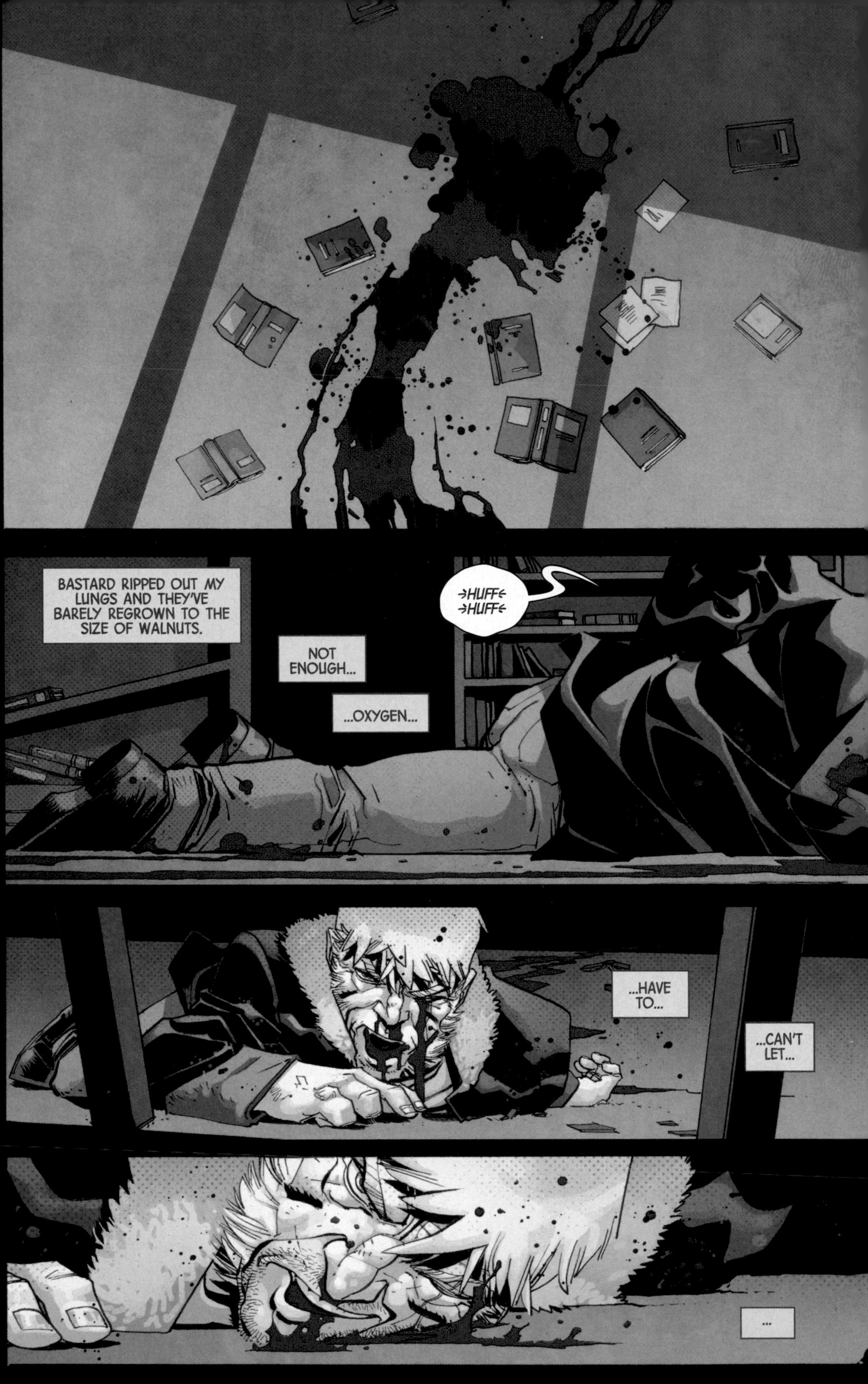

BASTARD RIPPED OUT MY LUNGS AND THEY'VE BARELY REGROWN TO THE SIZE OF WALNUTS.
HUFF HUFF
NOT ENOUGH...
...OXYGEN...
...HAVE TO...
...CAN'T LET...
...

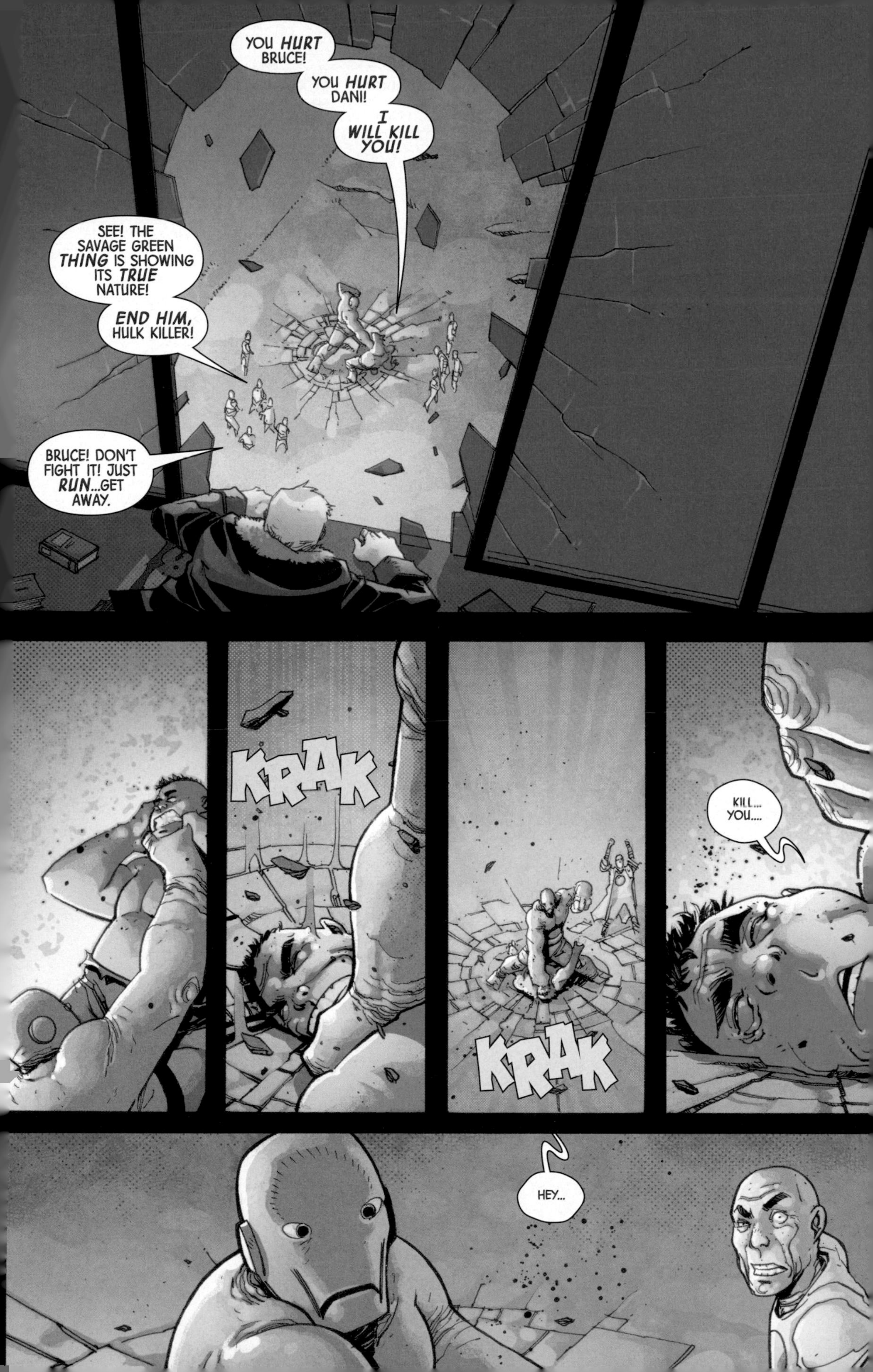
YOU HURT BRUCE!
YOU HURT DANI!
I WILL KILL YOU!
SEE! THE SAVAGE GREEN THING IS SHOWING ITS TRUE NATURE!
END HIM, HULK KILLER!
BRUCE! DON'T FIGHT IT! JUST RUN...GET AWAY.
KRAK
KRAK
KILL... YOU....
HEY...

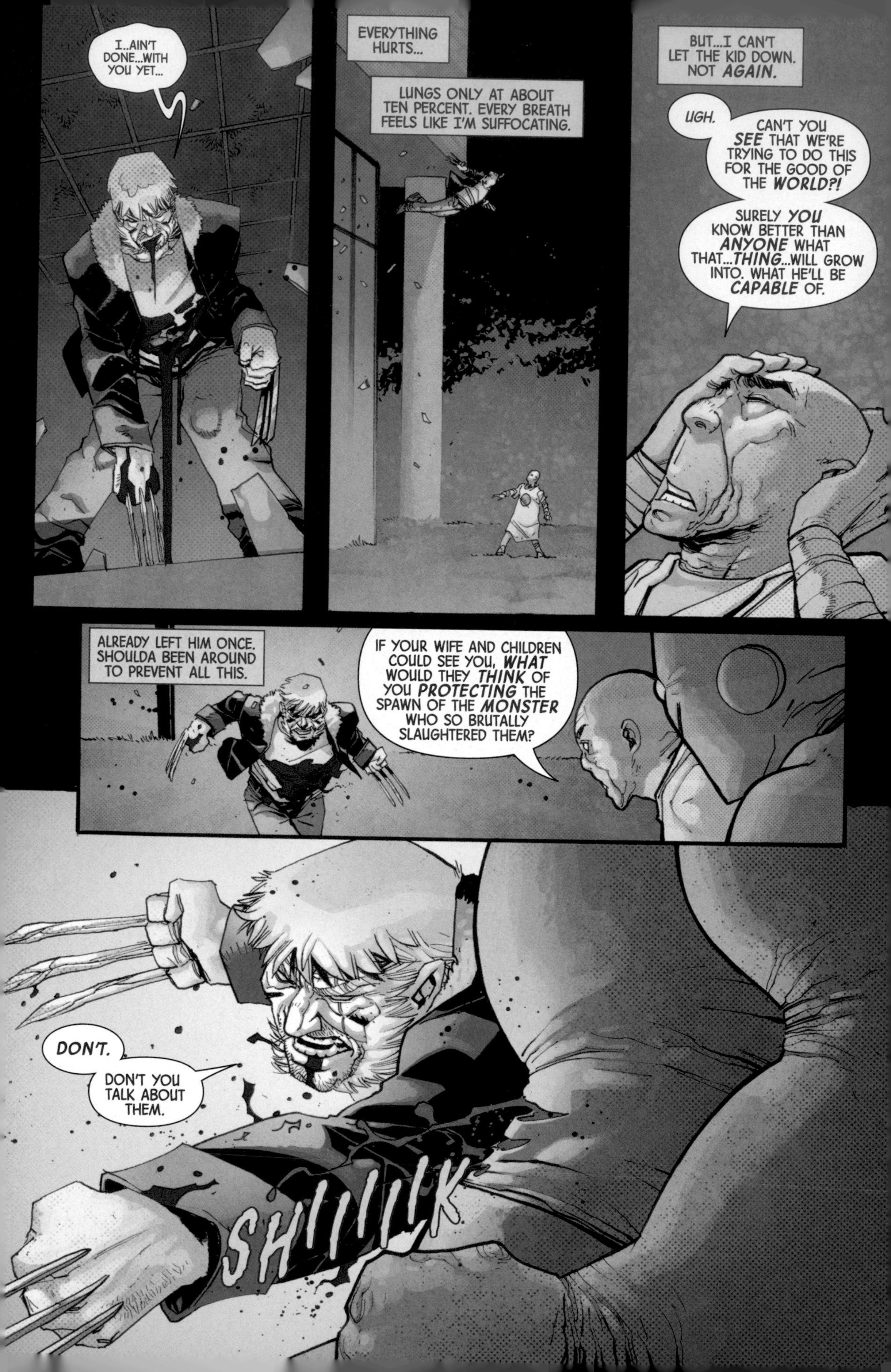
I..AIN'T DONE...WITH YOU YET...
EVERYTHING HURTS...
LUNGS ONLY AT ABOUT TEN PERCENT. EVERY BREATH FEELS LIKE I'M SUFFOCATING.
BUT...I CAN'T LET THE KID DOWN. NOT AGAIN.
UGH.
CAN'T YOU SEE THAT WE'RE TRYING TO DO THIS FOR THE GOOD OF THE WORLD?!
SURELY YOU KNOW BETTER THAN ANYONE WHAT THAT...THING...WILL GROW INTO. WHAT HE'LL BE CAPABLE OF.
ALREADY LEFT HIM ONCE. SHOULDA BEEN AROUND TO PREVENT ALL THIS.
IF YOUR WIFE AND CHILDREN COULD SEE YOU, WHAT WOULD THEY THINK OF YOU PROTECTING THE SPAWN OF THE MONSTER WHO SO BRUTALLY SLAUGHTERED THEM?
DON'T.
DON'T YOU TALK ABOUT THEM.
SHIIIIK

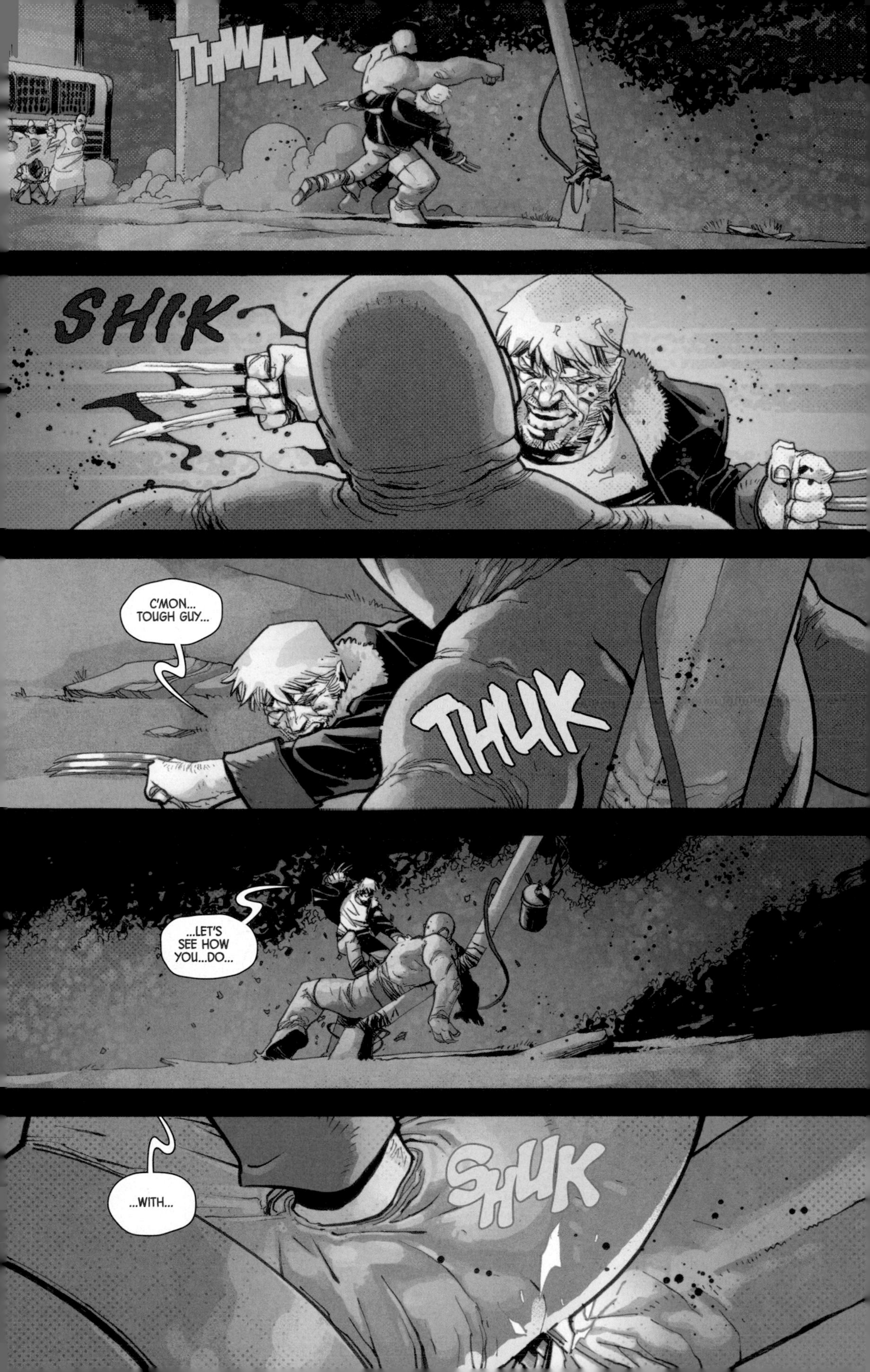
THWAK
SHIK
C'MON... TOUGH GUY...
THUK
...LET'S SEE HOW YOU...DO...
...WITH...
SHUK

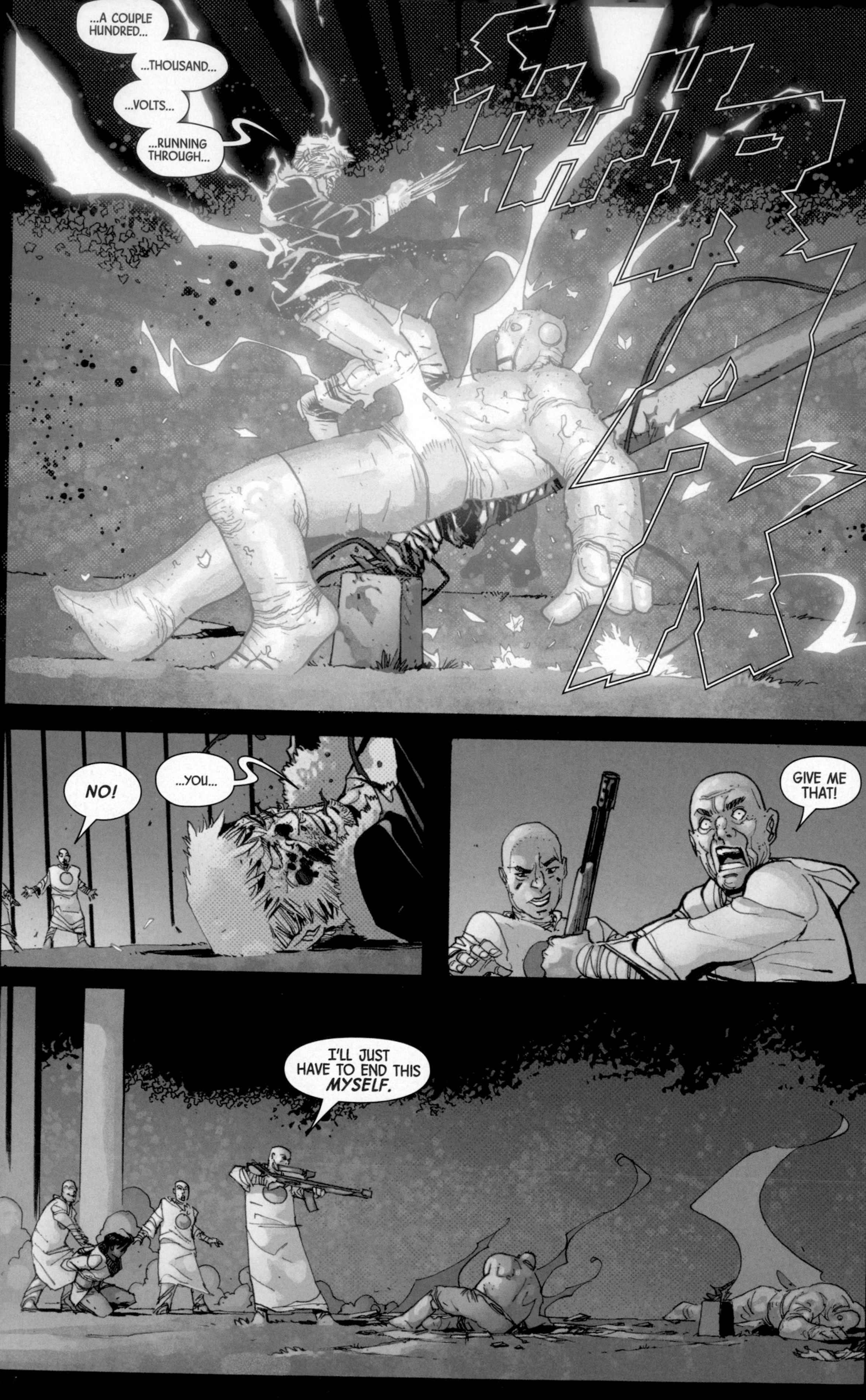
...A COUPLE HUNDRED...
...THOUSAND...
...VOLTS...
...RUNNING THROUGH...
NO!
...YOU...
GIVE ME THAT!
I'LL JUST HAVE TO END THIS MYSELF.

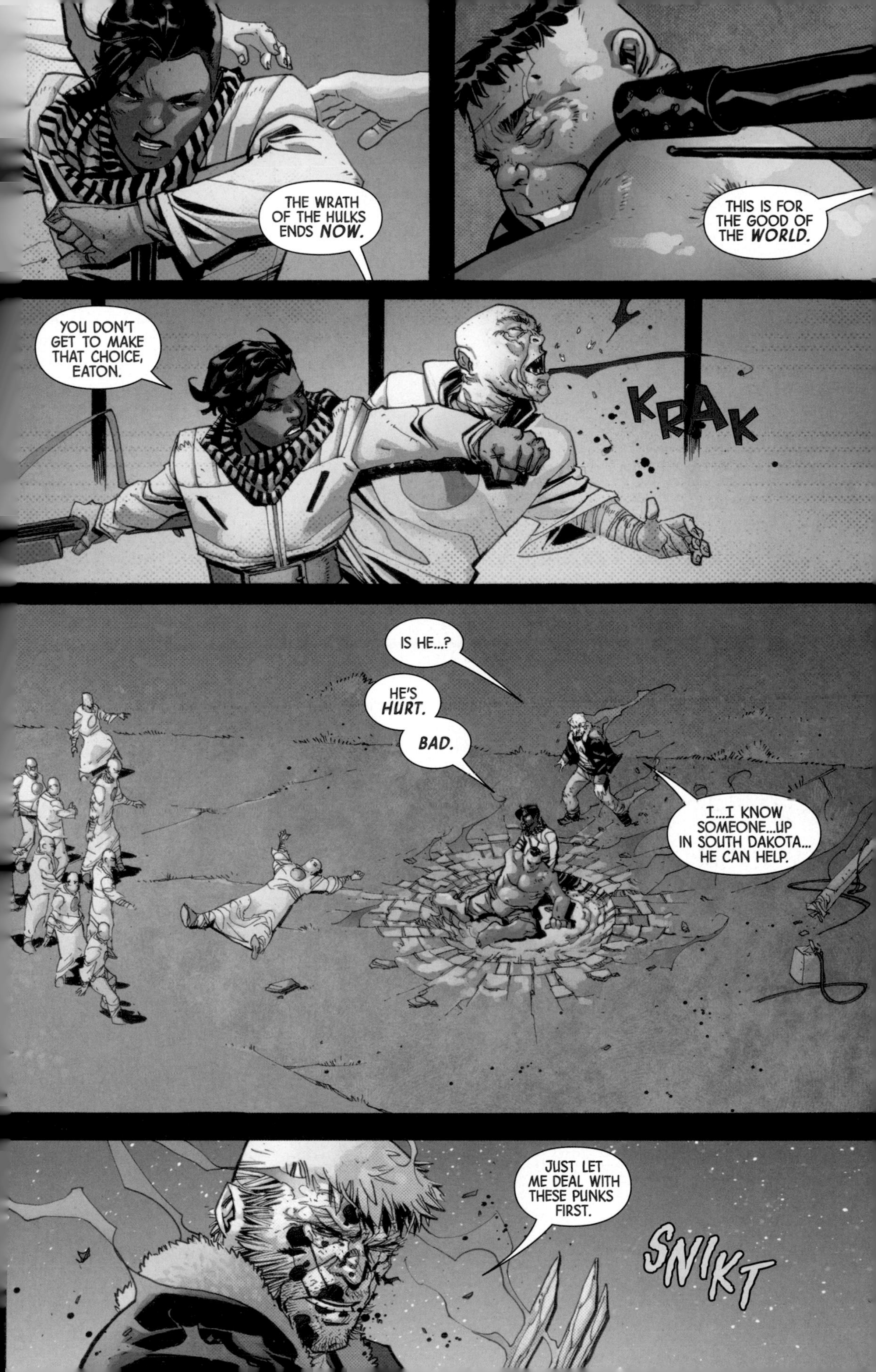

THE WRATH OF THE HULKS ENDS NOW.
THIS IS FOR THE GOOD OF THE WORLD.
YOU DON'T GET TO MAKE THAT CHOICE, EATON.
KRAK
IS HE...?
HE'S HURT.
BAD.
I...I KNOW SOMEONE...UP IN SOUTH DAKOTA... HE CAN HELP.
JUST LET ME DEAL WITH THESE PUNKS FIRST.
SNIKT

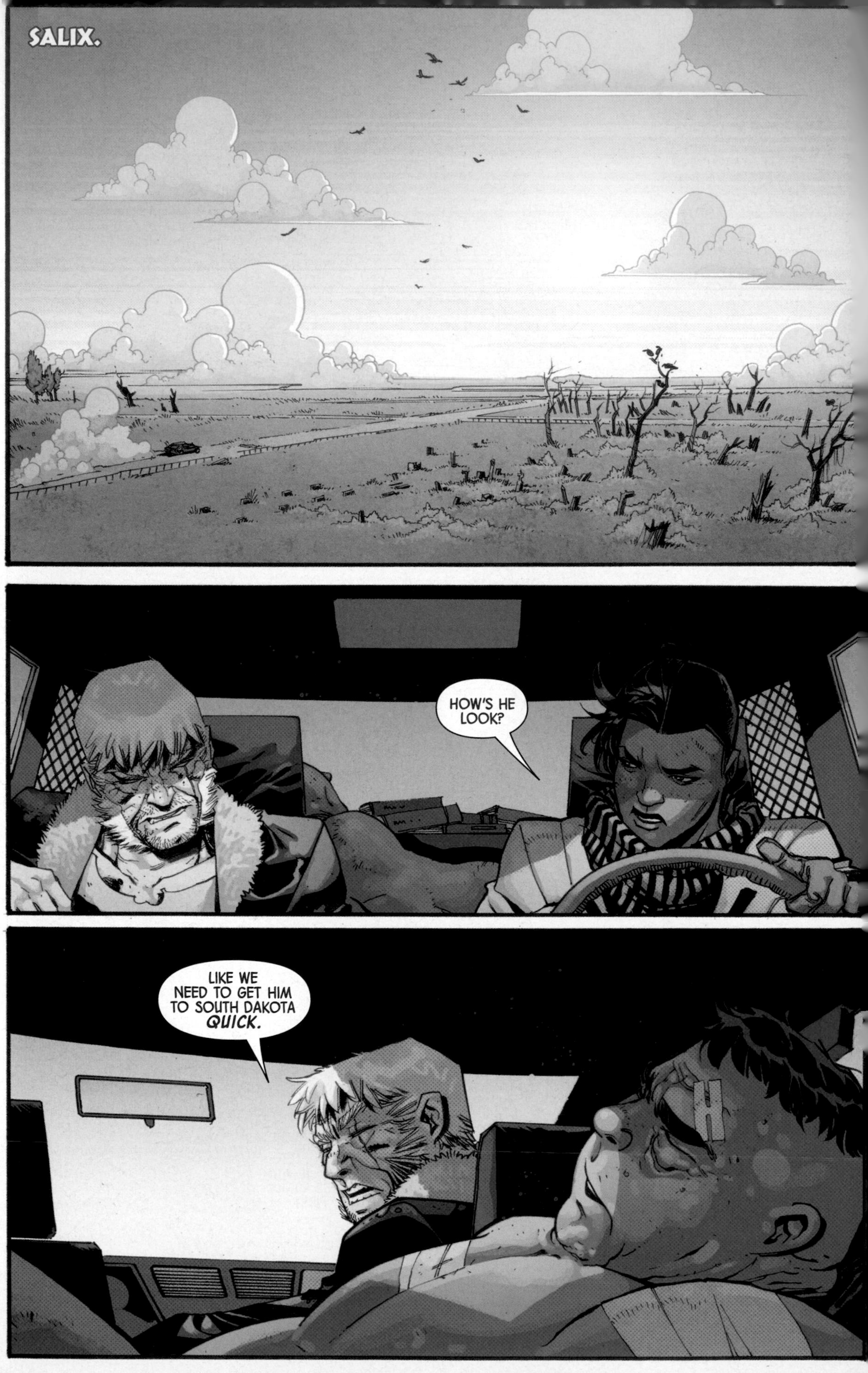
SALIX.
HOW'S HE LOOK?
LIKE WE NEED TO GET HIM TO SOUTH DAKOTA *QUICK.*

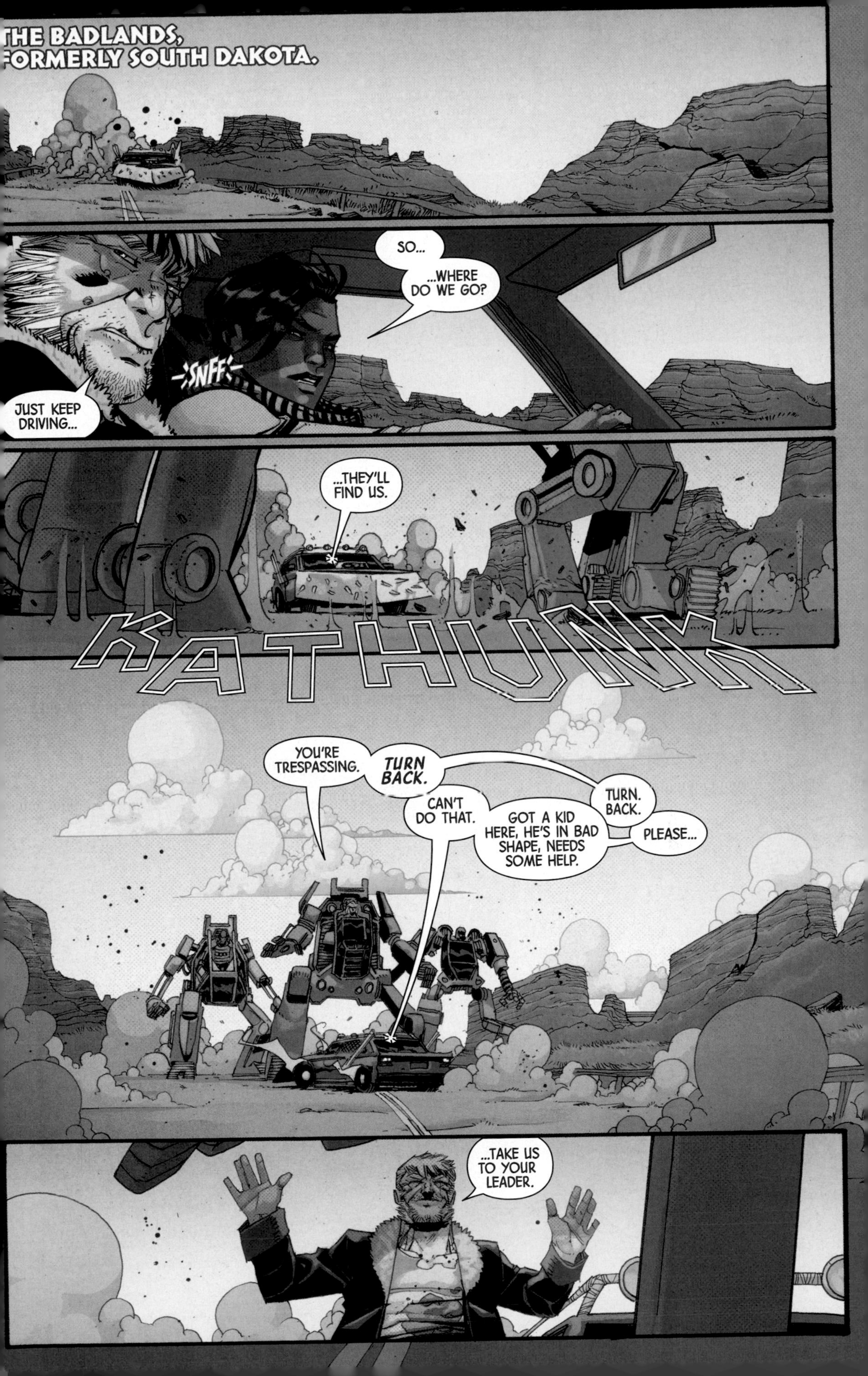
THE BADLANDS, FORMERLY SOUTH DAKOTA.
SO...
...WHERE DO WE GO?
-SNFF-
JUST KEEP DRIVING...
...THEY'LL FIND US.
KATHUNK
YOU'RE TRESPASSING.
TURN BACK.
CAN'T DO THAT.
GOT A KID HERE, HE'S IN BAD SHAPE, NEEDS SOME HELP.
TURN. BACK.
PLEASE...
...TAKE US TO YOUR LEADER.

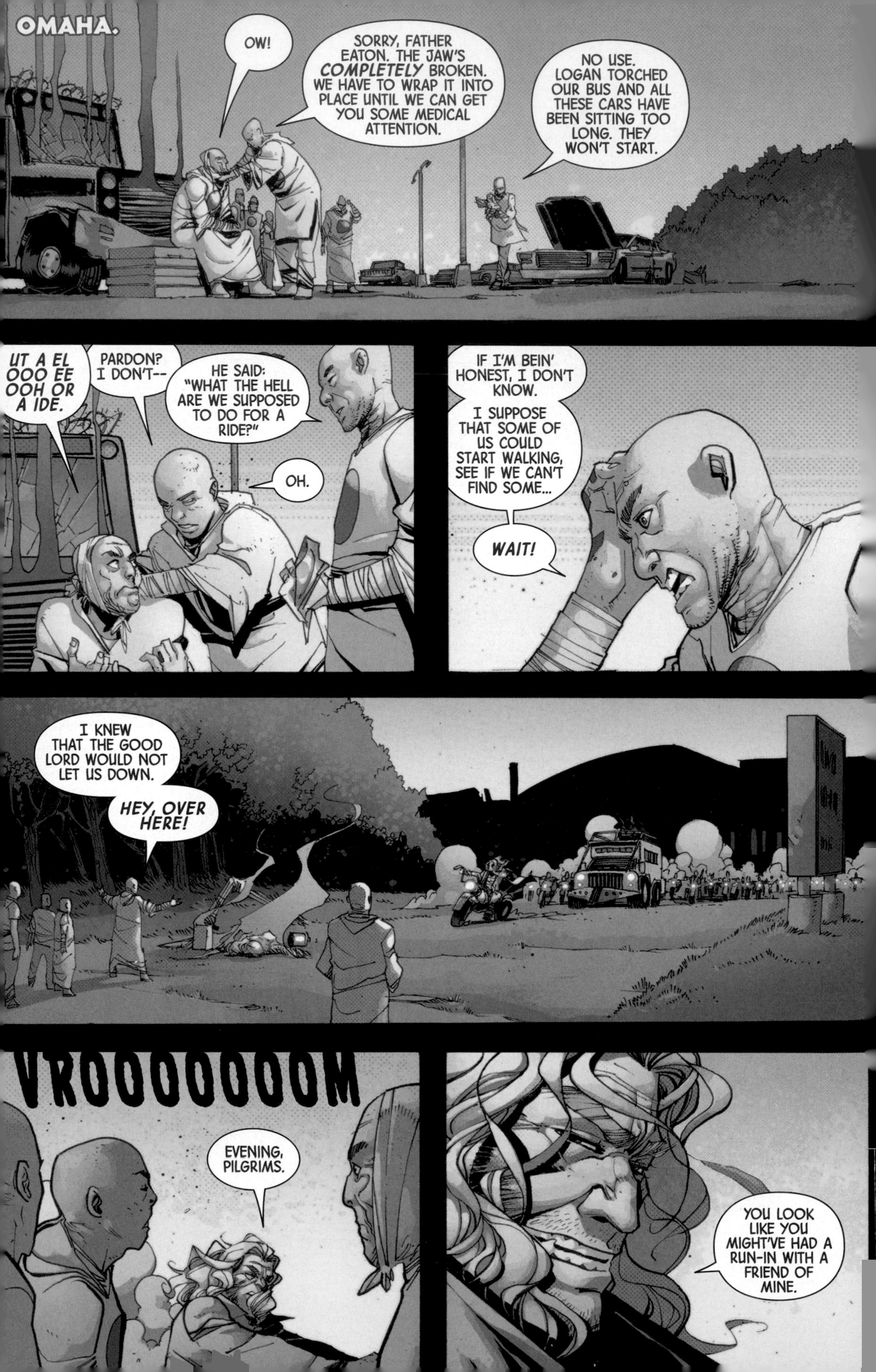
OMAHA.
OW!
SORRY, FATHER EATON. THE JAW'S COMPLETELY BROKEN. WE HAVE TO WRAP IT INTO PLACE UNTIL WE CAN GET YOU SOME MEDICAL ATTENTION.
NO USE. LOGAN TORCHED OUR BUS AND ALL THESE CARS HAVE BEEN SITTING TOO LONG. THEY WON'T START.
UT A EL OOO EE OOH OR A IDE.
PARDON? I DON'T--
HE SAID: "WHAT THE HELL ARE WE SUPPOSED TO DO FOR A RIDE?"
OH.
IF I'M BEIN' HONEST, I DON'T KNOW.
I SUPPOSE THAT SOME OF US COULD START WALKING, SEE IF WE CAN'T FIND SOME...
WAIT!
I KNEW THAT THE GOOD LORD WOULD NOT LET US DOWN.
HEY, OVER HERE!
VROOOOOOOOM
EVENING, PILGRIMS.
YOU LOOK LIKE YOU MIGHT'VE HAD A RUN-IN WITH A FRIEND OF MINE.

BEEP
BEEP
BEEP
BEEP

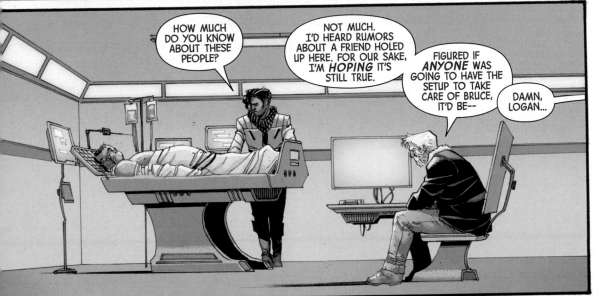

HOW MUCH DO YOU KNOW ABOUT THESE PEOPLE?

NOT MUCH. I'D HEARD RUMORS ABOUT A FRIEND HOLED UP HERE. FOR OUR SAKE, I'M *HOPING* IT'S STILL TRUE.

FIGURED IF *ANYONE* WAS GOING TO HAVE THE SETUP TO TAKE CARE OF BRUCE, IT'D BE--

DAMN, LOGAN...

...YOU GOT *OLD!*

YOU AIN'T NO SPRING CHICKEN EITHER, *FORGE.*

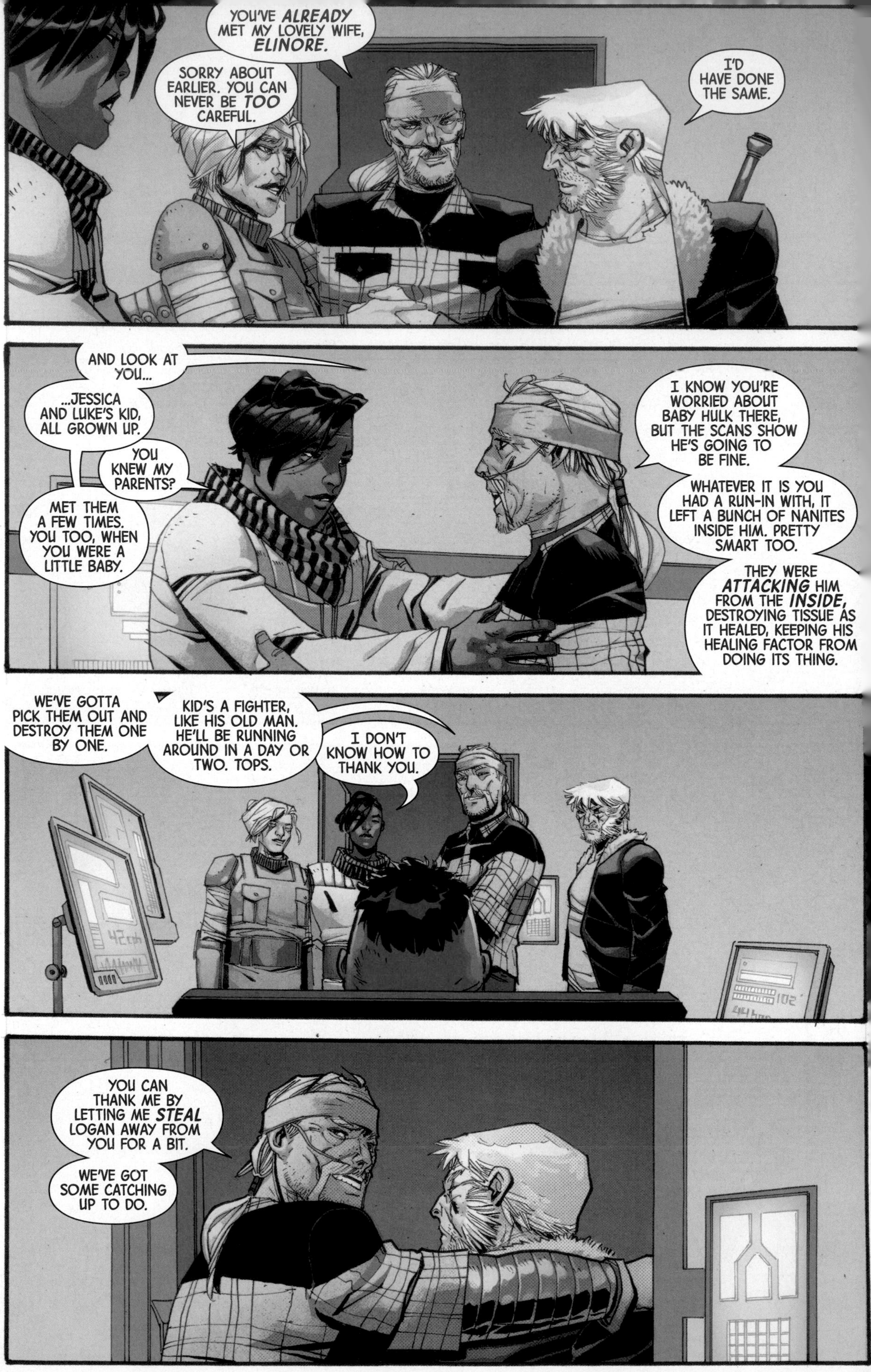
YOU'VE ALREADY MET MY LOVELY WIFE, ELINORE.
SORRY ABOUT EARLIER. YOU CAN NEVER BE TOO CAREFUL.
I'D HAVE DONE THE SAME.
AND LOOK AT YOU...
...JESSICA AND LUKE'S KID, ALL GROWN UP.
YOU KNEW MY PARENTS?
MET THEM A FEW TIMES. YOU TOO, WHEN YOU WERE A LITTLE BABY.
I KNOW YOU'RE WORRIED ABOUT BABY HULK THERE, BUT THE SCANS SHOW HE'S GOING TO BE FINE.
WHATEVER IT IS YOU HAD A RUN-IN WITH, IT LEFT A BUNCH OF NANITES INSIDE HIM. PRETTY SMART TOO.
THEY WERE ATTACKING HIM FROM THE INSIDE, DESTROYING TISSUE AS IT HEALED, KEEPING HIS HEALING FACTOR FROM DOING ITS THING.
WE'VE GOTTA PICK THEM OUT AND DESTROY THEM ONE BY ONE.
KID'S A FIGHTER, LIKE HIS OLD MAN. HE'LL BE RUNNING AROUND IN A DAY OR TWO. TOPS.
I DON'T KNOW HOW TO THANK YOU.
YOU CAN THANK ME BY LETTING ME STEAL LOGAN AWAY FROM YOU FOR A BIT.
WE'VE GOT SOME CATCHING UP TO DO.

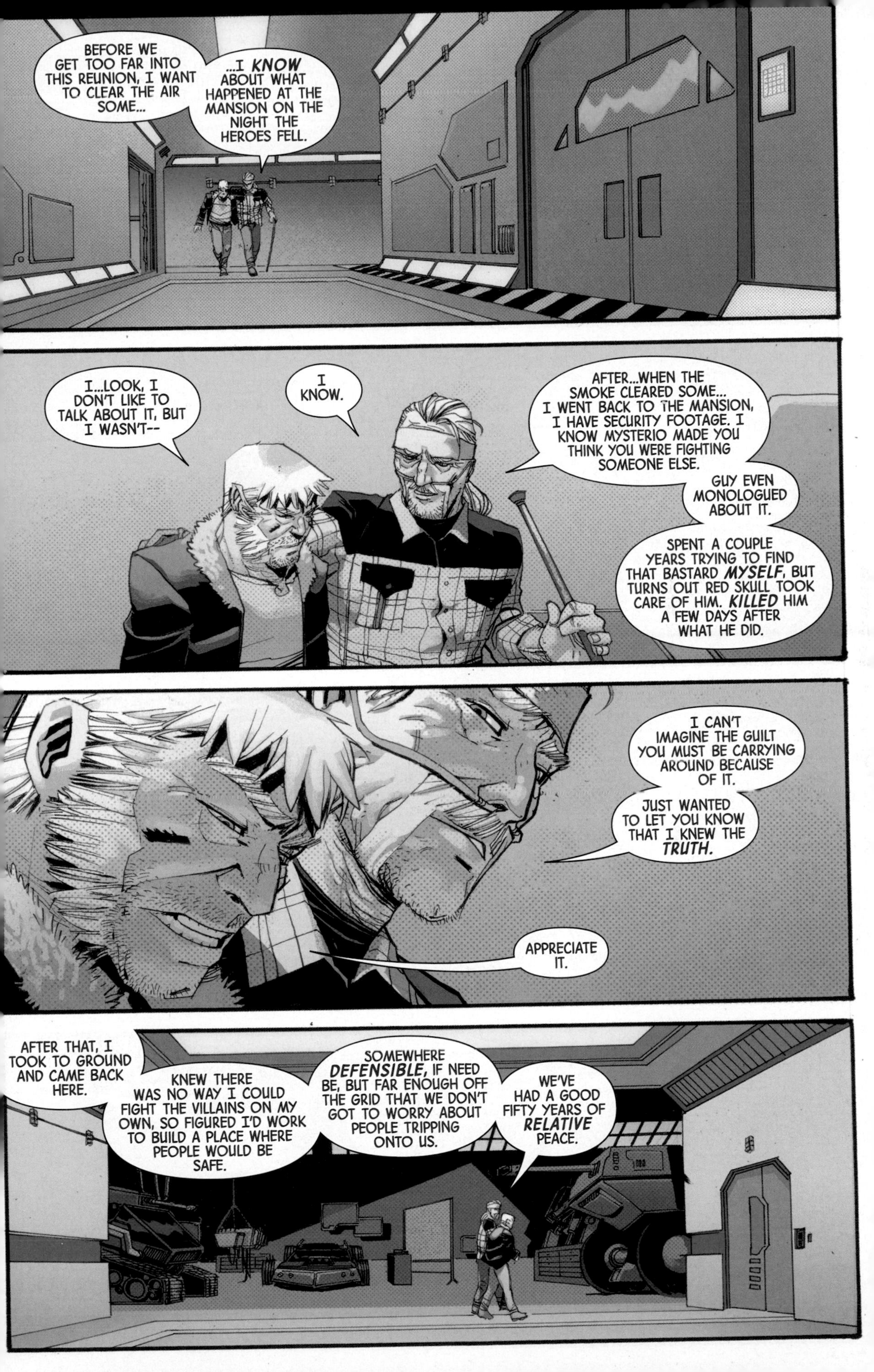
BEFORE WE GET TOO FAR INTO THIS REUNION, I WANT TO CLEAR THE AIR SOME...
...I KNOW ABOUT WHAT HAPPENED AT THE MANSION ON THE NIGHT THE HEROES FELL.
I...LOOK, I DON'T LIKE TO TALK ABOUT IT, BUT I WASN'T--
I KNOW.
AFTER...WHEN THE SMOKE CLEARED SOME... I WENT BACK TO THE MANSION. I HAVE SECURITY FOOTAGE. I KNOW MYSTERIO MADE YOU THINK YOU WERE FIGHTING SOMEONE ELSE.
GUY EVEN MONOLOGUED ABOUT IT.
SPENT A COUPLE YEARS TRYING TO FIND THAT BASTARD MYSELF, BUT TURNS OUT RED SKULL TOOK CARE OF HIM. KILLED HIM A FEW DAYS AFTER WHAT HE DID.
I CAN'T IMAGINE THE GUILT YOU MUST BE CARRYING AROUND BECAUSE OF IT.
JUST WANTED TO LET YOU KNOW THAT I KNEW THE TRUTH.
APPRECIATE IT.
AFTER THAT, I TOOK TO GROUND AND CAME BACK HERE.
KNEW THERE WAS NO WAY I COULD FIGHT THE VILLAINS ON MY OWN, SO FIGURED I'D WORK TO BUILD A PLACE WHERE PEOPLE WOULD BE SAFE.
SOMEWHERE DEFENSIBLE, IF NEED BE, BUT FAR ENOUGH OFF THE GRID THAT WE DON'T GOT TO WORRY ABOUT PEOPLE TRIPPING ONTO US.
WE'VE HAD A GOOD FIFTY YEARS OF RELATIVE PEACE.

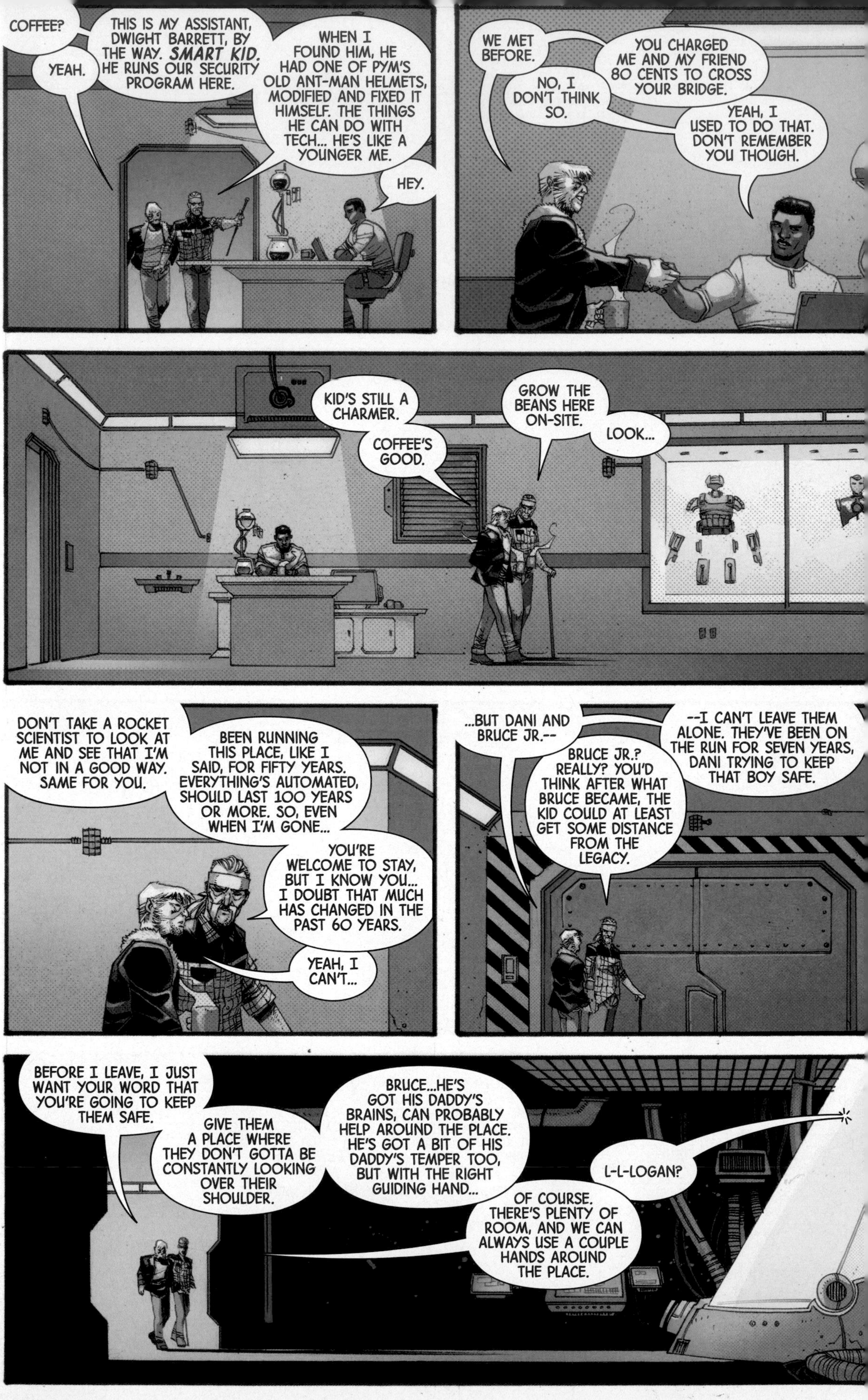
COFFEE?
THIS IS MY ASSISTANT, DWIGHT BARRETT, BY THE WAY. SMART KID. HE RUNS OUR SECURITY PROGRAM HERE.
YEAH.
WHEN I FOUND HIM, HE HAD ONE OF PYM'S OLD ANT-MAN HELMETS, MODIFIED AND FIXED IT HIMSELF. THE THINGS HE CAN DO WITH TECH... HE'S LIKE A YOUNGER ME.
HEY.
WE MET BEFORE.
NO, I DON'T THINK SO.
YOU CHARGED ME AND MY FRIEND 80 CENTS TO CROSS YOUR BRIDGE.
YEAH, I USED TO DO THAT. DON'T REMEMBER YOU THOUGH.
KID'S STILL A CHARMER.
COFFEE'S GOOD.
GROW THE BEANS HERE ON-SITE.
LOOK...
DON'T TAKE A ROCKET SCIENTIST TO LOOK AT ME AND SEE THAT I'M NOT IN A GOOD WAY. SAME FOR YOU.
BEEN RUNNING THIS PLACE, LIKE I SAID, FOR FIFTY YEARS. EVERYTHING'S AUTOMATED, SHOULD LAST 100 YEARS OR MORE. SO, EVEN WHEN I'M GONE...
YOU'RE WELCOME TO STAY, BUT I KNOW YOU... I DOUBT THAT MUCH HAS CHANGED IN THE PAST 60 YEARS.
YEAH, I CAN'T...
...BUT DANI AND BRUCE JR.--
--I CAN'T LEAVE THEM ALONE. THEY'VE BEEN ON THE RUN FOR SEVEN YEARS, DANI TRYING TO KEEP THAT BOY SAFE.
BRUCE JR.? REALLY? YOU'D THINK AFTER WHAT BRUCE BECAME, THE KID COULD AT LEAST GET SOME DISTANCE FROM THE LEGACY.
BEFORE I LEAVE, I JUST WANT YOUR WORD THAT YOU'RE GOING TO KEEP THEM SAFE.
GIVE THEM A PLACE WHERE THEY DON'T GOTTA BE CONSTANTLY LOOKING OVER THEIR SHOULDER.
BRUCE...HE'S GOT HIS DADDY'S BRAINS, CAN PROBABLY HELP AROUND THE PLACE. HE'S GOT A BIT OF HIS DADDY'S TEMPER TOO, BUT WITH THE RIGHT GUIDING HAND...
L-L-LOGAN?
OF COURSE. THERE'S PLENTY OF ROOM, AND WE CAN ALWAYS USE A COUPLE HANDS AROUND THE PLACE.

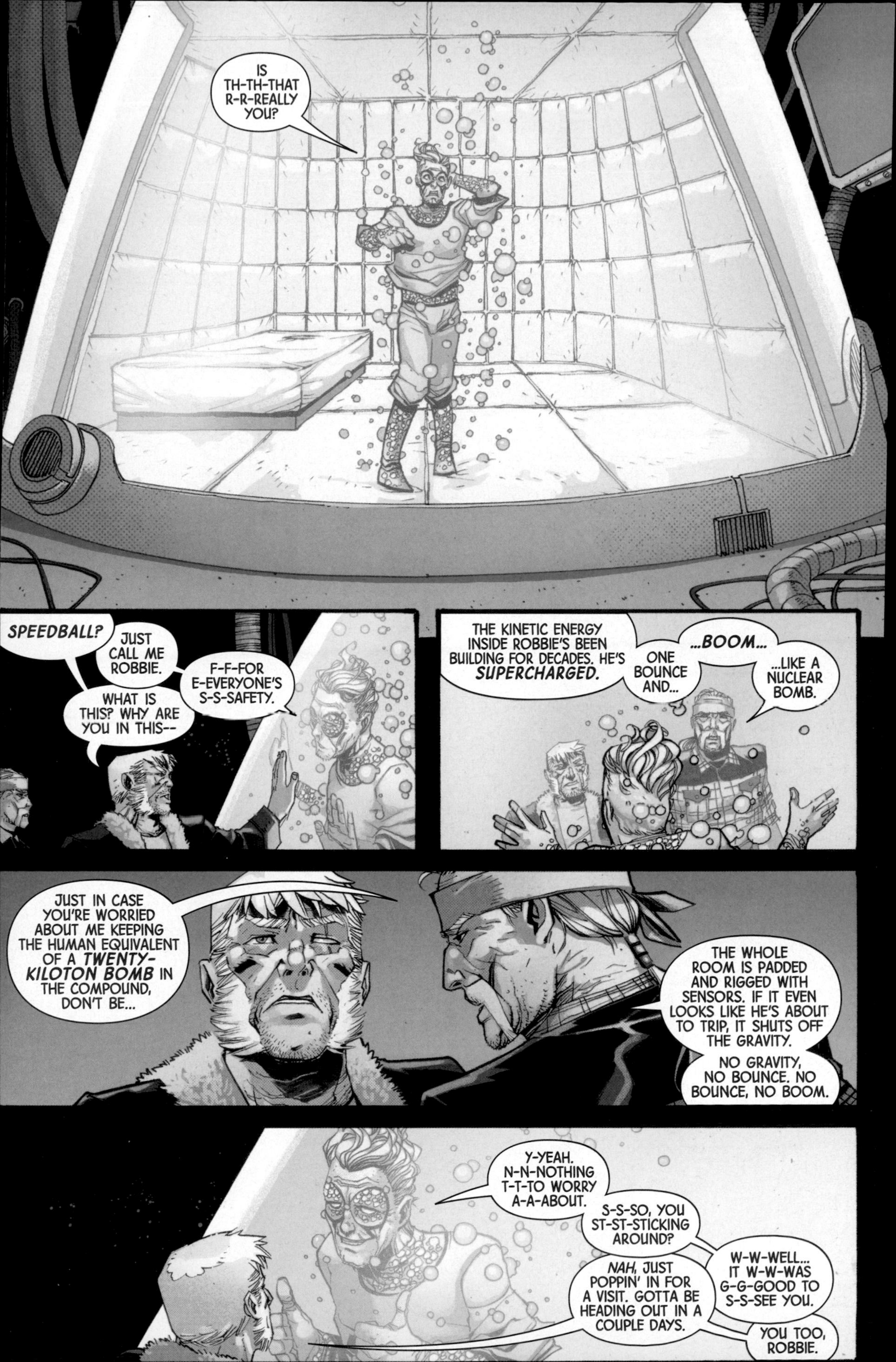
IS TH-TH-THAT R-R-REALLY YOU?
SPEEDBALL?
JUST CALL ME ROBBIE.
WHAT IS THIS? WHY ARE YOU IN THIS--
F-F-FOR E-EVERYONE'S S-S-SAFETY.
THE KINETIC ENERGY INSIDE ROBBIE'S BEEN BUILDING FOR DECADES. HE'S SUPERCHARGED.
ONE BOUNCE AND...
...BOOM...
...LIKE A NUCLEAR BOMB.
JUST IN CASE YOU'RE WORRIED ABOUT ME KEEPING THE HUMAN EQUIVALENT OF A TWENTY-KILOTON BOMB IN THE COMPOUND, DON'T BE...
THE WHOLE ROOM IS PADDED AND RIGGED WITH SENSORS. IF IT EVEN LOOKS LIKE HE'S ABOUT TO TRIP, IT SHUTS OFF THE GRAVITY.
NO GRAVITY, NO BOUNCE. NO BOUNCE, NO BOOM.
Y-YEAH. N-N-NOTHING T-T-TO WORRY A-A-ABOUT.
S-S-SO, YOU ST-ST-STICKING AROUND?
NAH, JUST POPPIN' IN FOR A VISIT. GOTTA BE HEADING OUT IN A COUPLE DAYS.
W-W-WELL... IT W-W-WAS G-G-GOOD TO S-S-SEE YOU.
YOU TOO, ROBBIE.

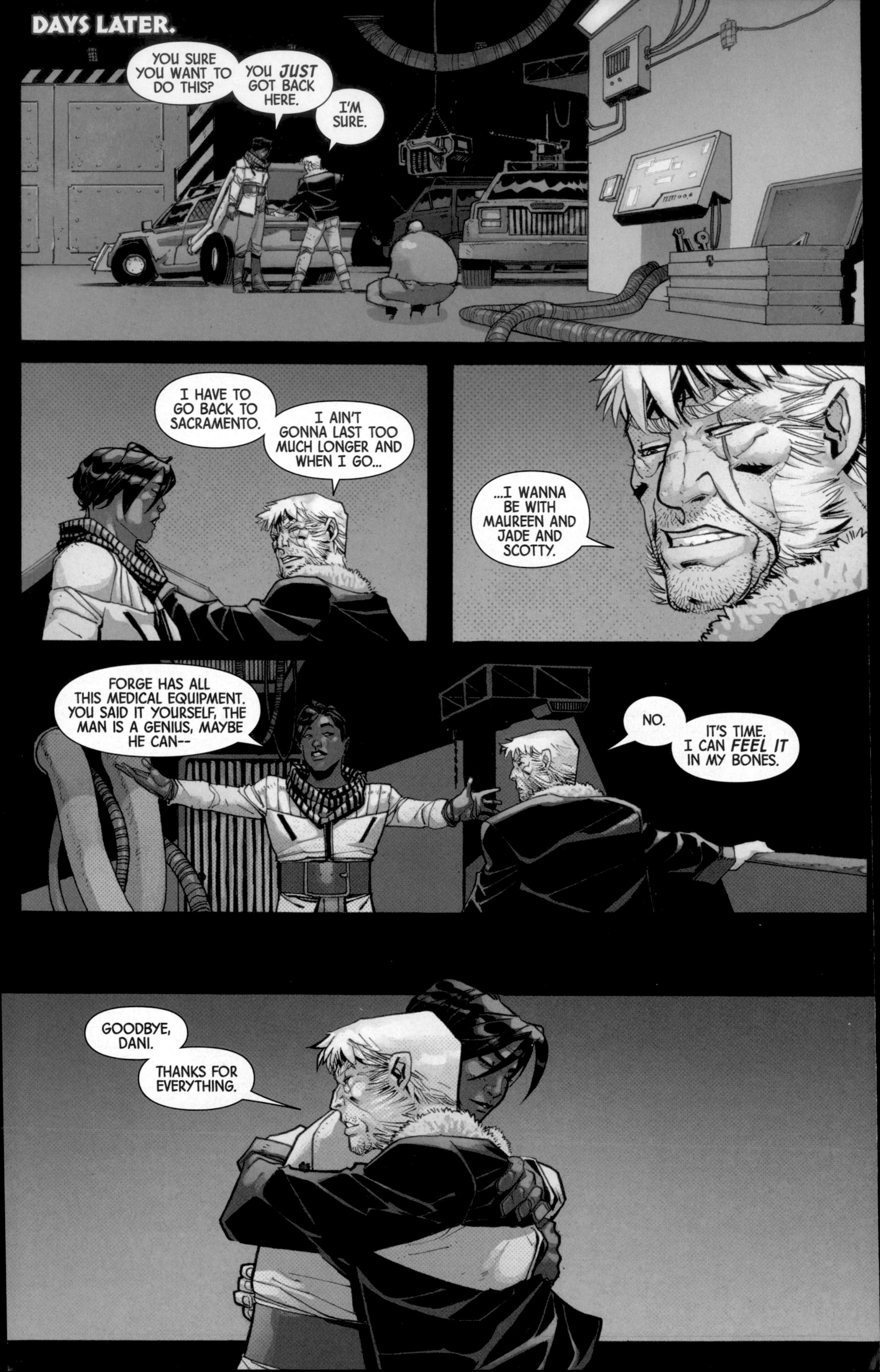
DAYS LATER.
YOU SURE YOU WANT TO DO THIS?
YOU JUST GOT BACK HERE.
I'M SURE.
I HAVE TO GO BACK TO SACRAMENTO.
I AIN'T GONNA LAST TOO MUCH LONGER AND WHEN I GO...
...I WANNA BE WITH MAUREEN AND JADE AND SCOTTY.
FORGE HAS ALL THIS MEDICAL EQUIPMENT. YOU SAID IT YOURSELF, THE MAN IS A GENIUS, MAYBE HE CAN--
NO.
IT'S TIME. I CAN FEEL IT IN MY BONES.
GOODBYE, DANI.
THANKS FOR EVERYTHING.

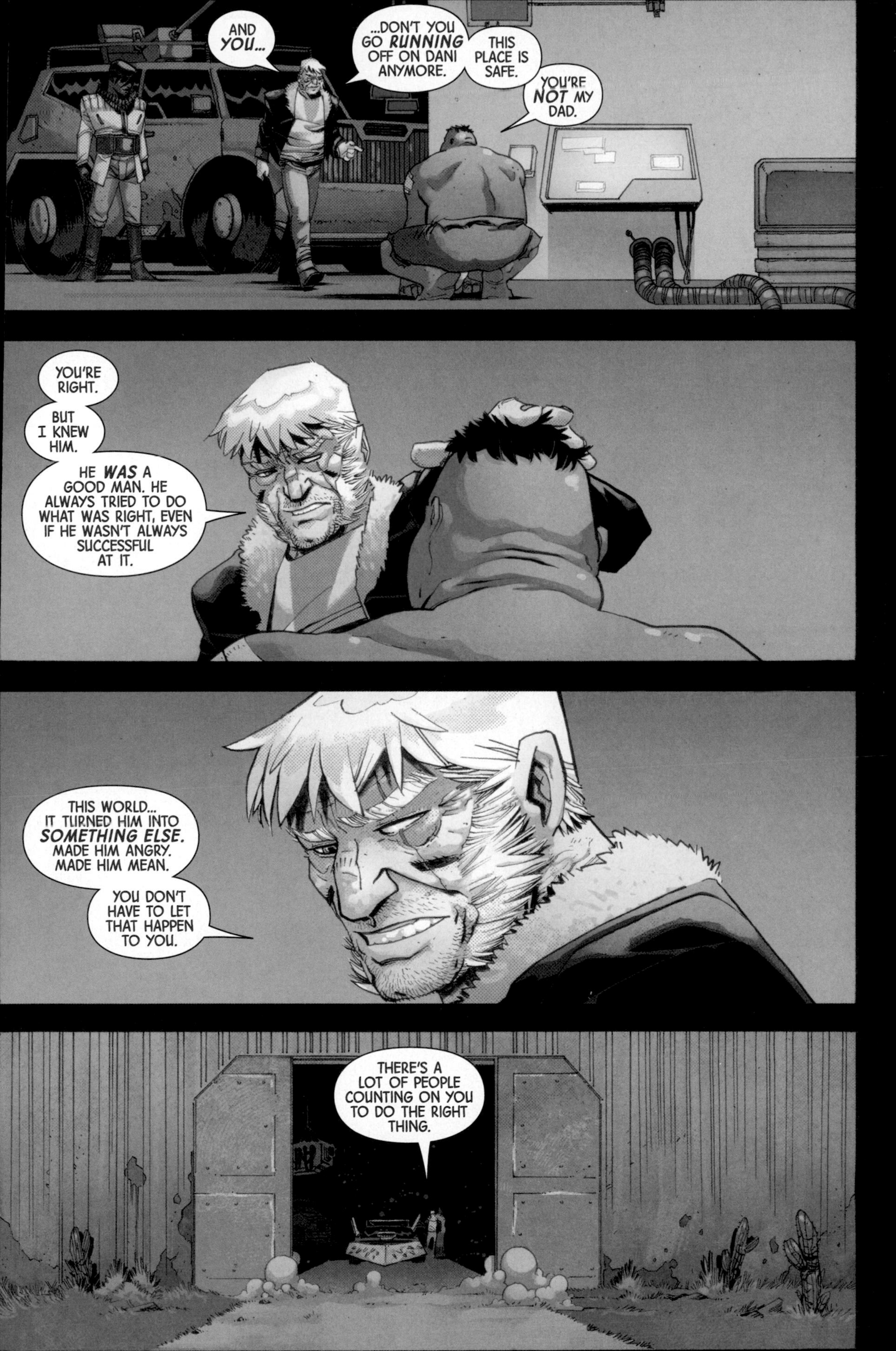
AND YOU...
...DON'T YOU GO RUNNING OFF ON DANI ANYMORE.
THIS PLACE IS SAFE.
YOU'RE NOT MY DAD.
YOU'RE RIGHT.
BUT I KNEW HIM.
HE WAS A GOOD MAN. HE ALWAYS TRIED TO DO WHAT WAS RIGHT, EVEN IF HE WASN'T ALWAYS SUCCESSFUL AT IT.
THIS WORLD... IT TURNED HIM INTO SOMETHING ELSE. MADE HIM ANGRY. MADE HIM MEAN.
YOU DON'T HAVE TO LET THAT HAPPEN TO YOU.
THERE'S A LOT OF PEOPLE COUNTING ON YOU TO DO THE RIGHT THING.

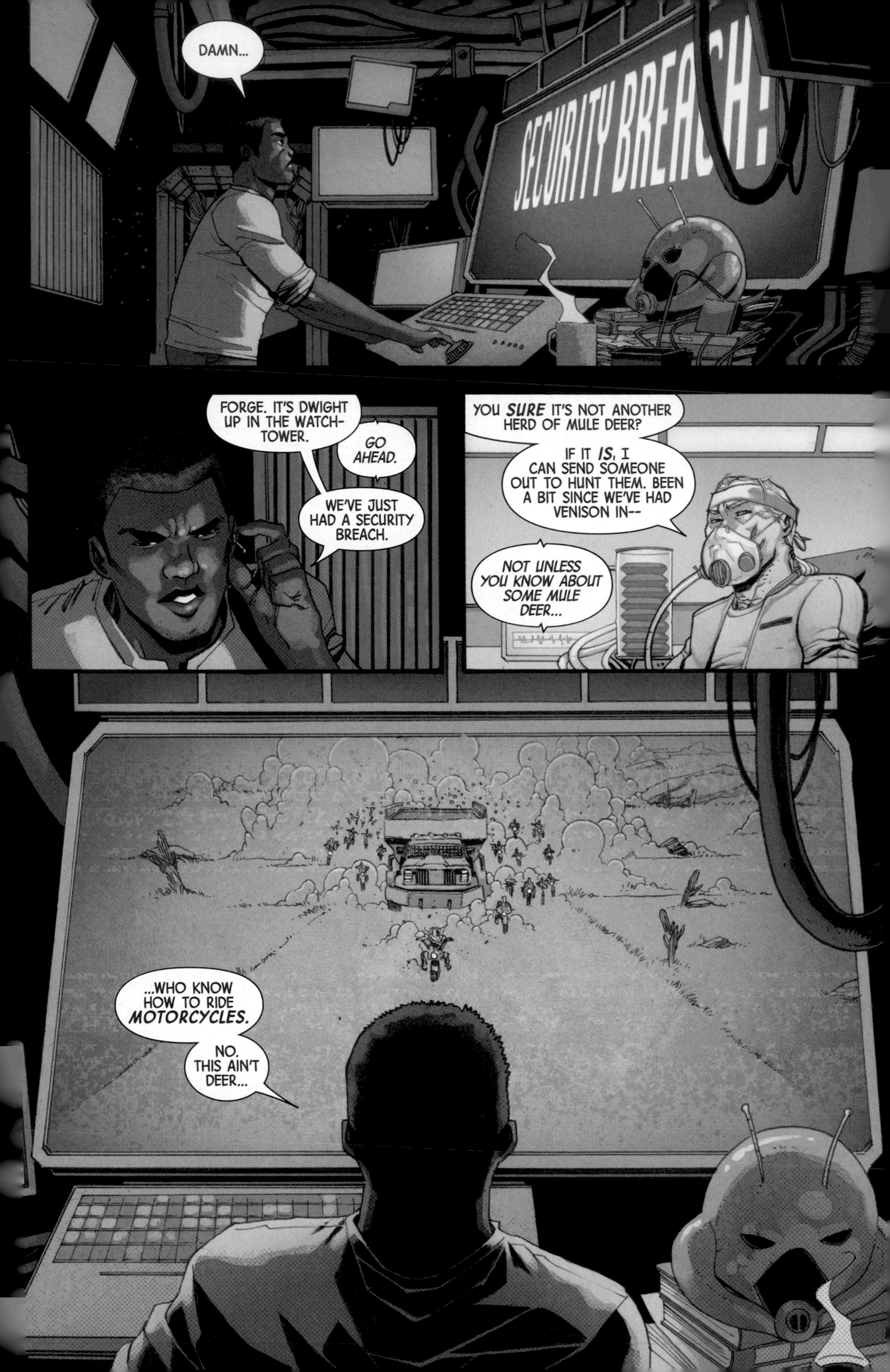
DAMN...
SECURITY BREACH!
FORGE. IT'S DWIGHT UP IN THE WATCH-TOWER.
GO AHEAD.
WE'VE JUST HAD A SECURITY BREACH.
YOU SURE IT'S NOT ANOTHER HERD OF MULE DEER?
IF IT IS, I CAN SEND SOMEONE OUT TO HUNT THEM. BEEN A BIT SINCE WE'VE HAD VENISON IN--
NOT UNLESS YOU KNOW ABOUT SOME MULE DEER...
...WHO KNOW HOW TO RIDE MOTORCYCLES.
NO. THIS AIN'T DEER...

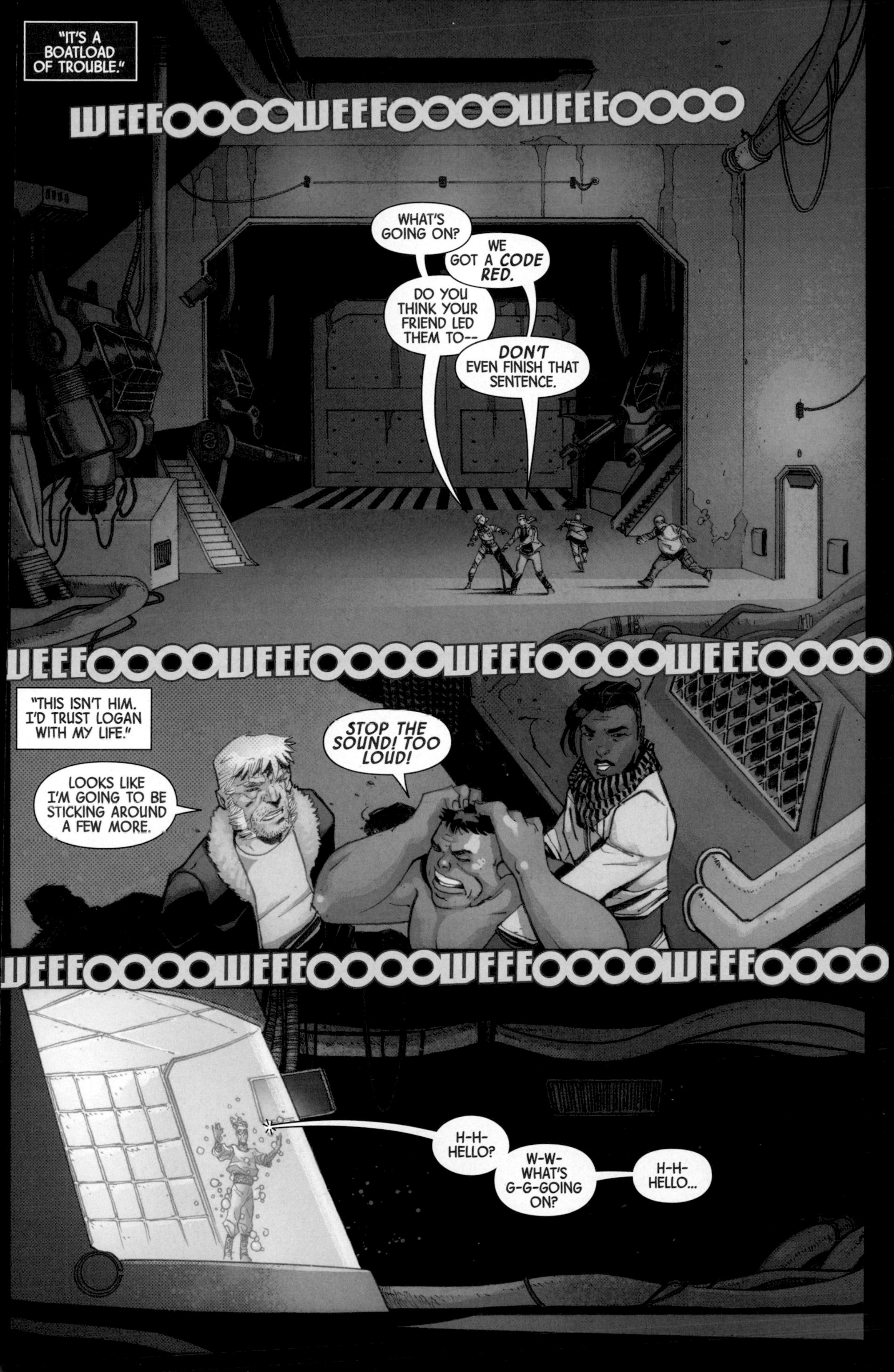
"IT'S A BOATLOAD OF TROUBLE."
WEEEOOOOWEEEOOOOWEEEOOOO
WHAT'S GOING ON?
WE GOT A CODE RED.
DO YOU THINK YOUR FRIEND LED THEM TO--
DON'T EVEN FINISH THAT SENTENCE.
WEEEOOOOWEEEOOOOWEEEOOOOWEEEOOOO
"THIS ISN'T HIM. I'D TRUST LOGAN WITH MY LIFE."
LOOKS LIKE I'M GOING TO BE STICKING AROUND A FEW MORE.
STOP THE SOUND! TOO LOUD!
WEEEOOOOWEEEOOOOWEEEOOOOWEEEOOOO
H-H-HELLO?
W-W-WHAT'S G-G-GOING ON?
H-H-HELLO...

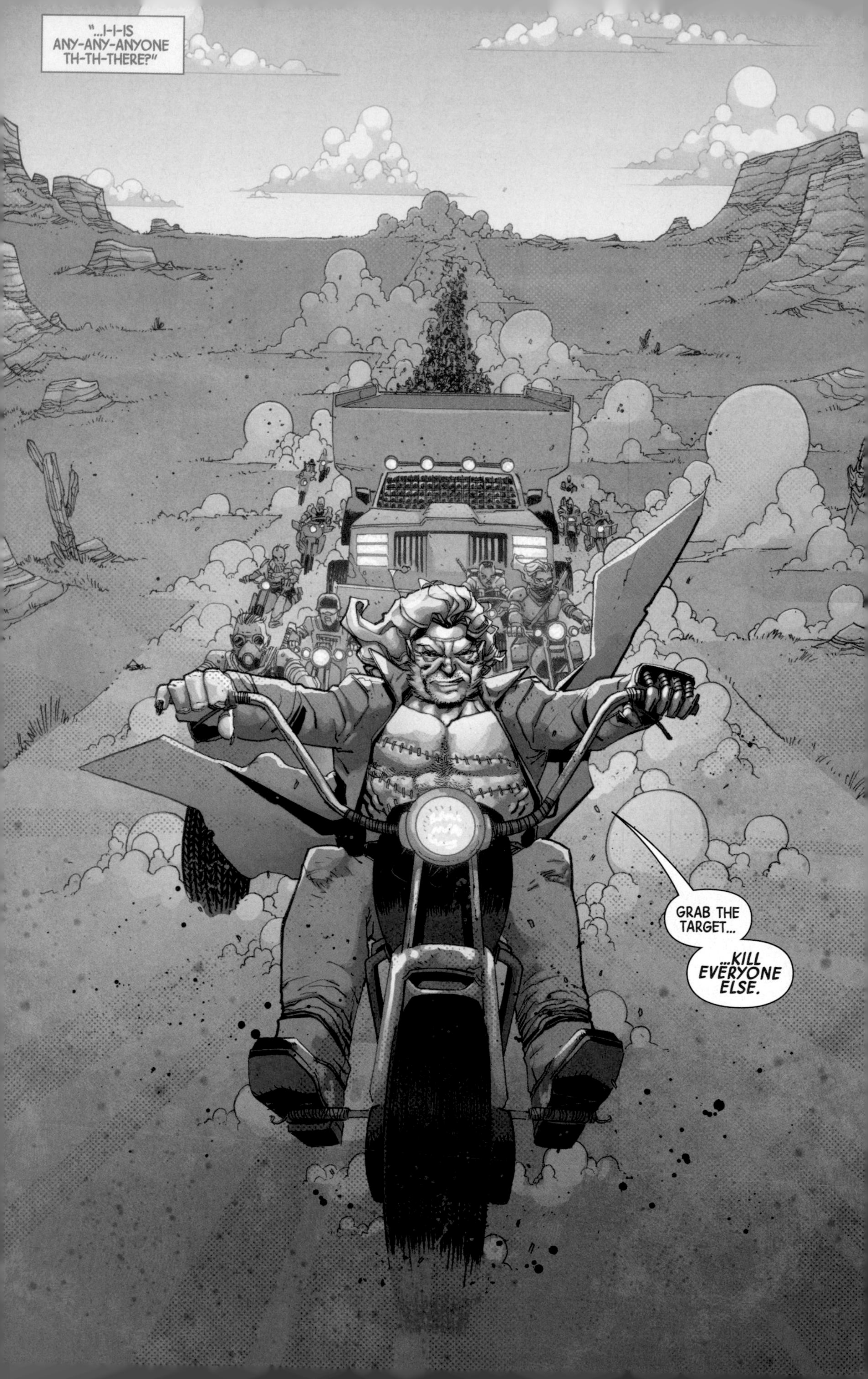
"...I-I-IS ANY-ANY-ANYONE TH-TH-THERE?"
GRAB THE TARGET...
...KILL EVERYONE ELSE.

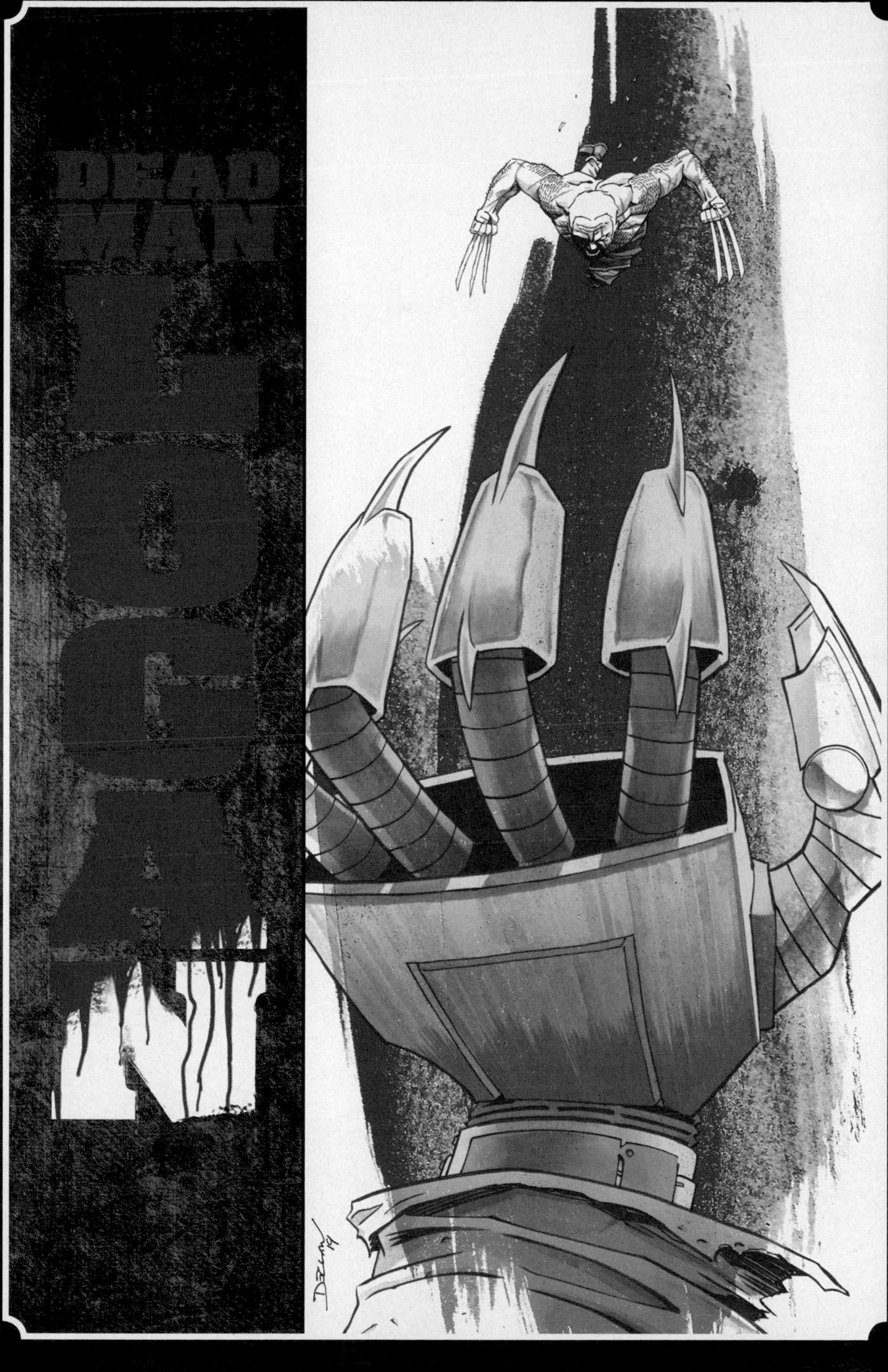
DEAD MAN
LOGAN

10

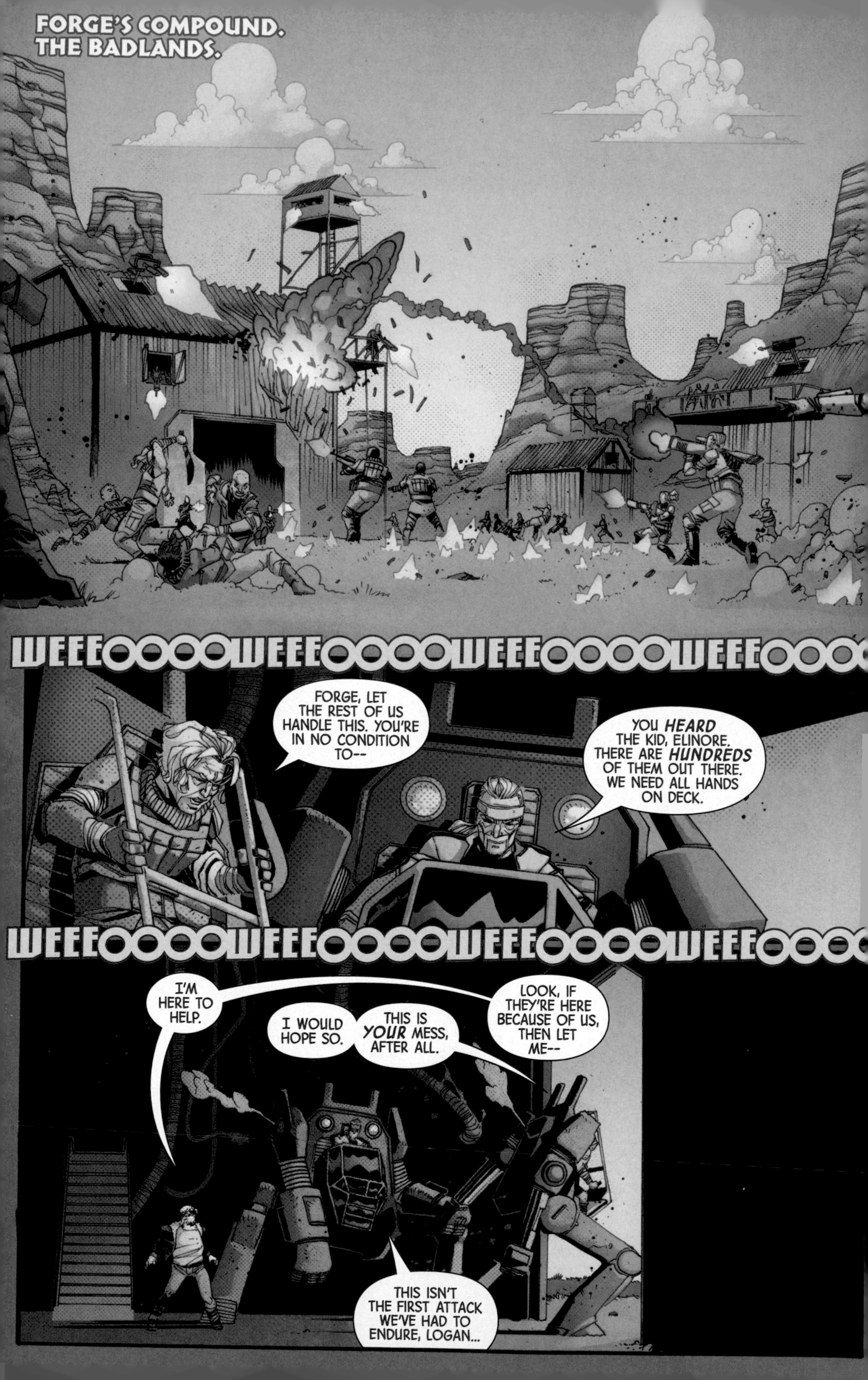
FORGE'S COMPOUND. THE BADLANDS.
WEEEOOOOWEEEOOOOWEEEOOOOWEEEOOOO
FORGE, LET THE REST OF US HANDLE THIS. YOU'RE IN NO CONDITION TO--
YOU HEARD THE KID, ELINORE. THERE ARE HUNDREDS OF THEM OUT THERE. WE NEED ALL HANDS ON DECK.
WEEEOOOOWEEEOOOOWEEEOOOOWEEEOOOO
I'M HERE TO HELP.
I WOULD HOPE SO.
THIS IS YOUR MESS, AFTER ALL.
LOOK, IF THEY'RE HERE BECAUSE OF US, THEN LET ME--
THIS ISN'T THE FIRST ATTACK WE'VE HAD TO ENDURE, LOGAN...

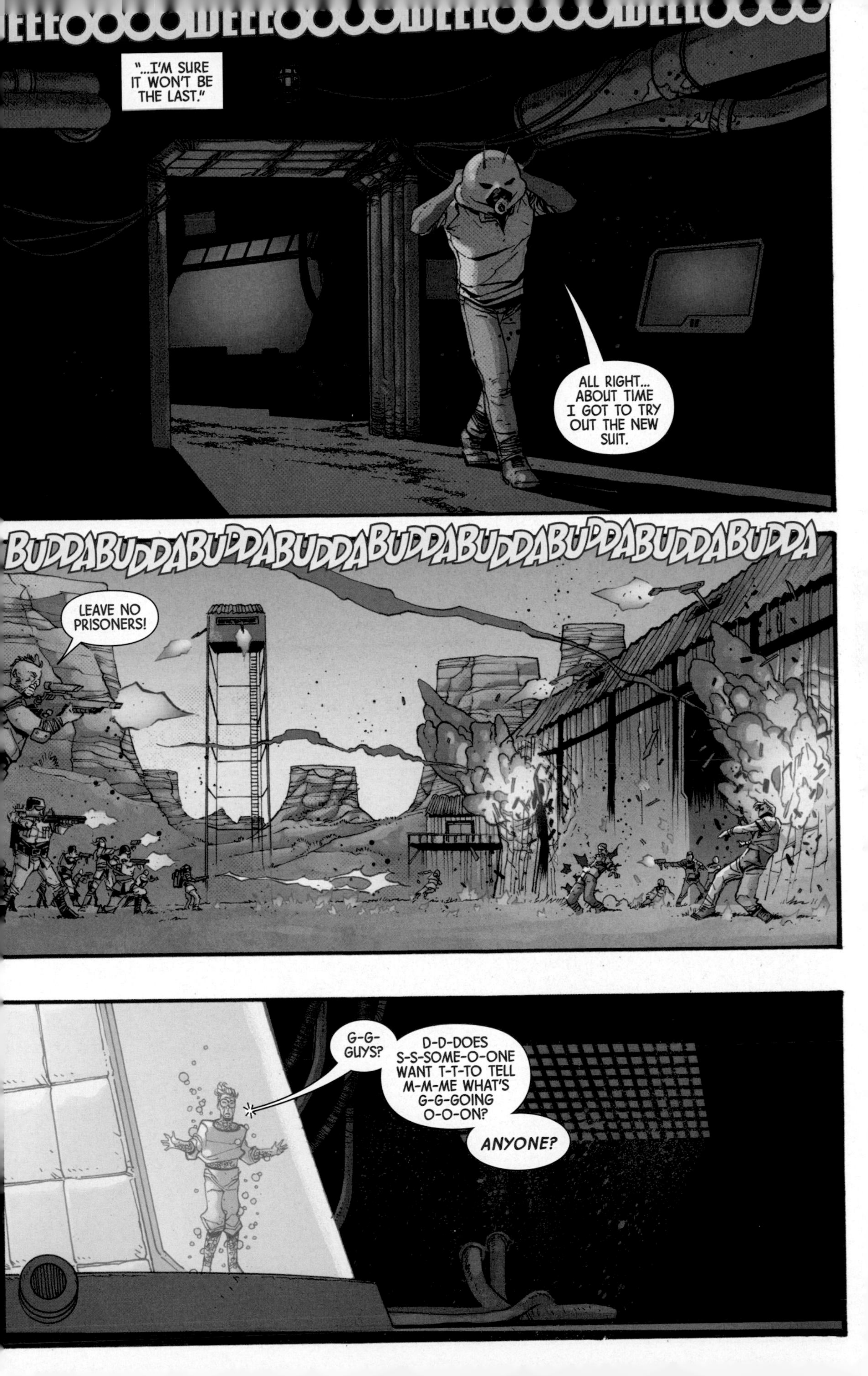
WEEEOOOOOWEEEOOOOOWEEEOOOOOWEEEOOOO
"...I'M SURE IT WON'T BE THE LAST."
ALL RIGHT... ABOUT TIME I GOT TO TRY OUT THE NEW SUIT.
BUDDABUDDABUDDABUDDABUDDABUDDABUDDABUDDABUDDABUDDA
LEAVE NO PRISONERS!
G-G-GUYS?
D-D-DOES S-S-SOME-O-ONE WANT T-T-TO TELL M-M-ME WHAT'S G-G-GOING O-O-ON?
ANYONE?

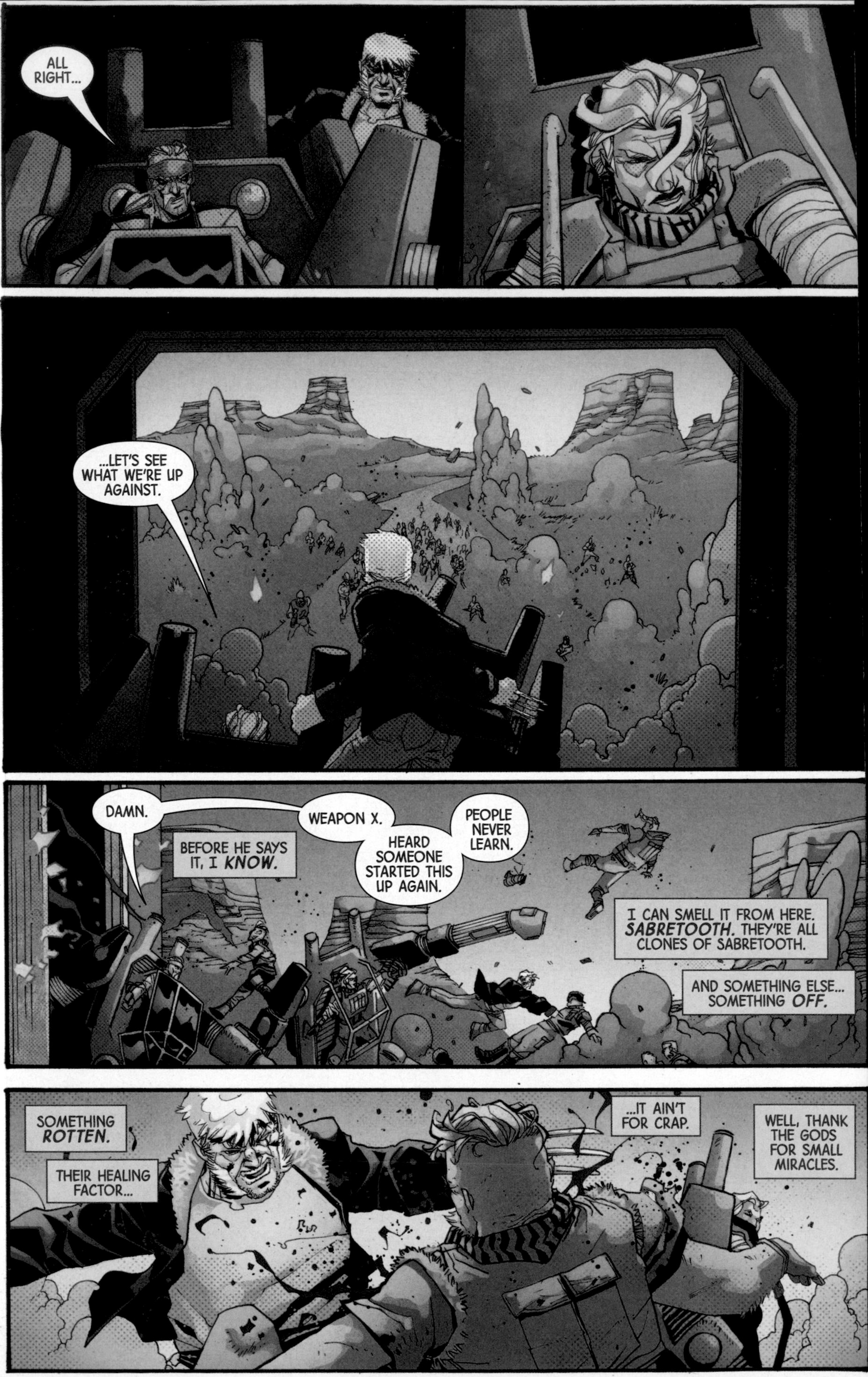
ALL RIGHT...
...LET'S SEE WHAT WE'RE UP AGAINST.
DAMN.
BEFORE HE SAYS IT, I *KNOW.*
WEAPON X.
HEARD SOMEONE STARTED THIS UP AGAIN.
PEOPLE NEVER LEARN.
I CAN SMELL IT FROM HERE. ***SABRETOOTH.*** THEY'RE ALL CLONES OF SABRETOOTH.
AND SOMETHING ELSE... SOMETHING ***OFF.***
SOMETHING ***ROTTEN.***
THEIR HEALING FACTOR...
...IT AIN'T FOR CRAP.
WELL, THANK THE GODS FOR SMALL MIRACLES.

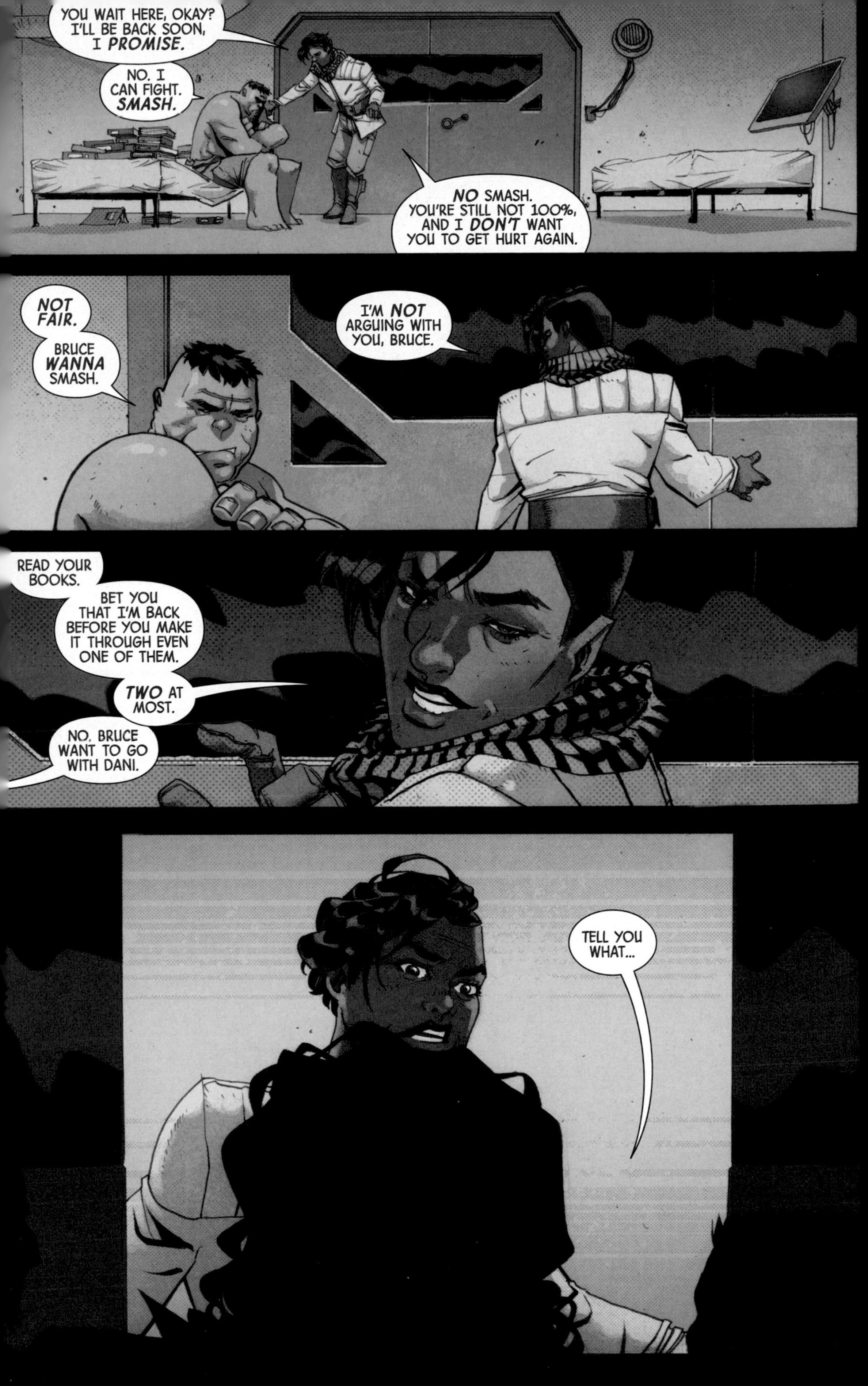
YOU WAIT HERE, OKAY? I'LL BE BACK SOON, I PROMISE.
NO. I CAN FIGHT. SMASH.
NO SMASH. YOU'RE STILL NOT 100%, AND I DON'T WANT YOU TO GET HURT AGAIN.
NOT FAIR.
BRUCE WANNA SMASH.
I'M NOT ARGUING WITH YOU, BRUCE.
READ YOUR BOOKS.
BET YOU THAT I'M BACK BEFORE YOU MAKE IT THROUGH EVEN ONE OF THEM.
TWO AT MOST.
NO, BRUCE WANT TO GO WITH DANI.
TELL YOU WHAT...

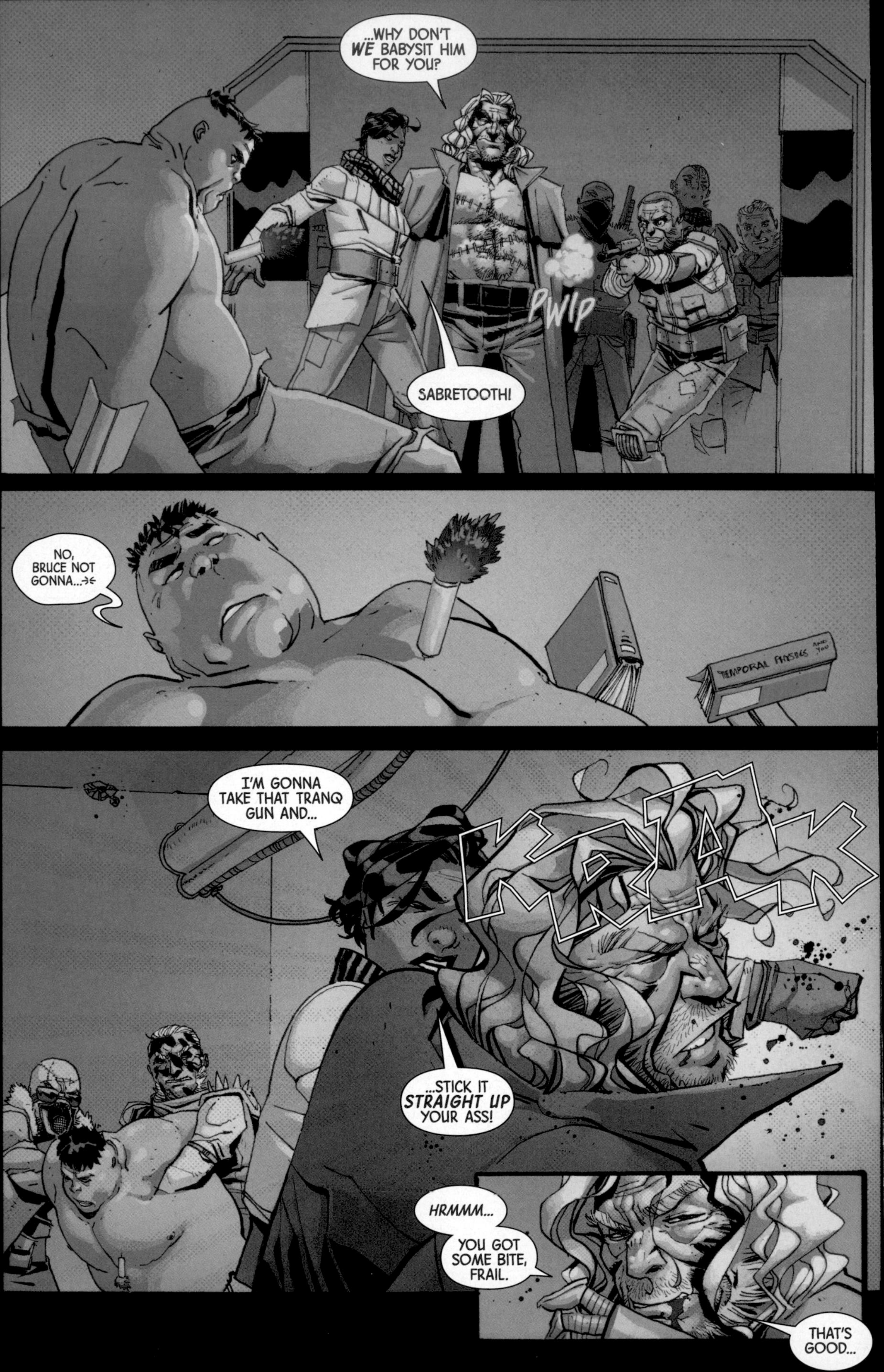
...WHY DON'T *WE* BABYSIT HIM FOR YOU?
PWIP
SABRETOOTH!
NO, BRUCE NOT GONNA...
TEMPORAL PHYSICS AND YOU
I'M GONNA TAKE THAT TRANQ GUN AND...
...STICK IT *STRAIGHT UP* YOUR ASS!
HRMMM...
YOU GOT SOME BITE, FRAIL.
THAT'S GOOD...

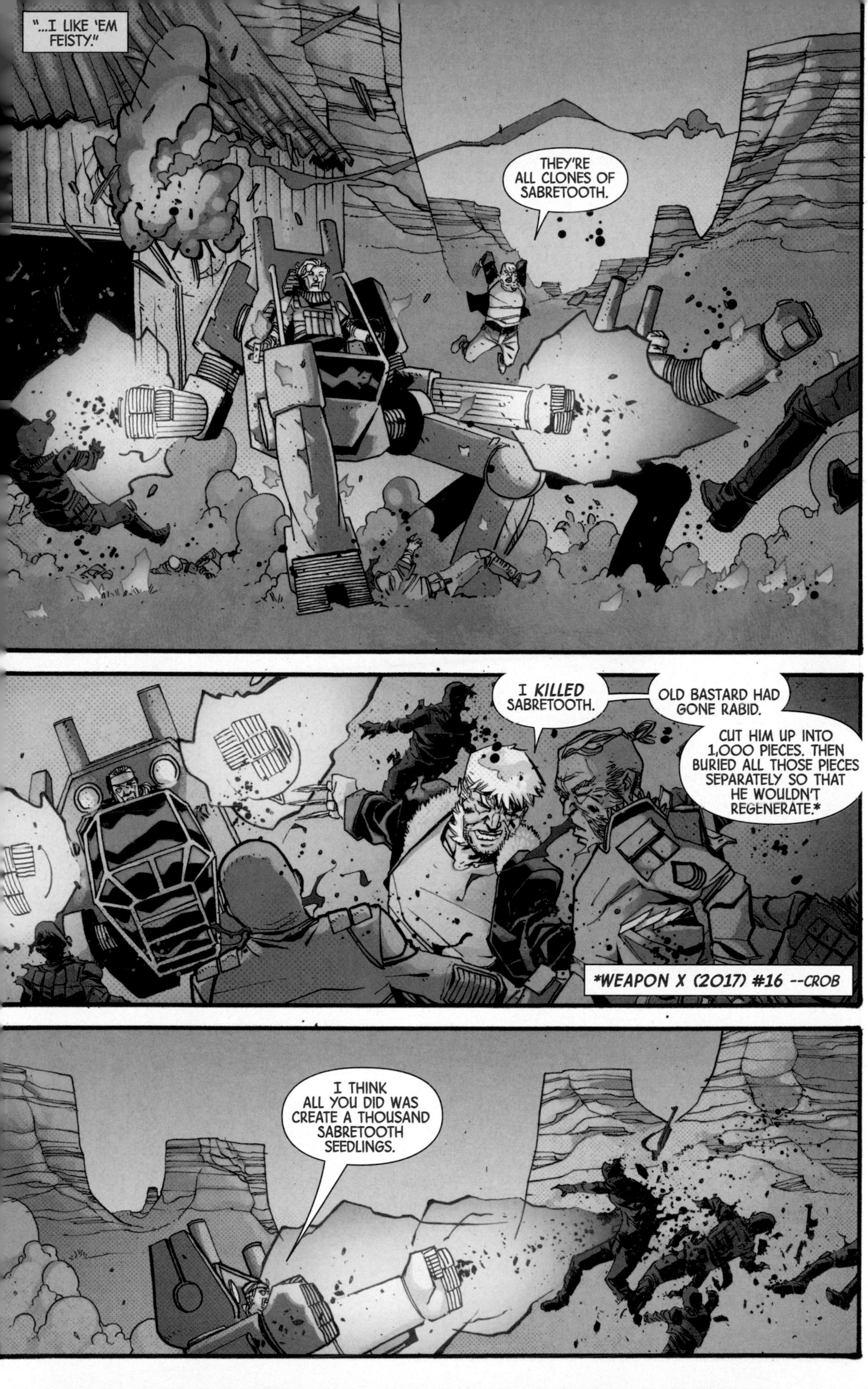
"...I LIKE 'EM FEISTY."
THEY'RE ALL CLONES OF SABRETOOTH.
I KILLED SABRETOOTH.
OLD BASTARD HAD GONE RABID.
CUT HIM UP INTO 1,000 PIECES. THEN BURIED ALL THOSE PIECES SEPARATELY SO THAT HE WOULDN'T REGENERATE.*
*WEAPON X (2017) #16 --CROB
I THINK ALL YOU DID WAS CREATE A THOUSAND SABRETOOTH SEEDLINGS.

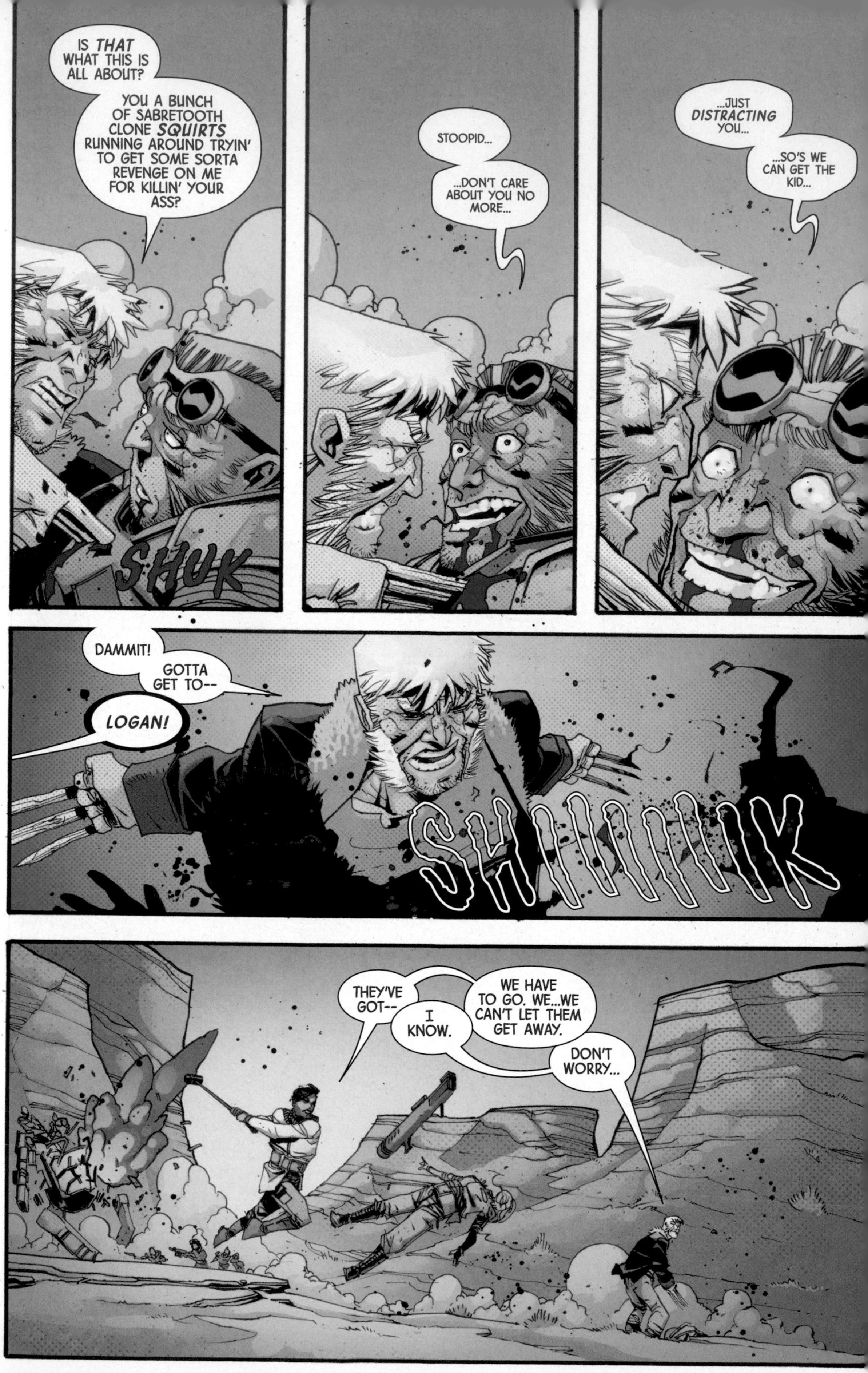

IS THAT WHAT THIS IS ALL ABOUT?
YOU A BUNCH OF SABRETOOTH CLONE SQUIRTS RUNNING AROUND TRYIN' TO GET SOME SORTA REVENGE ON ME FOR KILLIN' YOUR ASS?
SHUK
STOOPID...
...DON'T CARE ABOUT YOU NO MORE...
...JUST DISTRACTING YOU...
...SO'S WE CAN GET THE KID...
DAMMIT!
GOTTA GET TO--
LOGAN!
SHHHHHK
THEY'VE GOT--
WE HAVE TO GO. WE...WE CAN'T LET THEM GET AWAY.
I KNOW.
DON'T WORRY...

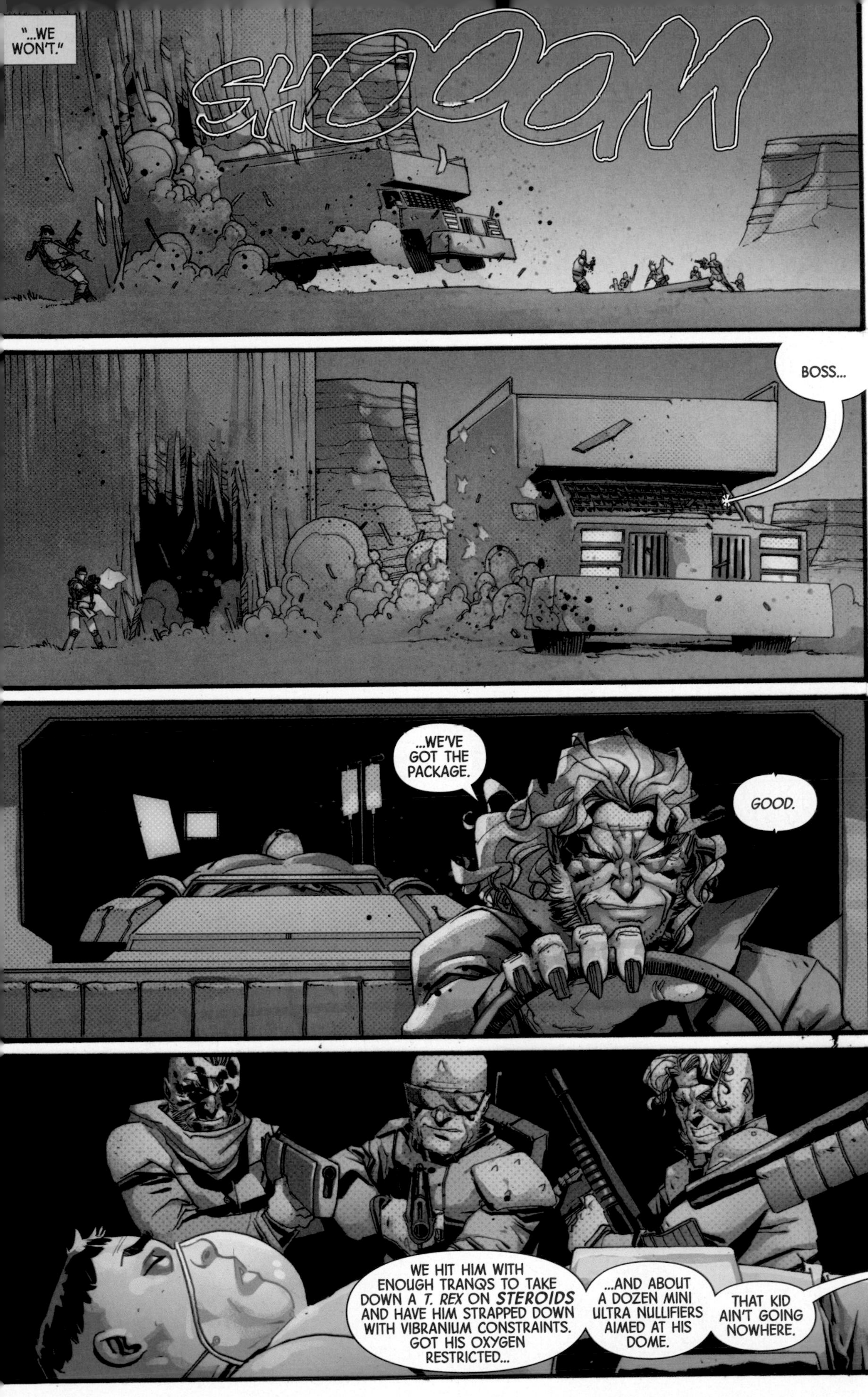
"...WE WON'T."
SHOOOOM
BOSS...
...WE'VE GOT THE PACKAGE.
GOOD.
WE HIT HIM WITH ENOUGH TRANQS TO TAKE DOWN A *T. REX* ON ***STEROIDS*** AND HAVE HIM STRAPPED DOWN WITH VIBRANIUM CONSTRAINTS. GOT HIS OXYGEN RESTRICTED...
...AND ABOUT A DOZEN MINI ULTRA NULLIFIERS AIMED AT HIS DOME.
THAT KID AIN'T GOING NOWHERE.

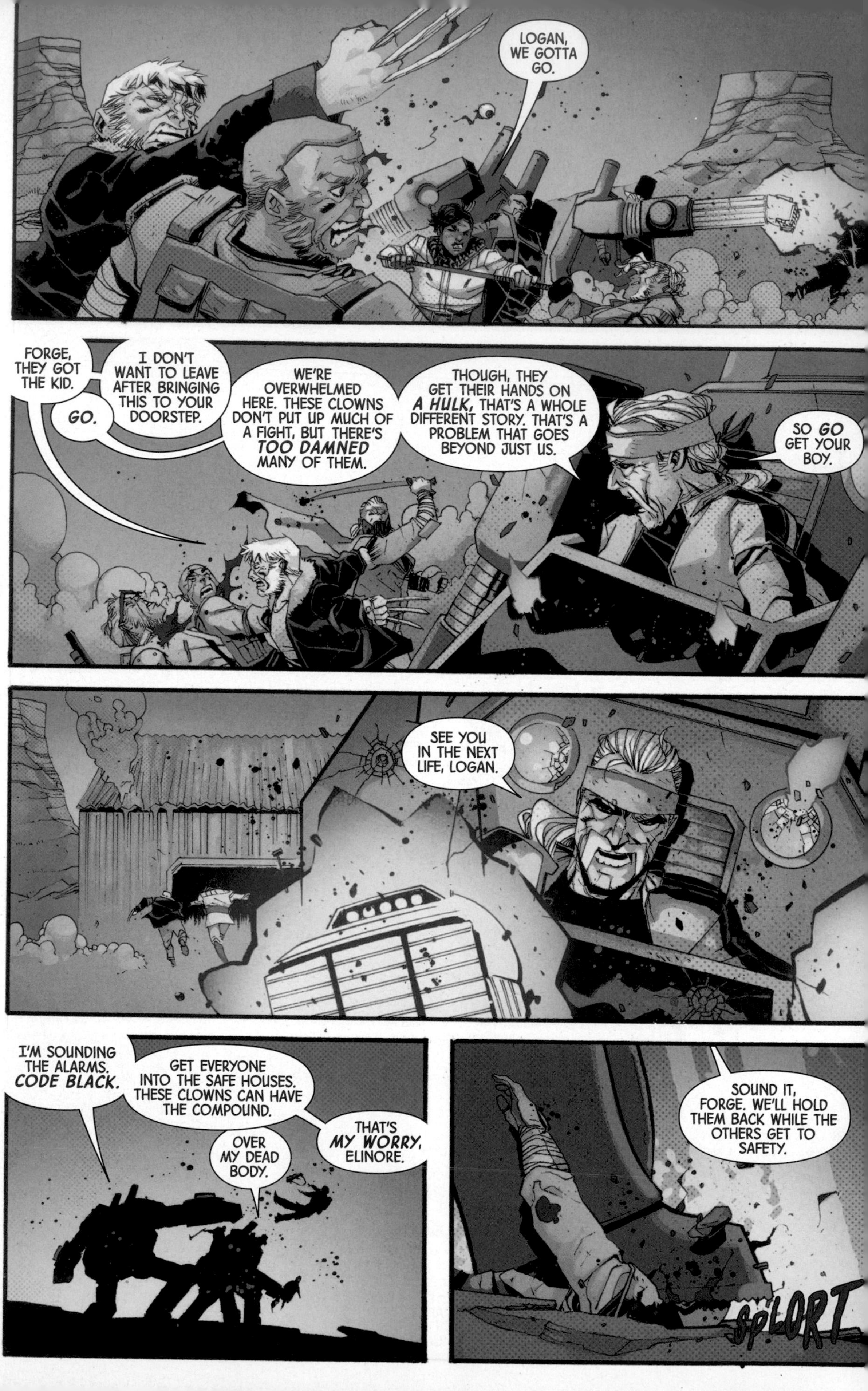

LOGAN, WE GOTTA GO.
FORGE, THEY GOT THE KID.
I DON'T WANT TO LEAVE AFTER BRINGING THIS TO YOUR DOORSTEP.
GO.
WE'RE OVERWHELMED HERE. THESE CLOWNS DON'T PUT UP MUCH OF A FIGHT, BUT THERE'S TOO DAMNED MANY OF THEM.
THOUGH, THEY GET THEIR HANDS ON A HULK, THAT'S A WHOLE DIFFERENT STORY. THAT'S A PROBLEM THAT GOES BEYOND JUST US.
SO GO GET YOUR BOY.
SEE YOU IN THE NEXT LIFE, LOGAN.
I'M SOUNDING THE ALARMS. CODE BLACK.
GET EVERYONE INTO THE SAFE HOUSES. THESE CLOWNS CAN HAVE THE COMPOUND.
OVER MY DEAD BODY.
THAT'S MY WORRY, ELINORE.
SOUND IT, FORGE. WE'LL HOLD THEM BACK WHILE THE OTHERS GET TO SAFETY.
SPLORT

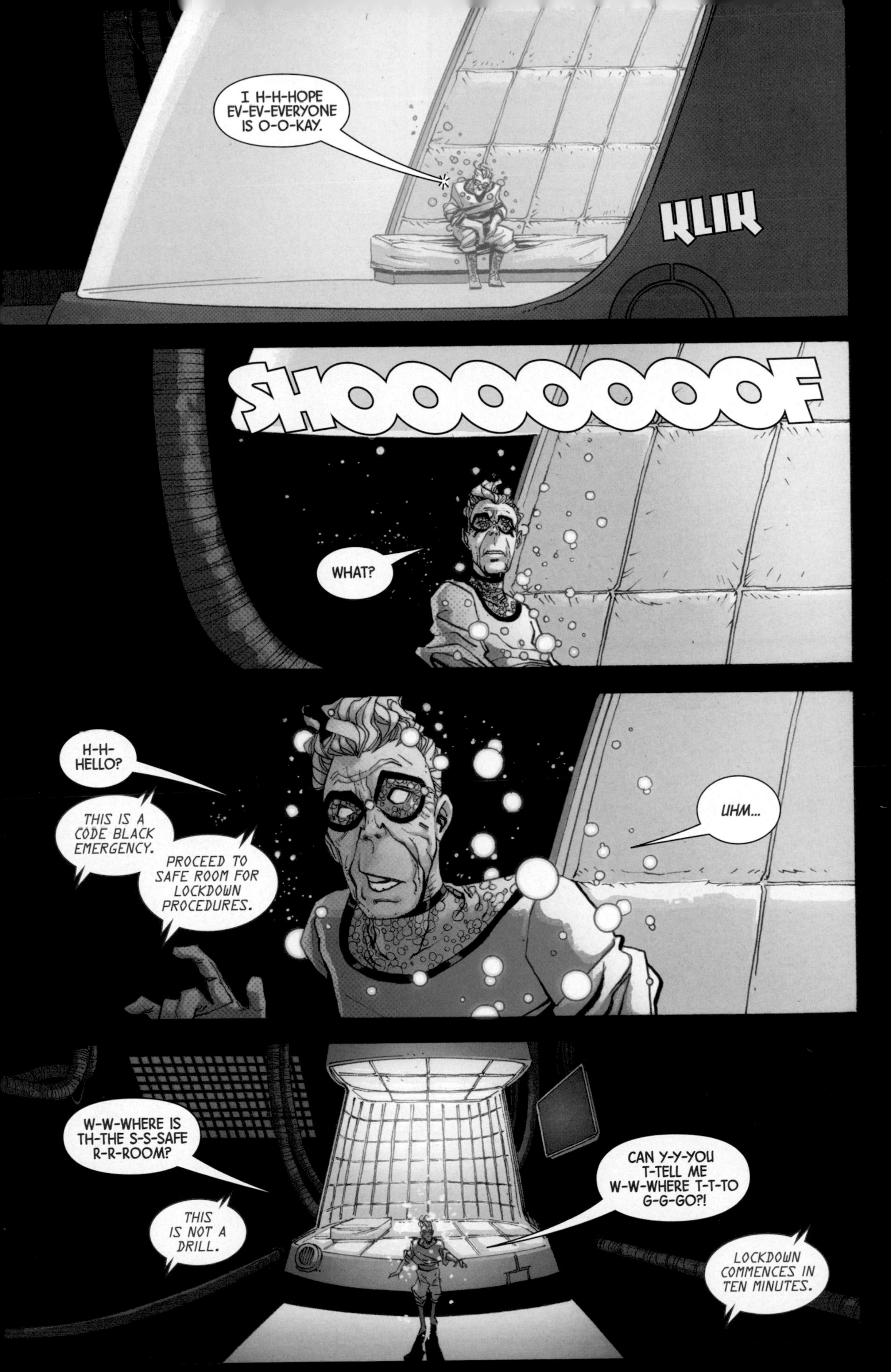
I H-H-HOPE EV-EV-EVERYONE IS O-O-KAY.
KLIK
SHOOOOOOOF
WHAT?
H-H-HELLO?
THIS IS A CODE BLACK EMERGENCY.
PROCEED TO SAFE ROOM FOR LOCKDOWN PROCEDURES.
UHM...
W-W-WHERE IS TH-THE S-S-SAFE R-R-ROOM?
THIS IS NOT A DRILL.
CAN Y-Y-YOU T-TELL ME W-W-WHERE T-T-TO G-G-GO?!
LOCKDOWN COMMENCES IN TEN MINUTES.

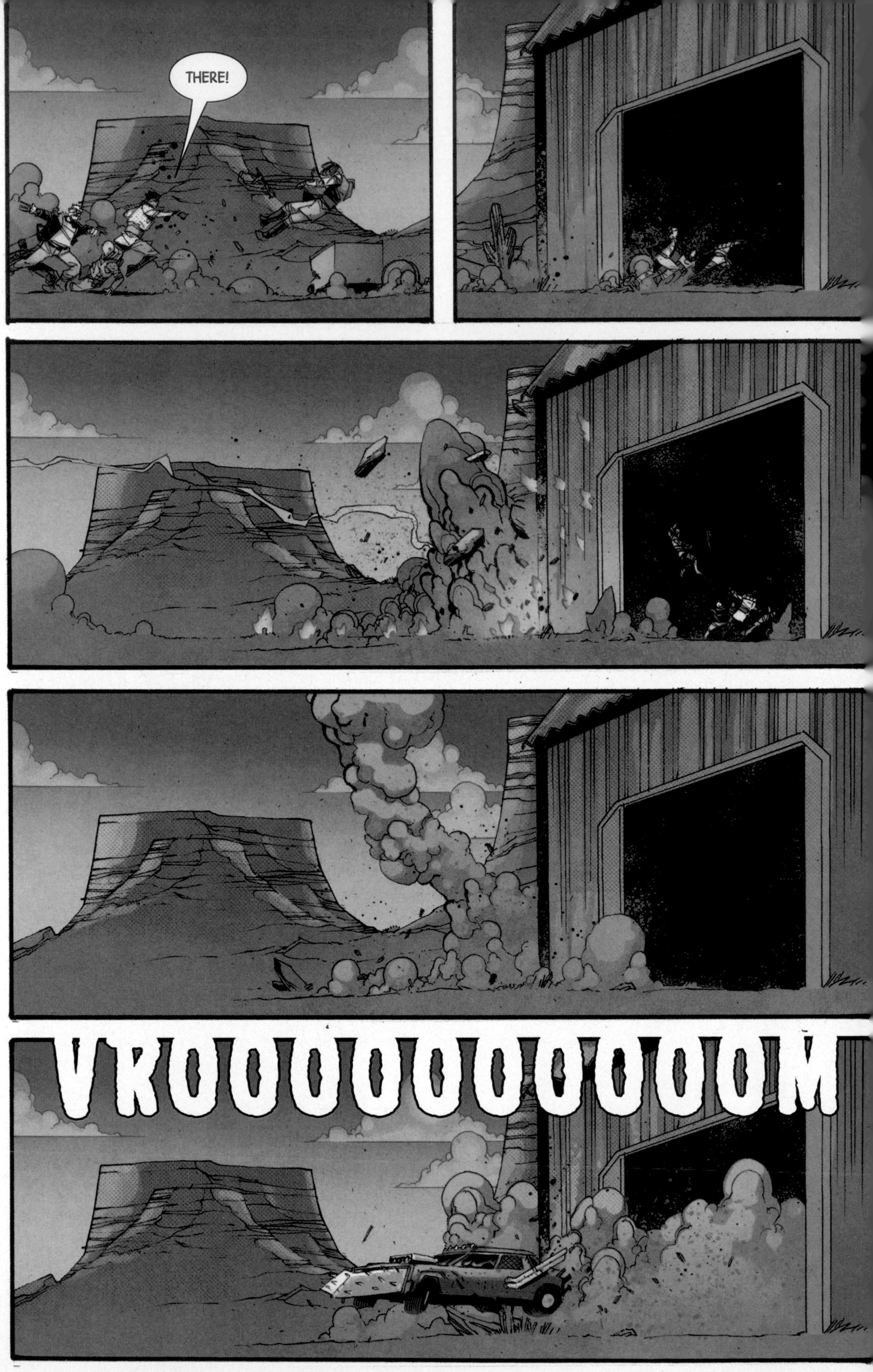
THERE!
VROOOOOOOOOOOM

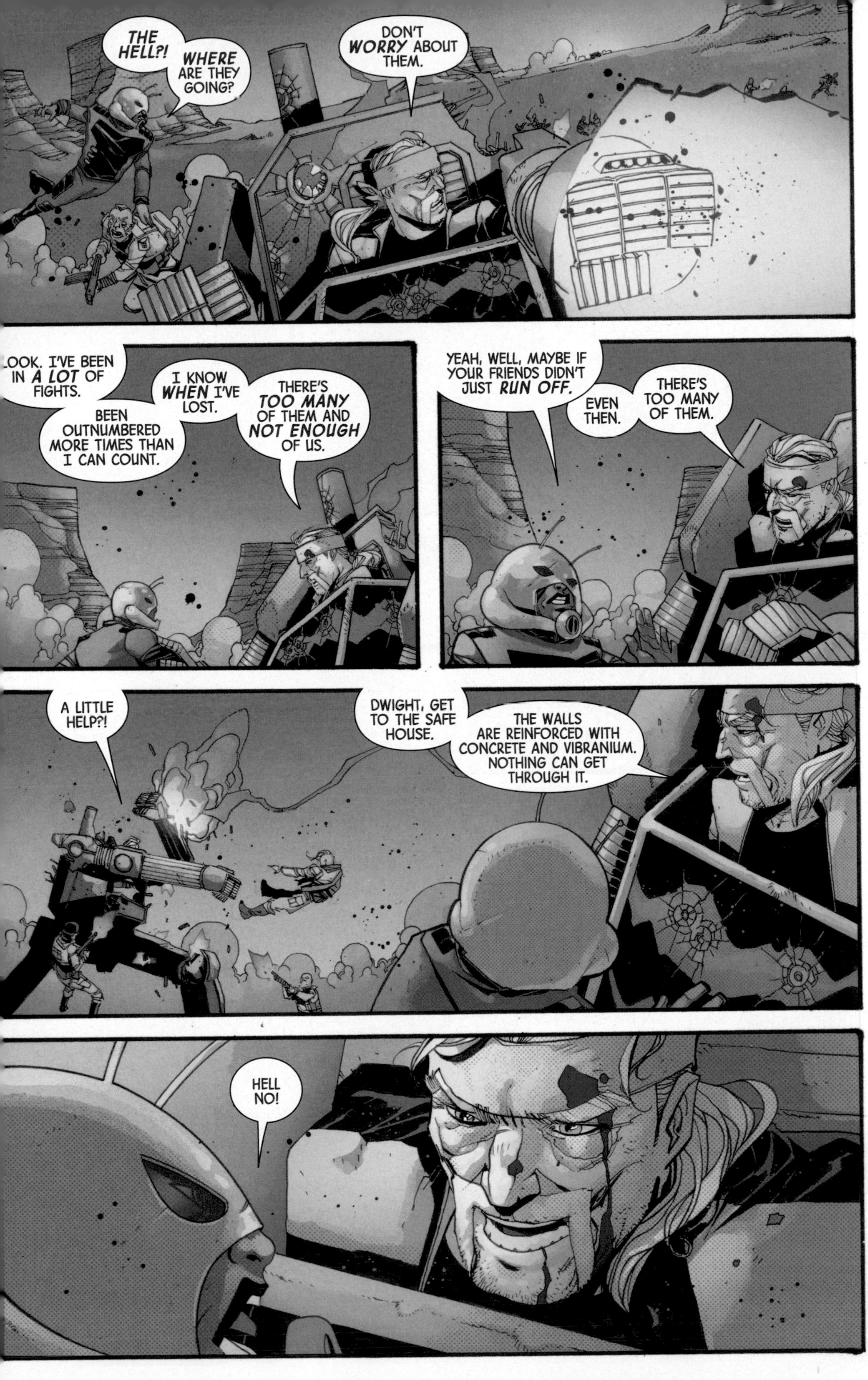
THE HELL?! WHERE ARE THEY GOING?
DON'T WORRY ABOUT THEM.
LOOK. I'VE BEEN IN A LOT OF FIGHTS.
I KNOW WHEN I'VE LOST.
BEEN OUTNUMBERED MORE TIMES THAN I CAN COUNT.
THERE'S TOO MANY OF THEM AND NOT ENOUGH OF US.
YEAH, WELL, MAYBE IF YOUR FRIENDS DIDN'T JUST RUN OFF.
EVEN THEN.
THERE'S TOO MANY OF THEM.
A LITTLE HELP?!
DWIGHT, GET TO THE SAFE HOUSE.
THE WALLS ARE REINFORCED WITH CONCRETE AND VIBRANIUM. NOTHING CAN GET THROUGH IT.
HELL NO!

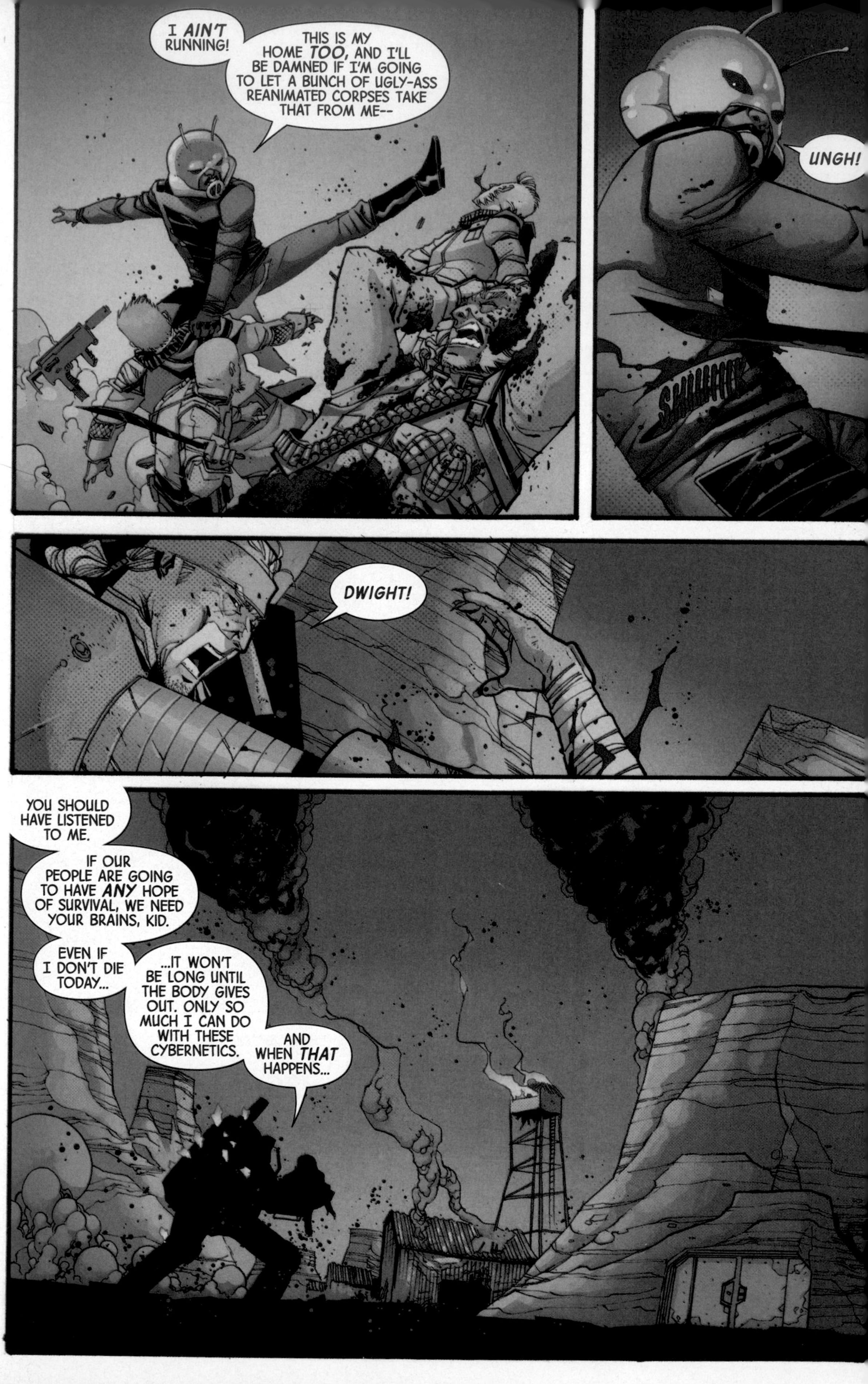
I AIN'T RUNNING!
THIS IS MY HOME TOO, AND I'LL BE DAMNED IF I'M GOING TO LET A BUNCH OF UGLY-ASS REANIMATED CORPSES TAKE THAT FROM ME--
UNGH!
DWIGHT!
YOU SHOULD HAVE LISTENED TO ME.
IF OUR PEOPLE ARE GOING TO HAVE ANY HOPE OF SURVIVAL, WE NEED YOUR BRAINS, KID.
EVEN IF I DON'T DIE TODAY...
...IT WON'T BE LONG UNTIL THE BODY GIVES OUT. ONLY SO MUCH I CAN DO WITH THESE CYBERNETICS.
AND WHEN THAT HAPPENS...

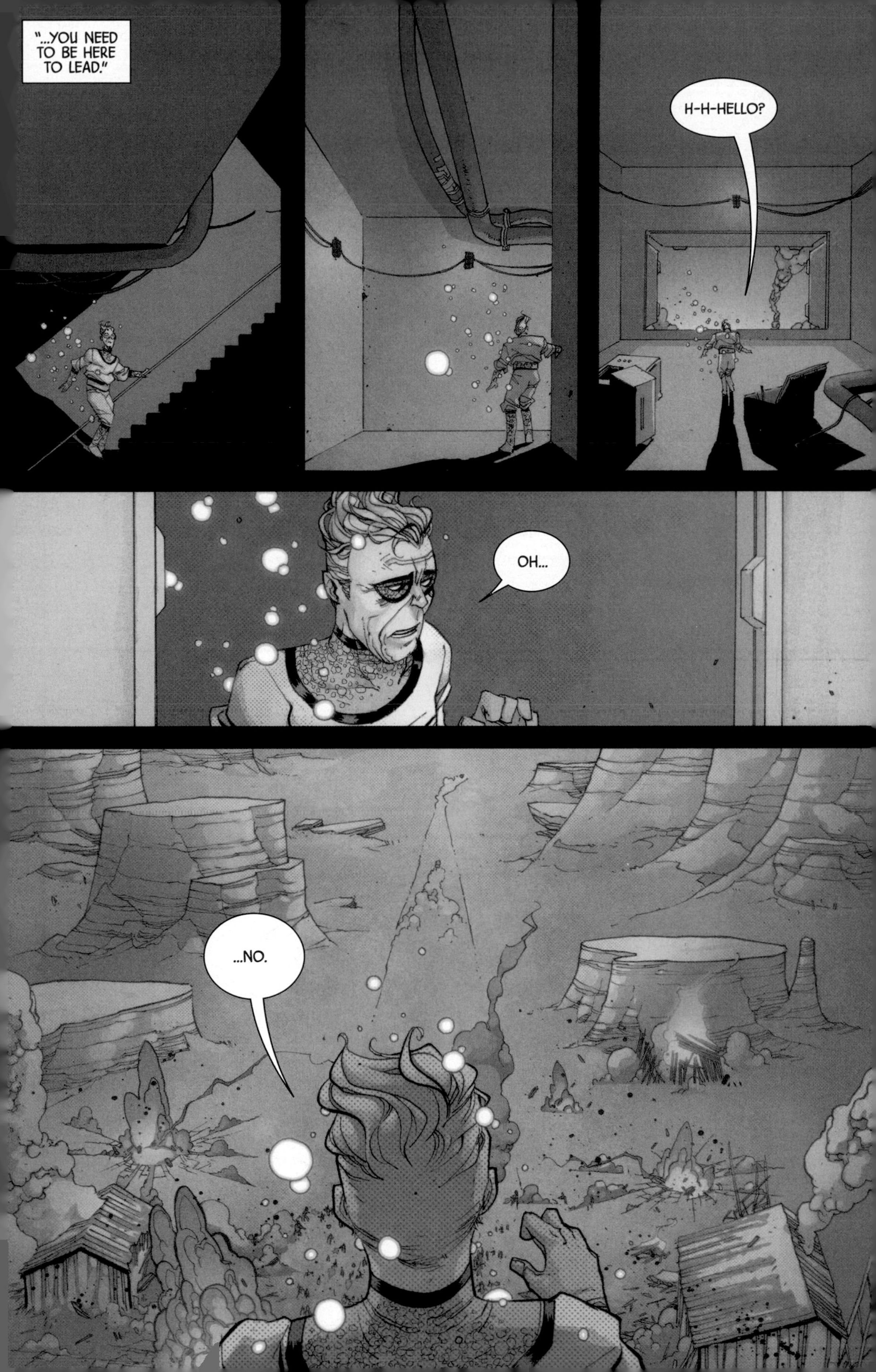
"...YOU NEED TO BE HERE TO LEAD."
H-H-HELLO?
OH...
...NO.

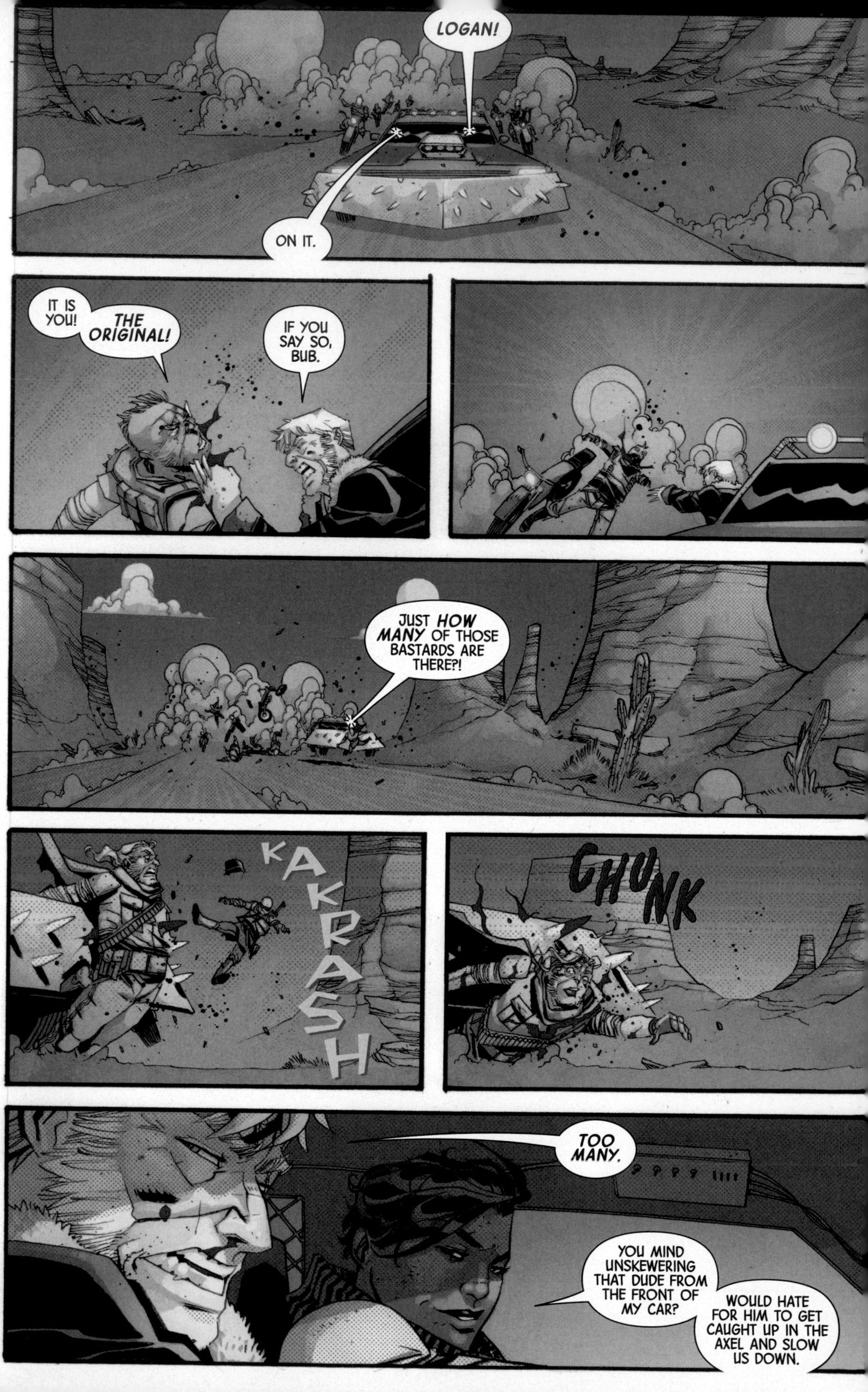
LOGAN!
ON IT.
IT IS YOU!
THE ORIGINAL!
IF YOU SAY SO, BUB.
JUST HOW MANY OF THOSE BASTARDS ARE THERE?!
KAKRASH
CHUNK
TOO MANY.
YOU MIND UNSKEWERING THAT DUDE FROM THE FRONT OF MY CAR?
WOULD HATE FOR HIM TO GET CAUGHT UP IN THE AXEL AND SLOW US DOWN.

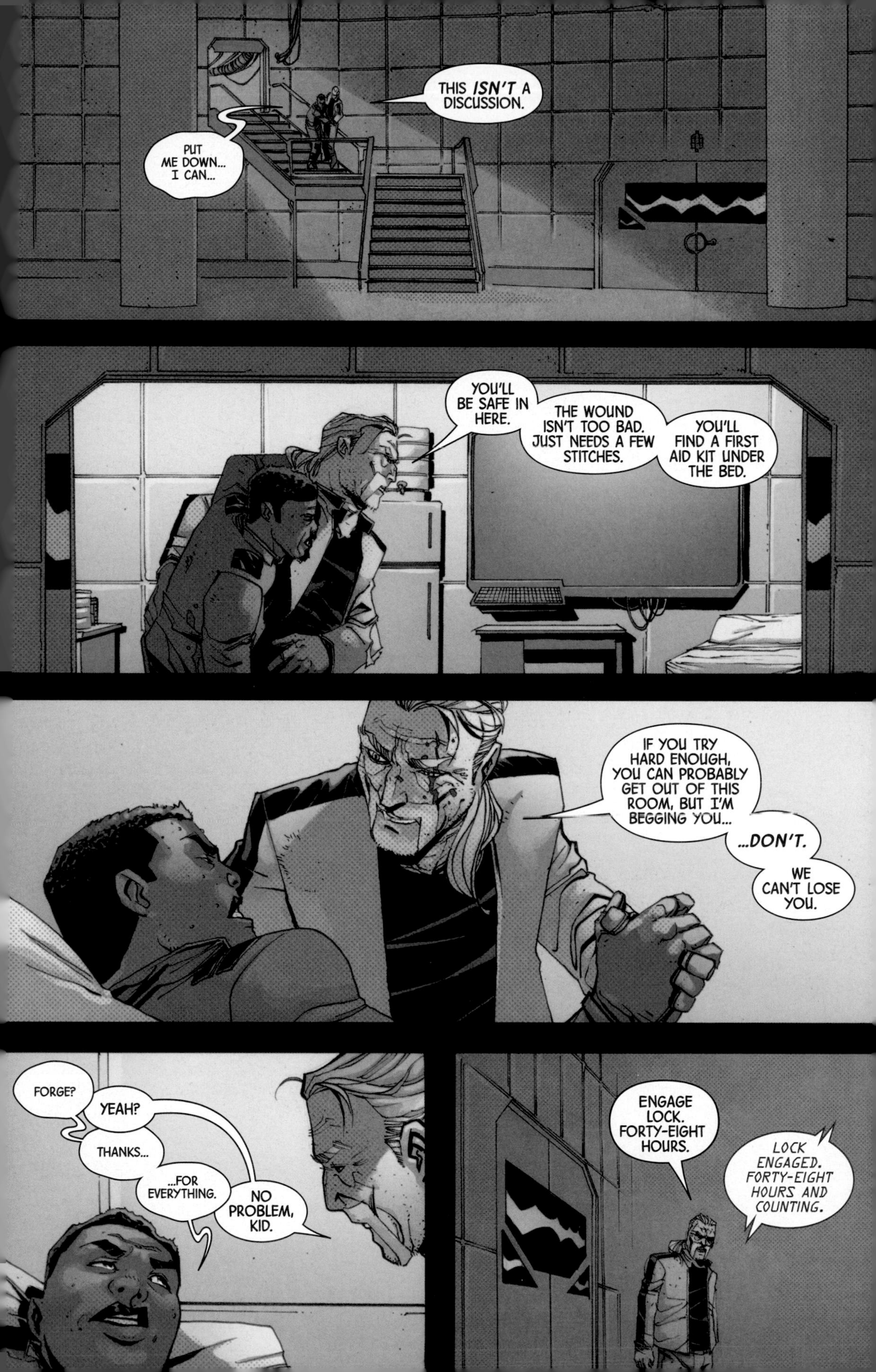
PUT ME DOWN... I CAN...
THIS ISN'T A DISCUSSION.
YOU'LL BE SAFE IN HERE.
THE WOUND ISN'T TOO BAD. JUST NEEDS A FEW STITCHES.
YOU'LL FIND A FIRST AID KIT UNDER THE BED.
IF YOU TRY HARD ENOUGH, YOU CAN PROBABLY GET OUT OF THIS ROOM, BUT I'M BEGGING YOU...
...DON'T.
WE CAN'T LOSE YOU.
FORGE?
YEAH?
THANKS...
...FOR EVERYTHING.
NO PROBLEM, KID.
ENGAGE LOCK. FORTY-EIGHT HOURS.
LOCK ENGAGED. FORTY-EIGHT HOURS AND COUNTING.

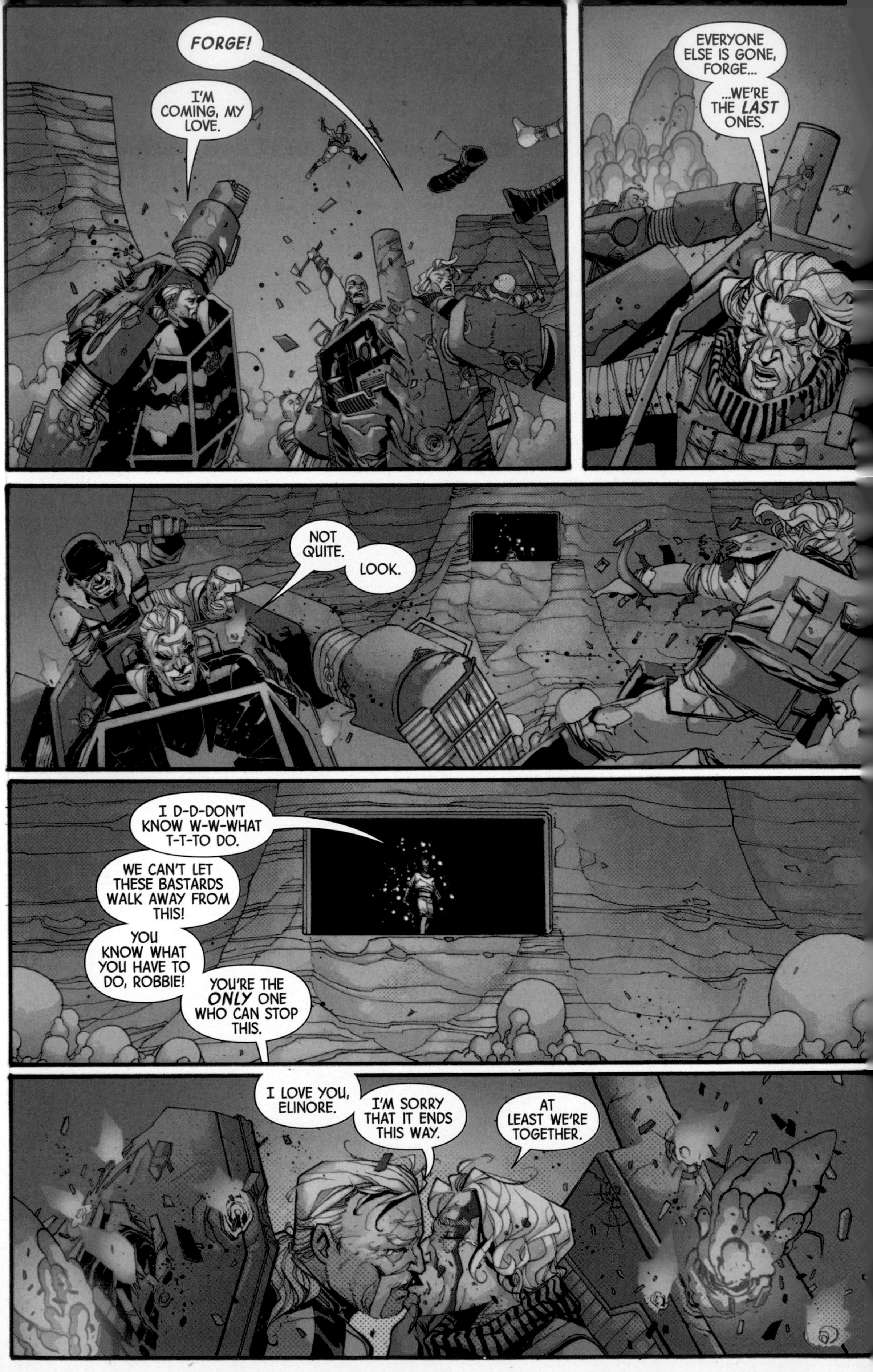
FORGE!
I'M COMING, MY LOVE.
EVERYONE ELSE IS GONE, FORGE...
...WE'RE THE LAST ONES.
NOT QUITE.
LOOK.
I D-D-DON'T KNOW W-W-WHAT T-T-TO DO.
WE CAN'T LET THESE BASTARDS WALK AWAY FROM THIS!
YOU KNOW WHAT YOU HAVE TO DO, ROBBIE!
YOU'RE THE ONLY ONE WHO CAN STOP THIS.
I LOVE YOU, ELINORE.
I'M SORRY THAT IT ENDS THIS WAY.
AT LEAST WE'RE TOGETHER.

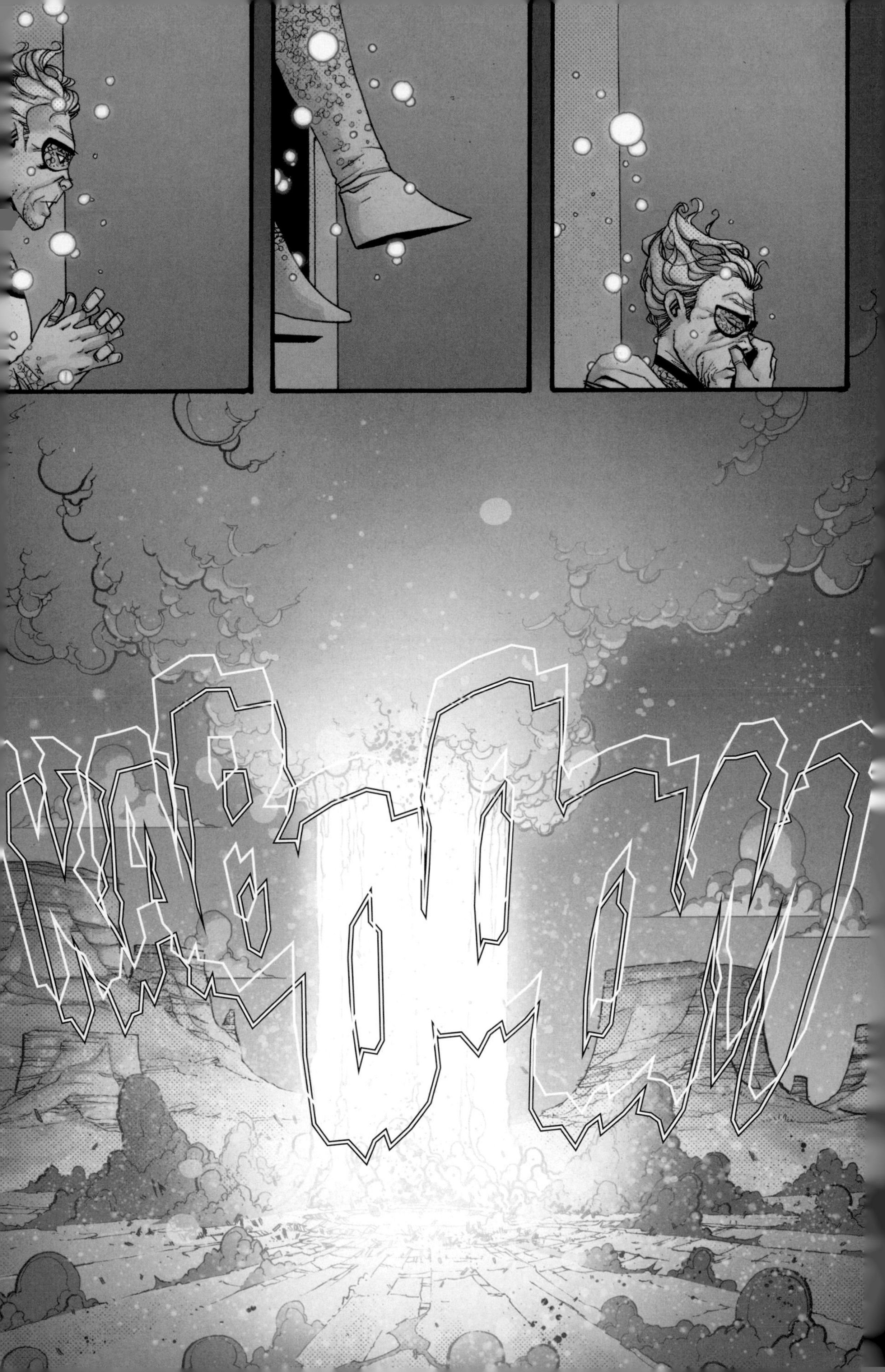

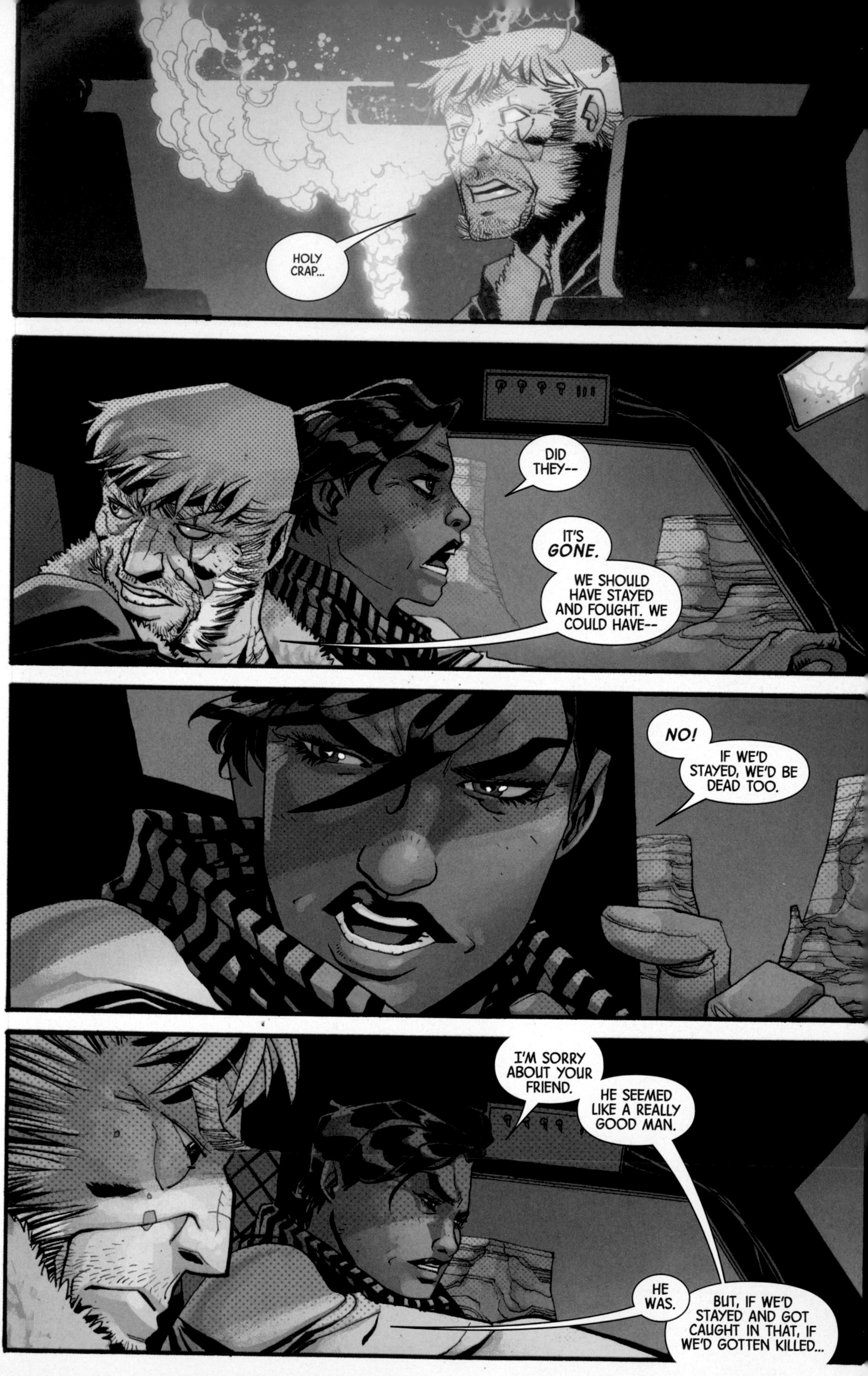
HOLY CRAP...
DID THEY--
IT'S GONE.
WE SHOULD HAVE STAYED AND FOUGHT. WE COULD HAVE--
NO!
IF WE'D STAYED, WE'D BE DEAD TOO.
I'M SORRY ABOUT YOUR FRIEND.
HE SEEMED LIKE A REALLY GOOD MAN.
HE WAS.
BUT, IF WE'D STAYED AND GOT CAUGHT IN THAT, IF WE'D GOTTEN KILLED...

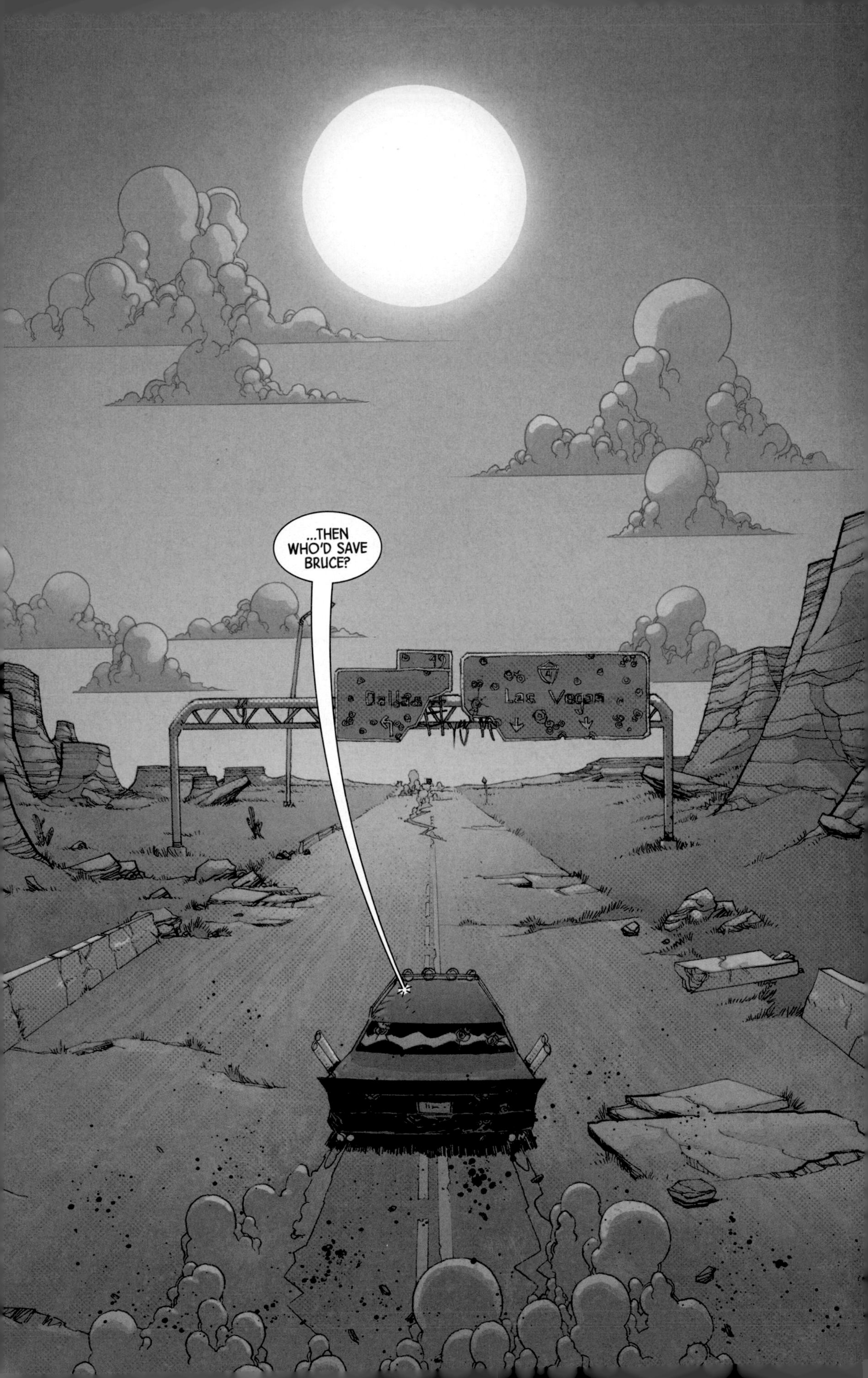
...THEN WHO'D SAVE BRUCE?
Dallas
Las Vegas

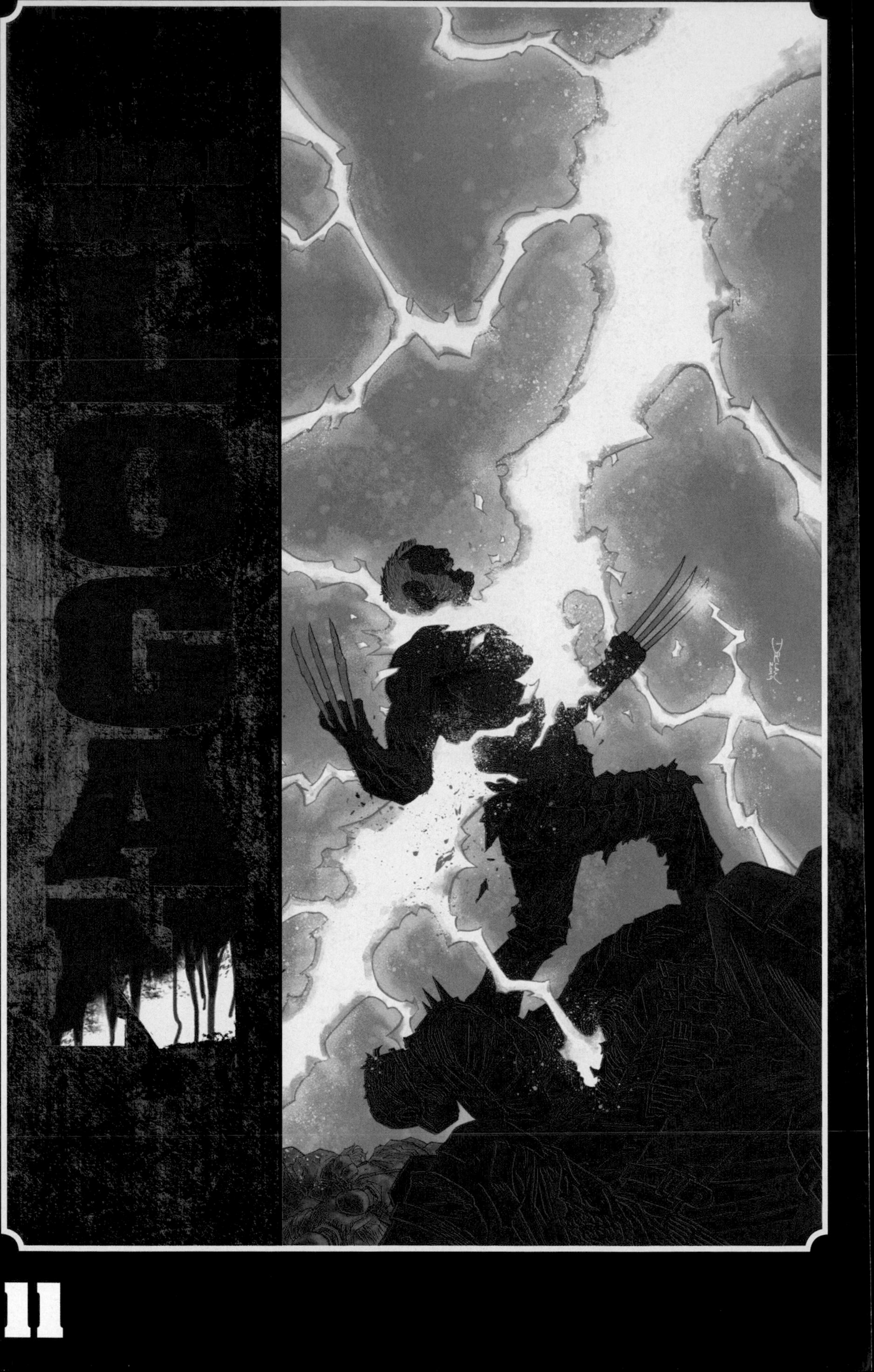
LOGAN
11

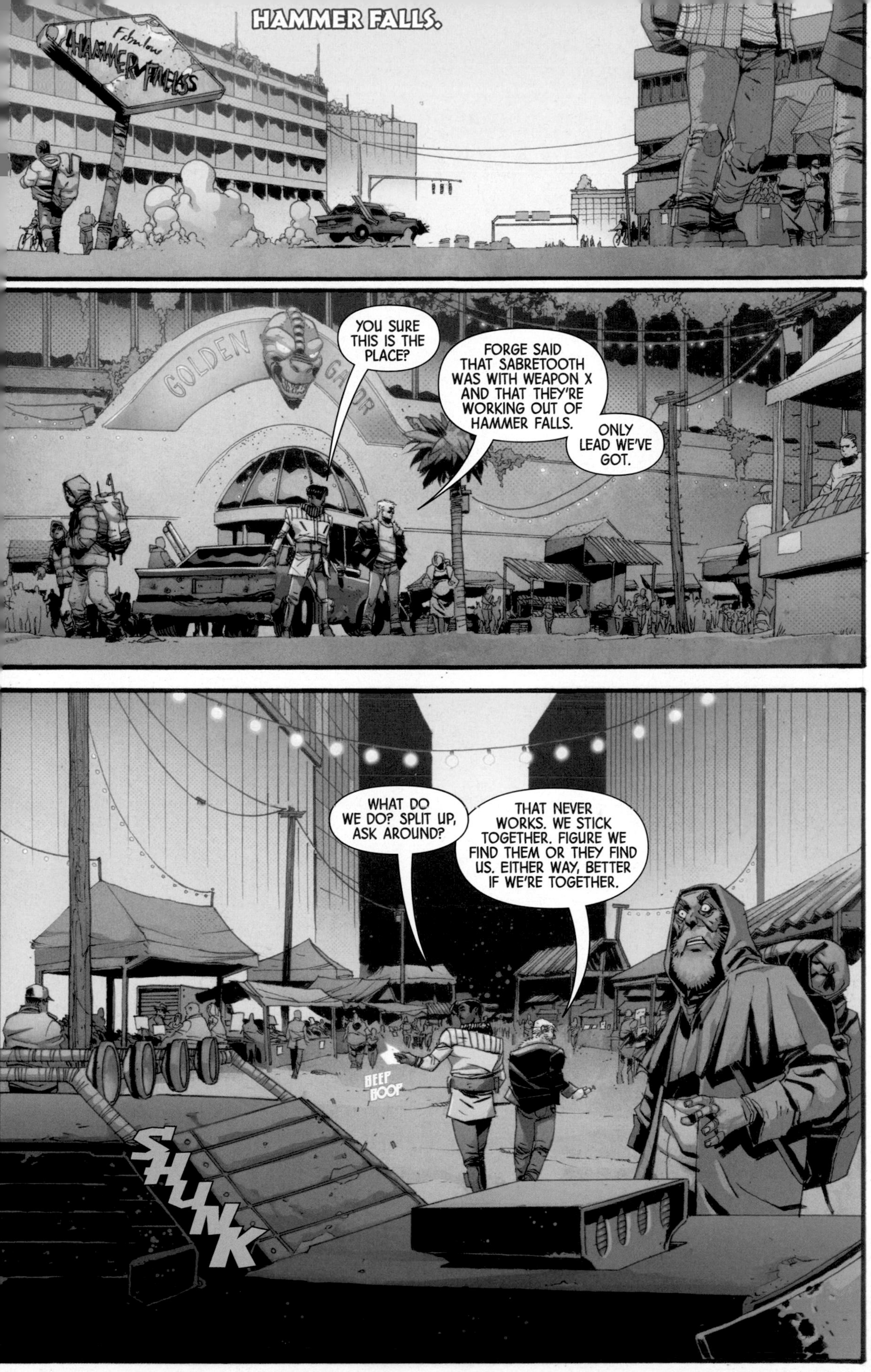
HAMMER FALLS.
Fabulous HAMMER FALLS
GOLDEN GATOR
YOU SURE THIS IS THE PLACE?
FORGE SAID THAT SABRETOOTH WAS WITH WEAPON X AND THAT THEY'RE WORKING OUT OF HAMMER FALLS.
ONLY LEAD WE'VE GOT.
WHAT DO WE DO? SPLIT UP, ASK AROUND?
THAT NEVER WORKS. WE STICK TOGETHER. FIGURE WE FIND THEM OR THEY FIND US. EITHER WAY, BETTER IF WE'RE TOGETHER.
BEEP BOOP
SHUNK

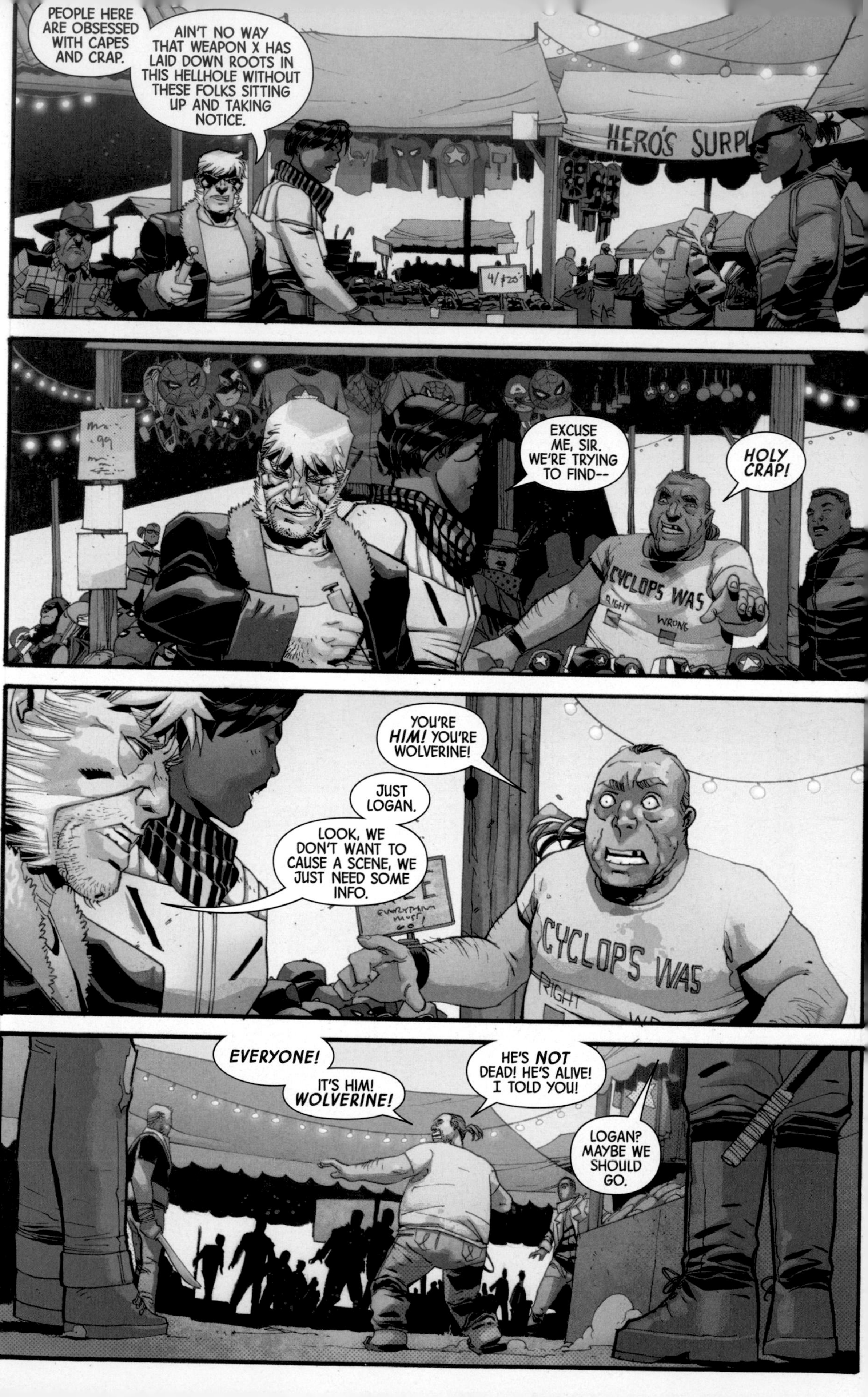
PEOPLE HERE ARE OBSESSED WITH CAPES AND CRAP.
AIN'T NO WAY THAT WEAPON X HAS LAID DOWN ROOTS IN THIS HELLHOLE WITHOUT THESE FOLKS SITTING UP AND TAKING NOTICE.
HERO'S SURPL
4/$20
EXCUSE ME, SIR. WE'RE TRYING TO FIND--
HOLY CRAP!
CYCLOPS WAS RIGHT WRONG
YOU'RE HIM! YOU'RE WOLVERINE!
JUST LOGAN.
LOOK, WE DON'T WANT TO CAUSE A SCENE, WE JUST NEED SOME INFO.
CYCLOPS WAS RIGHT
EVERYONE!
IT'S HIM! WOLVERINE!
HE'S NOT DEAD! HE'S ALIVE! I TOLD YOU!
LOGAN? MAYBE WE SHOULD GO.

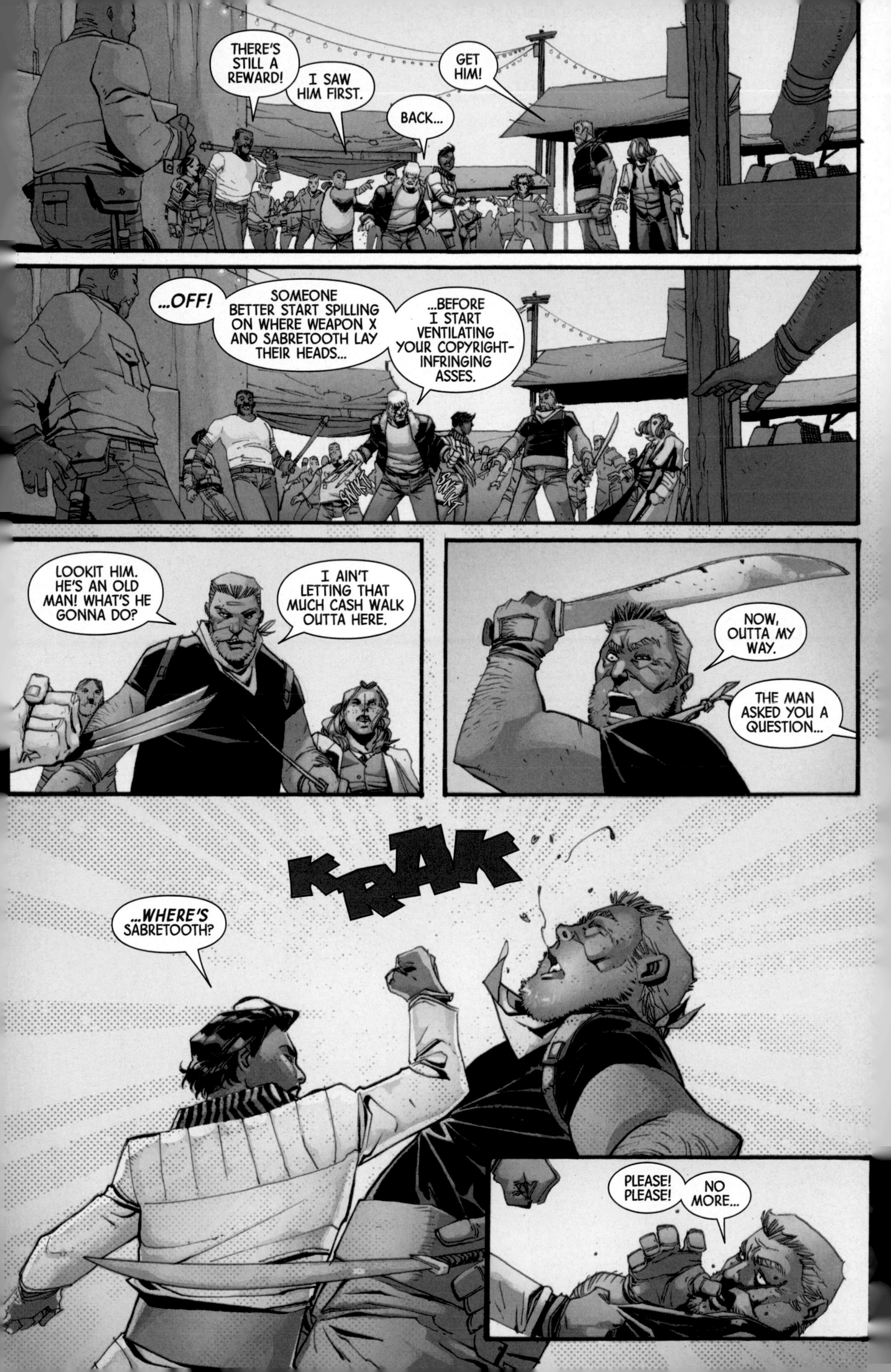
THERE'S STILL A REWARD!
I SAW HIM FIRST.
BACK...
GET HIM!
...OFF!
SOMEONE BETTER START SPILLING ON WHERE WEAPON X AND SABRETOOTH LAY THEIR HEADS...
...BEFORE I START VENTILATING YOUR COPYRIGHT-INFRINGING ASSES.
SNIKT
SNIKT
LOOKIT HIM. HE'S AN OLD MAN! WHAT'S HE GONNA DO?
I AIN'T LETTING THAT MUCH CASH WALK OUTTA HERE.
NOW, OUTTA MY WAY.
THE MAN ASKED YOU A QUESTION...
KRAK
...WHERE'S SABRETOOTH?
PLEASE! PLEASE!
NO MORE...

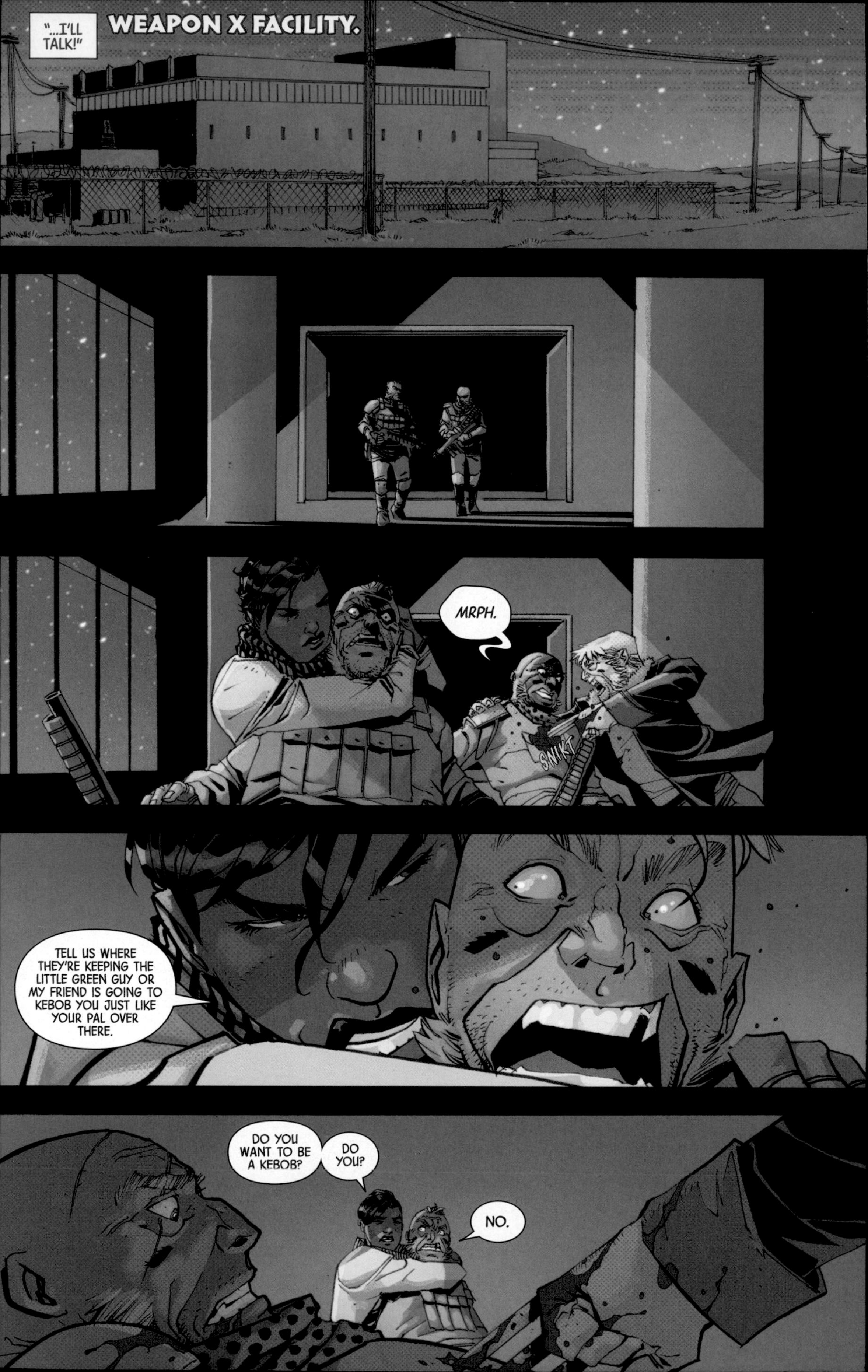
"...I'LL TALK!"
WEAPON X FACILITY.
MRPH.
SNIKT
TELL US WHERE THEY'RE KEEPING THE LITTLE GREEN GUY OR MY FRIEND IS GOING TO KEBOB YOU JUST LIKE YOUR PAL OVER THERE.
DO YOU WANT TO BE A KEBOB?
DO YOU?
NO.

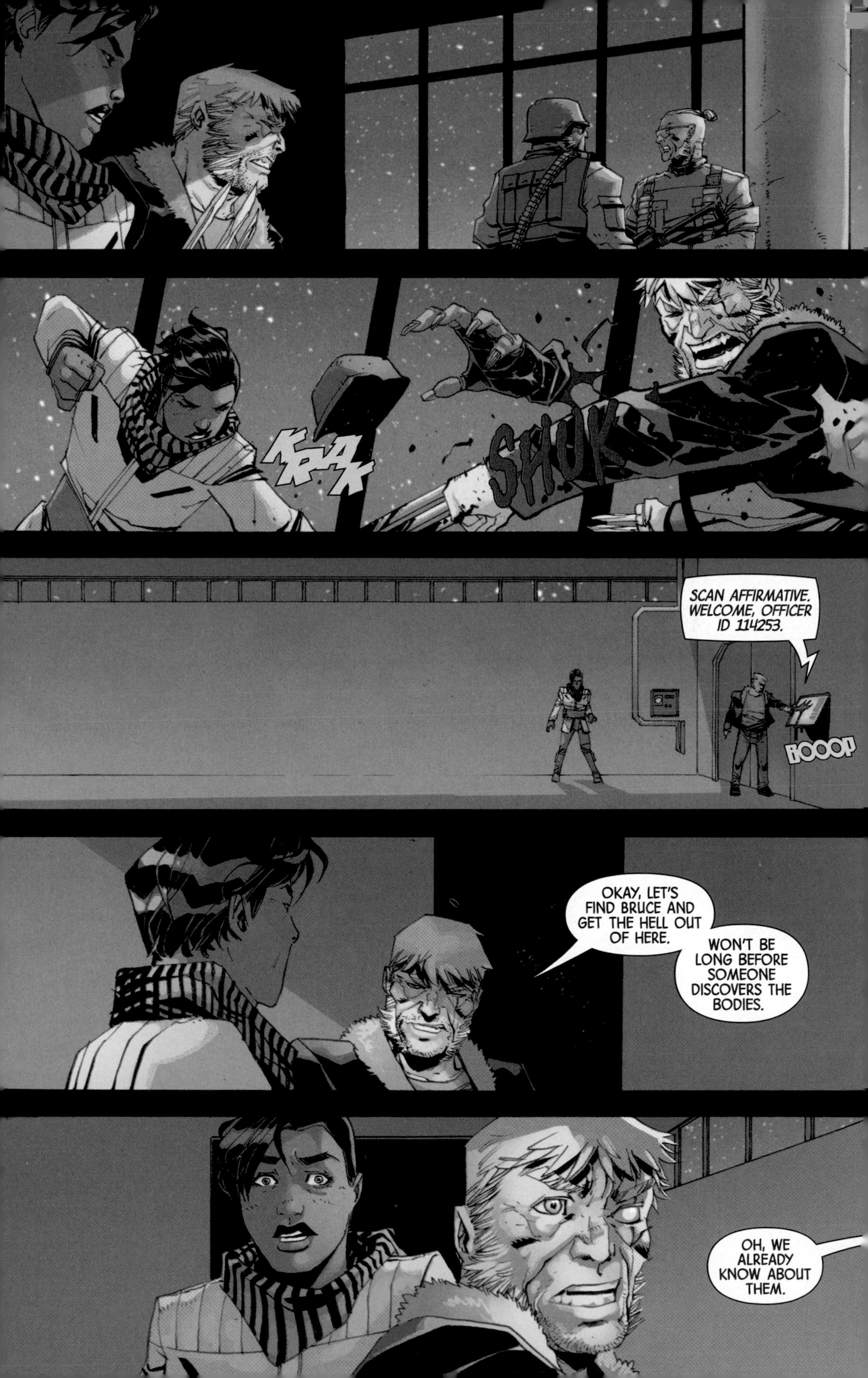
KRAK
SHUK
SCAN AFFIRMATIVE. WELCOME, OFFICER ID 114253.
BOOOP
OKAY, LET'S FIND BRUCE AND GET THE HELL OUT OF HERE.
WON'T BE LONG BEFORE SOMEONE DISCOVERS THE BODIES.
OH, WE ALREADY KNOW ABOUT THEM.

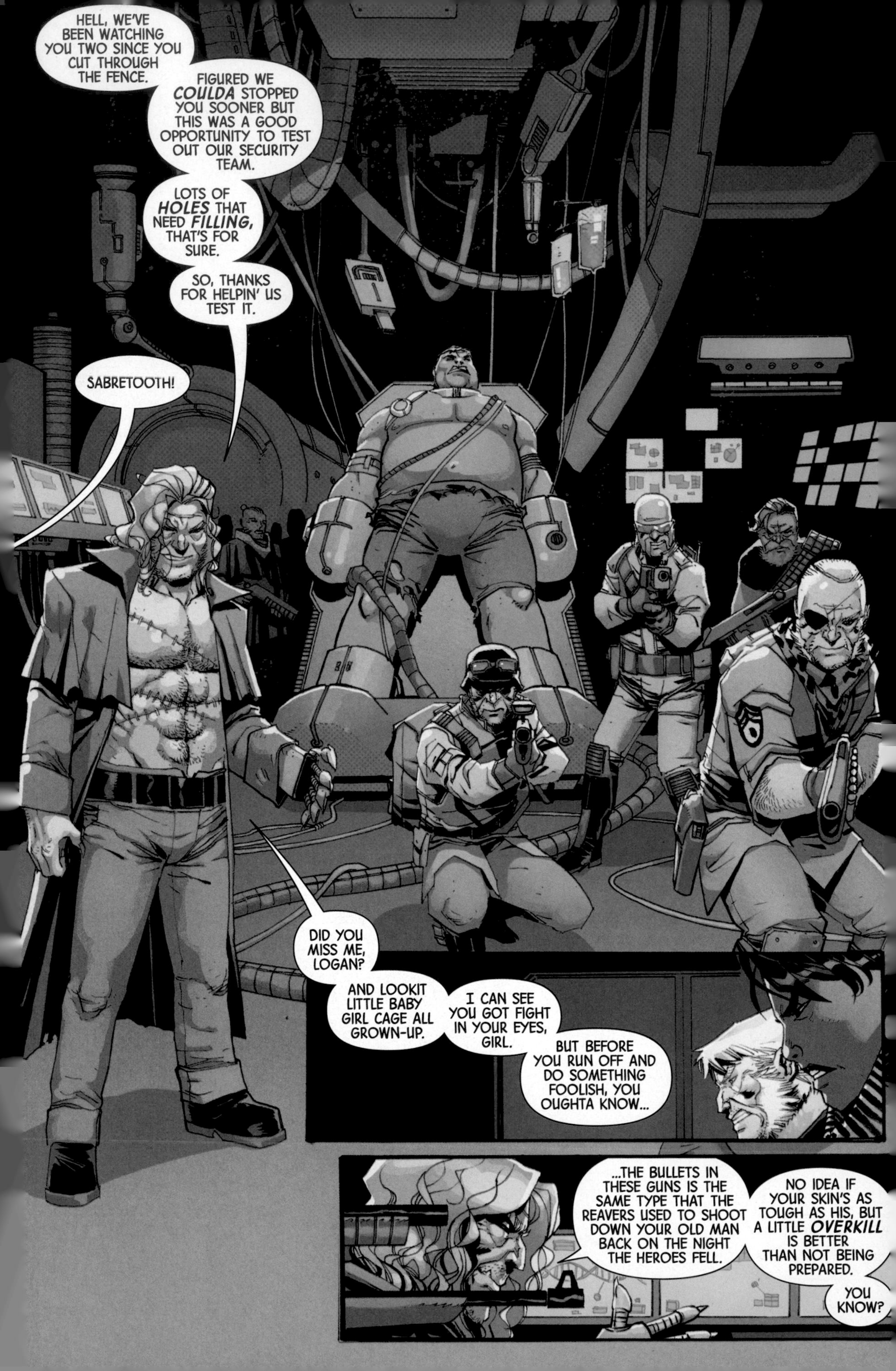
HELL, WE'VE BEEN WATCHING YOU TWO SINCE YOU CUT THROUGH THE FENCE.
FIGURED WE *COULDA* STOPPED YOU SOONER BUT THIS WAS A GOOD OPPORTUNITY TO TEST OUT OUR SECURITY TEAM.
LOTS OF *HOLES* THAT NEED *FILLING,* THAT'S FOR SURE.
SO, THANKS FOR HELPIN' US TEST IT.
SABRETOOTH!
DID YOU MISS ME, LOGAN?
AND LOOKIT LITTLE BABY GIRL CAGE ALL GROWN-UP.
I CAN SEE YOU GOT FIGHT IN YOUR EYES, GIRL.
BUT BEFORE YOU RUN OFF AND DO SOMETHING FOOLISH, YOU OUGHTA KNOW...
...THE BULLETS IN THESE GUNS IS THE SAME TYPE THAT THE REAVERS USED TO SHOOT DOWN YOUR OLD MAN BACK ON THE NIGHT THE HEROES FELL.
NO IDEA IF YOUR SKIN'S AS TOUGH AS HIS, BUT A LITTLE *OVERKILL* IS BETTER THAN NOT BEING PREPARED.
YOU KNOW?

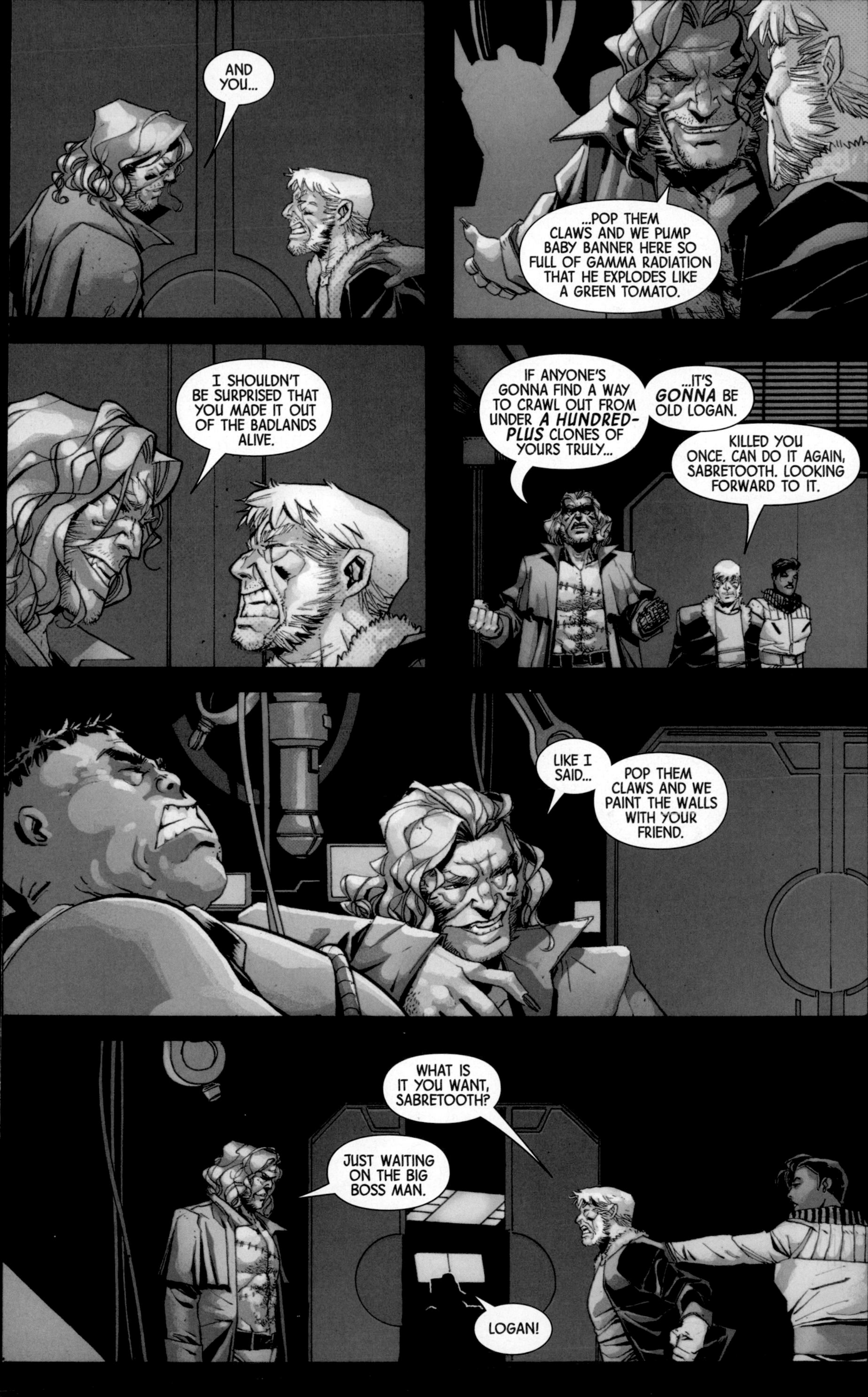
AND YOU...
...POP THEM CLAWS AND WE PUMP BABY BANNER HERE SO FULL OF GAMMA RADIATION THAT HE EXPLODES LIKE A GREEN TOMATO.
I SHOULDN'T BE SURPRISED THAT YOU MADE IT OUT OF THE BADLANDS ALIVE.
IF ANYONE'S GONNA FIND A WAY TO CRAWL OUT FROM UNDER A HUNDRED-PLUS CLONES OF YOURS TRULY...
...IT'S GONNA BE OLD LOGAN.
KILLED YOU ONCE. CAN DO IT AGAIN, SABRETOOTH. LOOKING FORWARD TO IT.
LIKE I SAID...
POP THEM CLAWS AND WE PAINT THE WALLS WITH YOUR FRIEND.
WHAT IS IT YOU WANT, SABRETOOTH?
JUST WAITING ON THE BIG BOSS MAN.
LOGAN!

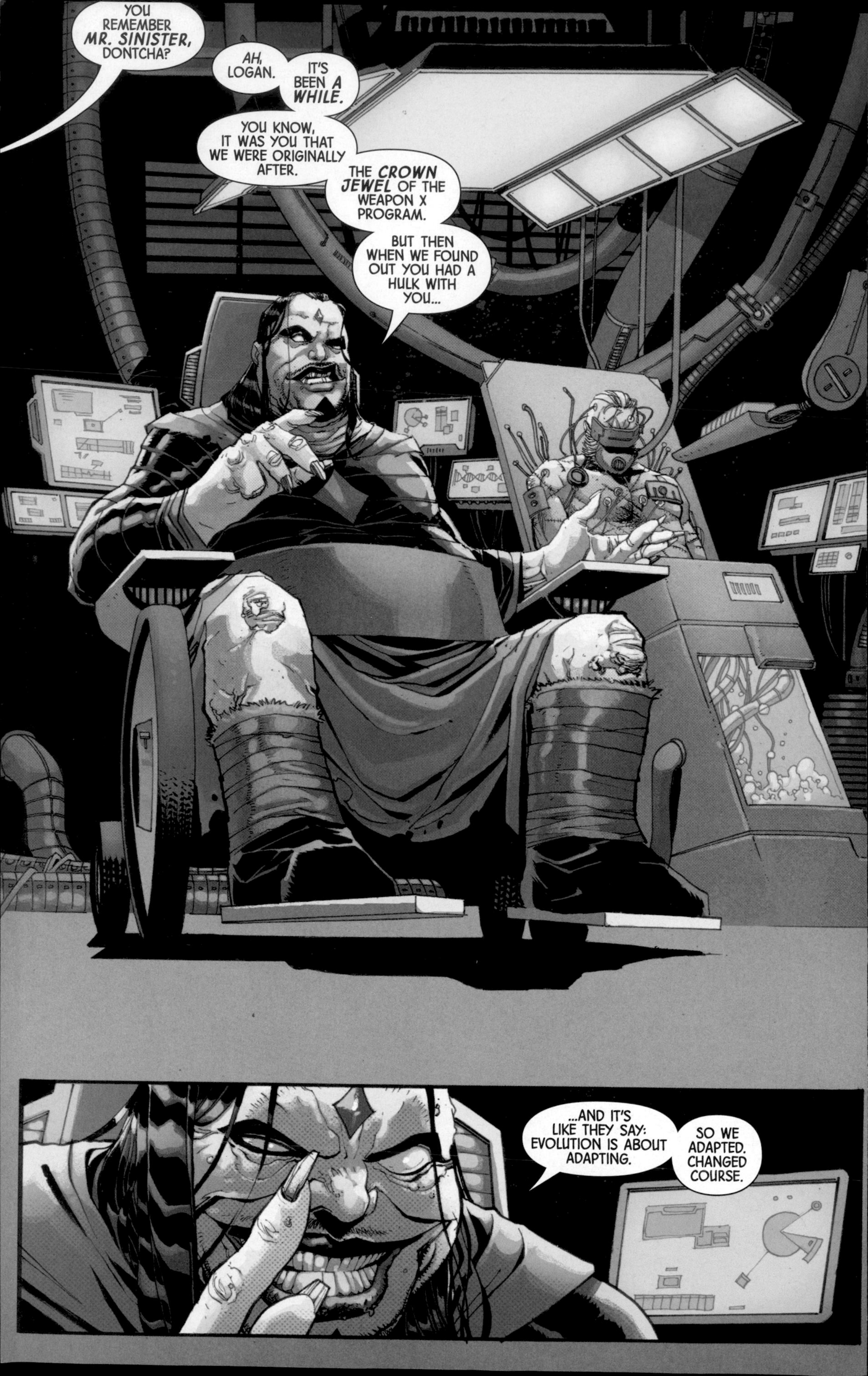
YOU REMEMBER MR. SINISTER, DONTCHA?
AH, LOGAN.
IT'S BEEN A WHILE.
YOU KNOW, IT WAS YOU THAT WE WERE ORIGINALLY AFTER.
THE CROWN JEWEL OF THE WEAPON X PROGRAM.
BUT THEN WHEN WE FOUND OUT YOU HAD A HULK WITH YOU...
...AND IT'S LIKE THEY SAY: EVOLUTION IS ABOUT ADAPTING.
SO WE ADAPTED. CHANGED COURSE.

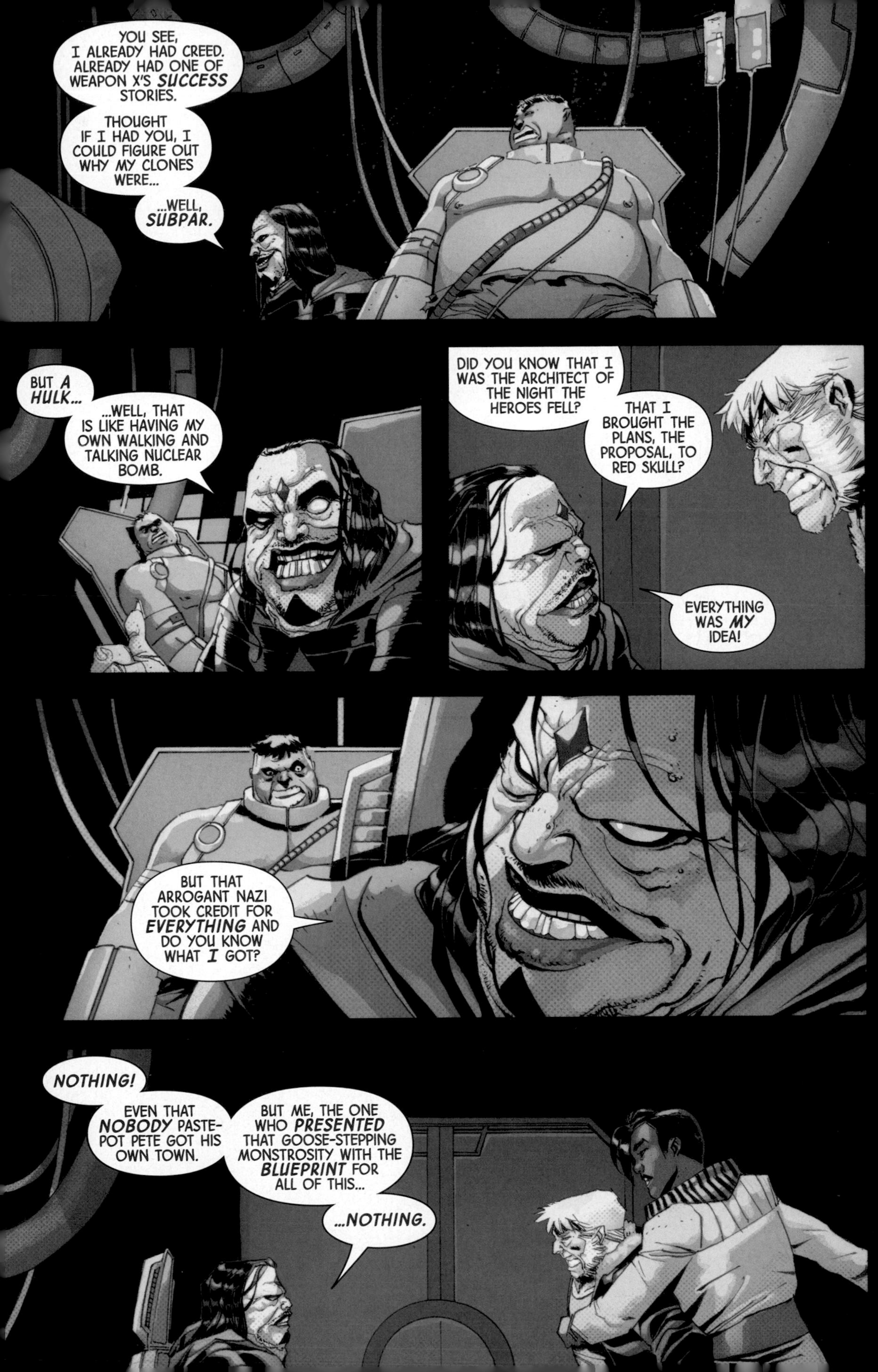
YOU SEE, I ALREADY HAD CREED. ALREADY HAD ONE OF WEAPON X'S SUCCESS STORIES.
THOUGHT IF I HAD YOU, I COULD FIGURE OUT WHY MY CLONES WERE...
...WELL, SUBPAR.
BUT A HULK...
...WELL, THAT IS LIKE HAVING MY OWN WALKING AND TALKING NUCLEAR BOMB.
DID YOU KNOW THAT I WAS THE ARCHITECT OF THE NIGHT THE HEROES FELL?
THAT I BROUGHT THE PLANS, THE PROPOSAL, TO RED SKULL?
EVERYTHING WAS MY IDEA!
BUT THAT ARROGANT NAZI TOOK CREDIT FOR EVERYTHING AND DO YOU KNOW WHAT I GOT?
NOTHING!
EVEN THAT NOBODY PASTE-POT PETE GOT HIS OWN TOWN.
BUT ME, THE ONE WHO PRESENTED THAT GOOSE-STEPPING MONSTROSITY WITH THE BLUEPRINT FOR ALL OF THIS...
...NOTHING.

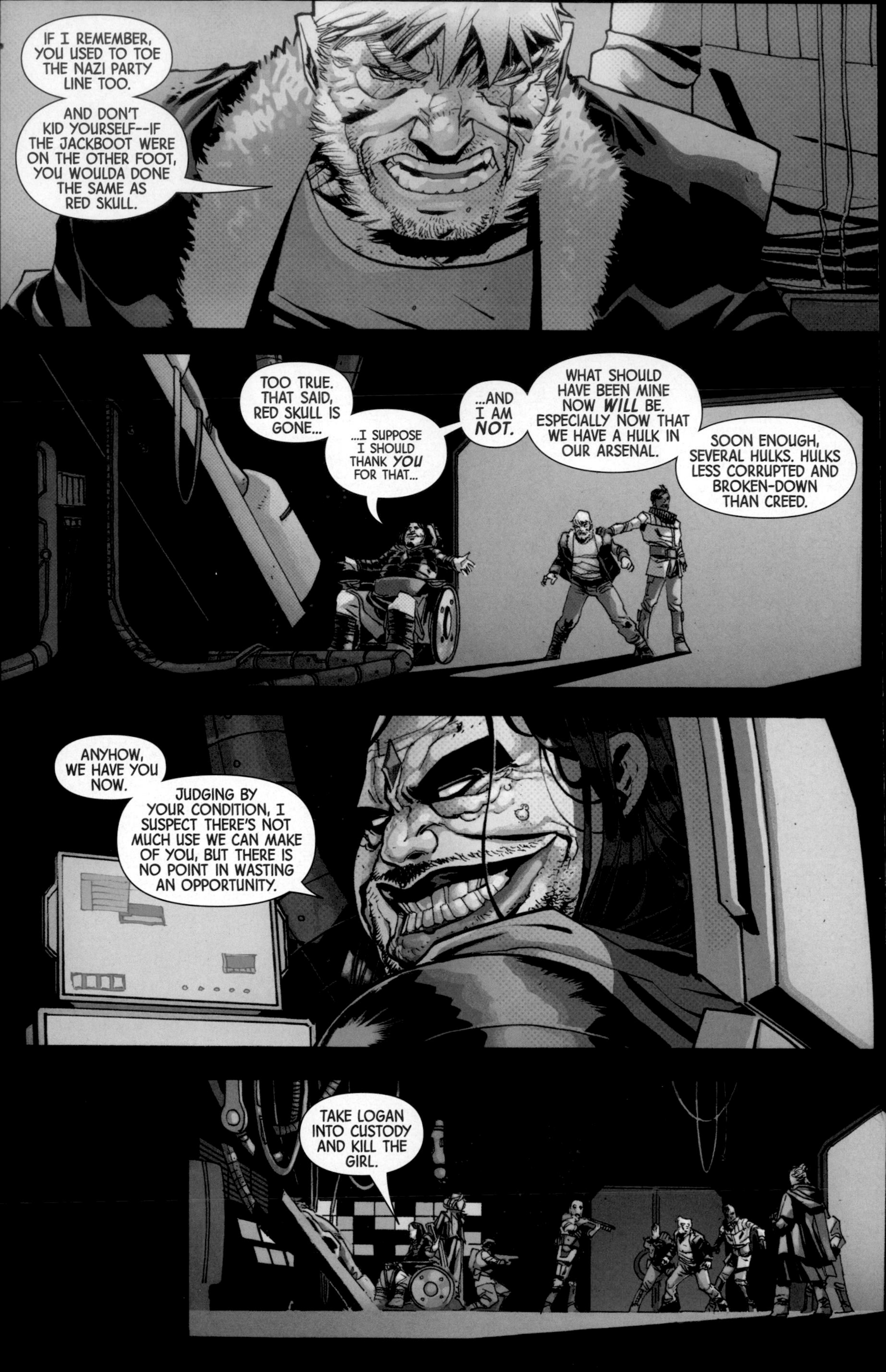
IF I REMEMBER, YOU USED TO TOE THE NAZI PARTY LINE TOO.
AND DON'T KID YOURSELF--IF THE JACKBOOT WERE ON THE OTHER FOOT, YOU WOULDA DONE THE SAME AS RED SKULL.
TOO TRUE. THAT SAID, RED SKULL IS GONE...
...I SUPPOSE I SHOULD THANK YOU FOR THAT...
...AND I AM NOT.
WHAT SHOULD HAVE BEEN MINE NOW WILL BE. ESPECIALLY NOW THAT WE HAVE A HULK IN OUR ARSENAL.
SOON ENOUGH, SEVERAL HULKS. HULKS LESS CORRUPTED AND BROKEN-DOWN THAN CREED.
ANYHOW, WE HAVE YOU NOW.
JUDGING BY YOUR CONDITION, I SUSPECT THERE'S NOT MUCH USE WE CAN MAKE OF YOU, BUT THERE IS NO POINT IN WASTING AN OPPORTUNITY.
TAKE LOGAN INTO CUSTODY AND KILL THE GIRL.

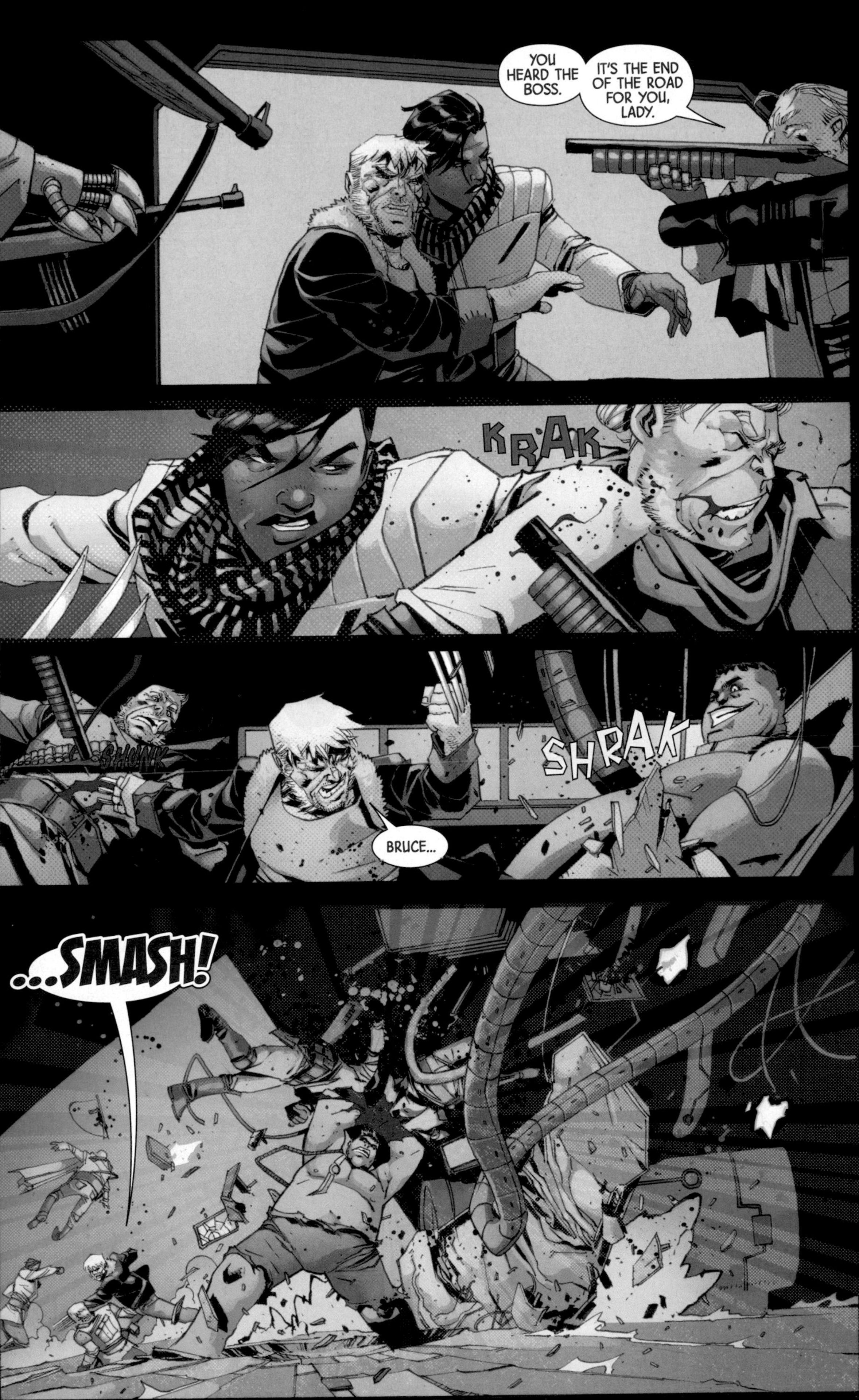
YOU HEARD THE BOSS.
IT'S THE END OF THE ROAD FOR YOU, LADY.
KRAK
SHUNK
SHRAK
BRUCE...
...SMASH!

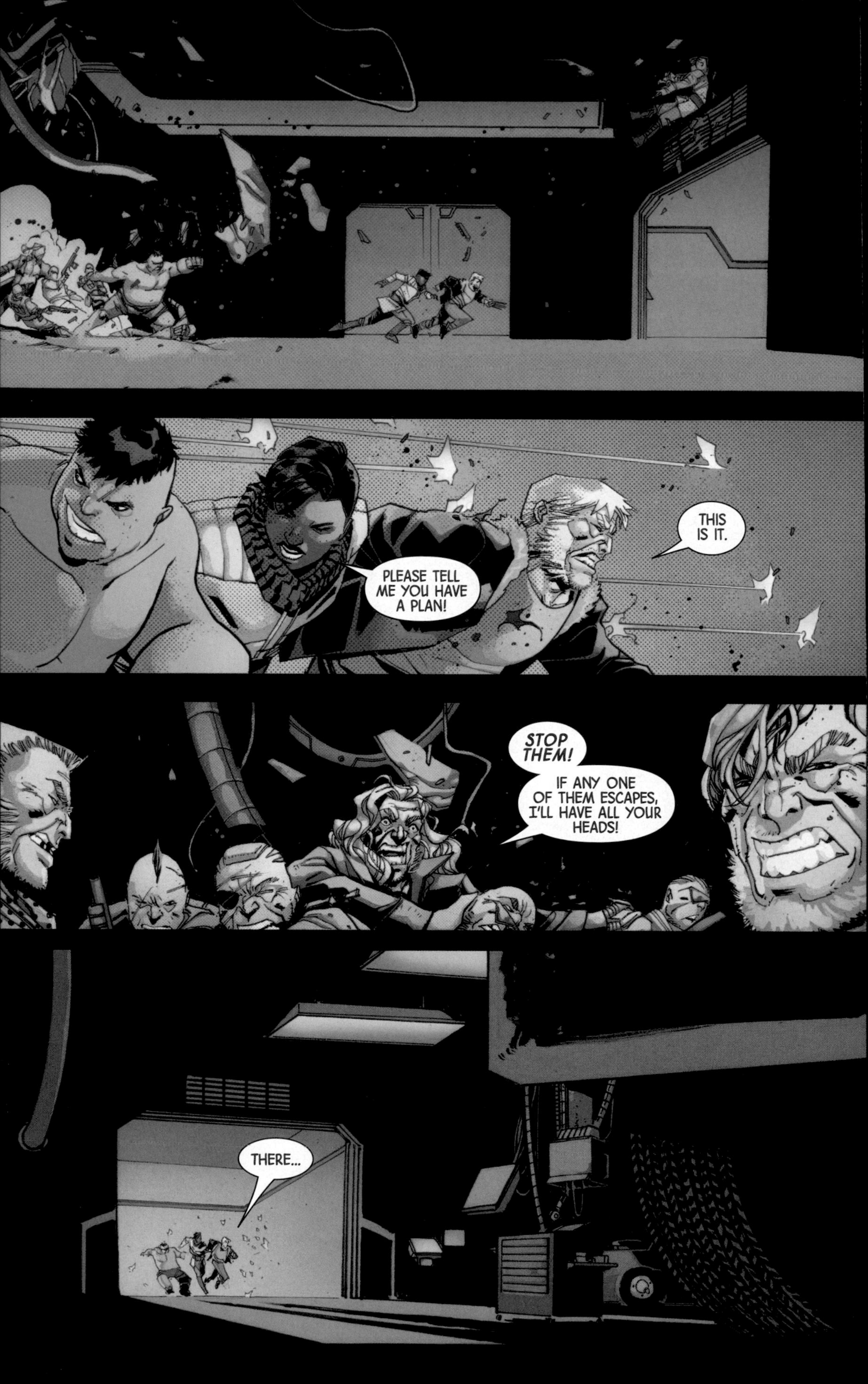
PLEASE TELL ME YOU HAVE A PLAN!
THIS IS IT.
STOP THEM!
IF ANY ONE OF THEM ESCAPES, I'LL HAVE ALL YOUR HEADS!
THERE...

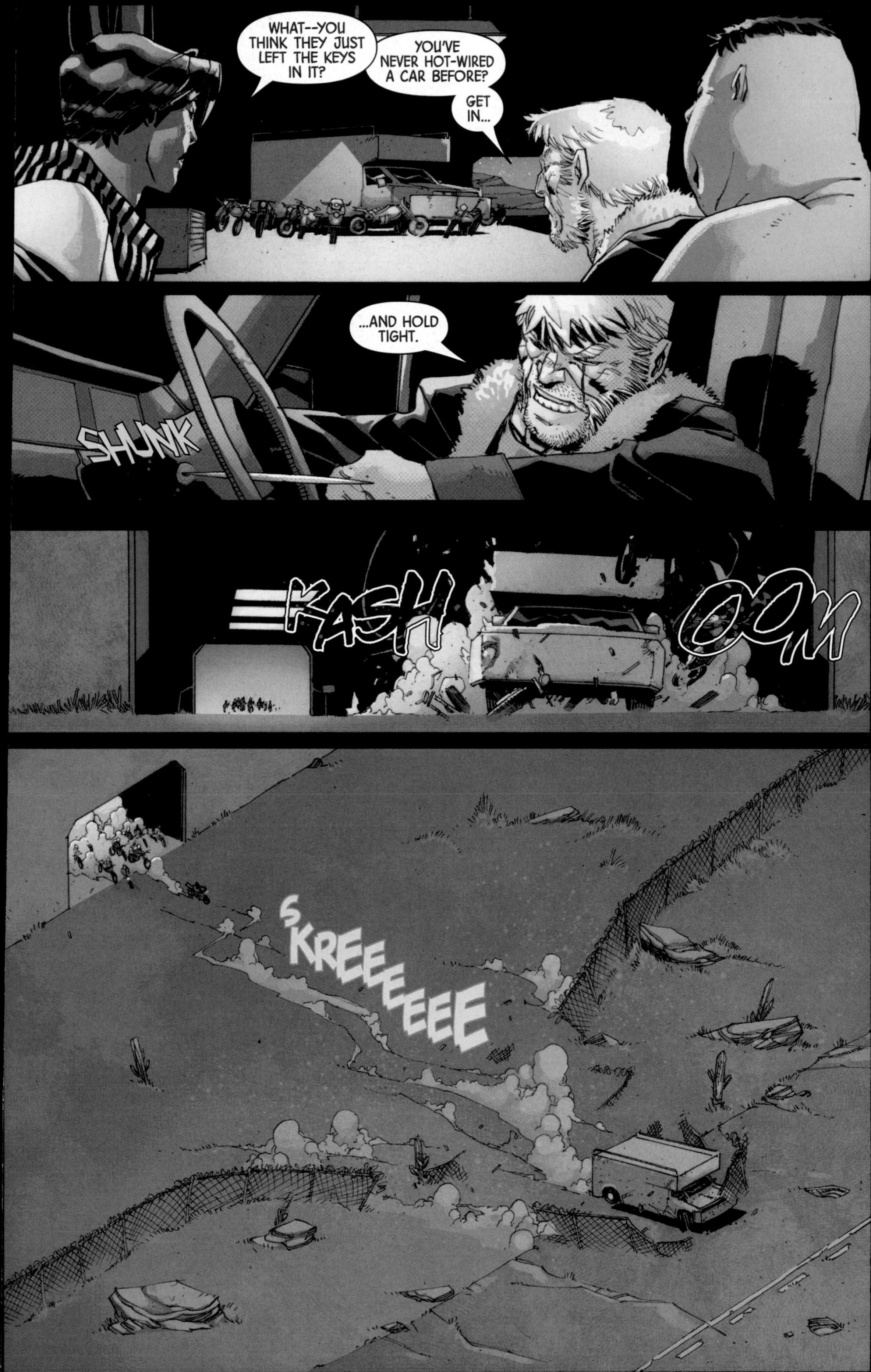
WHAT--YOU THINK THEY JUST LEFT THE KEYS IN IT?
YOU'VE NEVER HOT-WIRED A CAR BEFORE?
GET IN...
...AND HOLD TIGHT.
SHUNK
KASH
OOM
SKREEEEEE

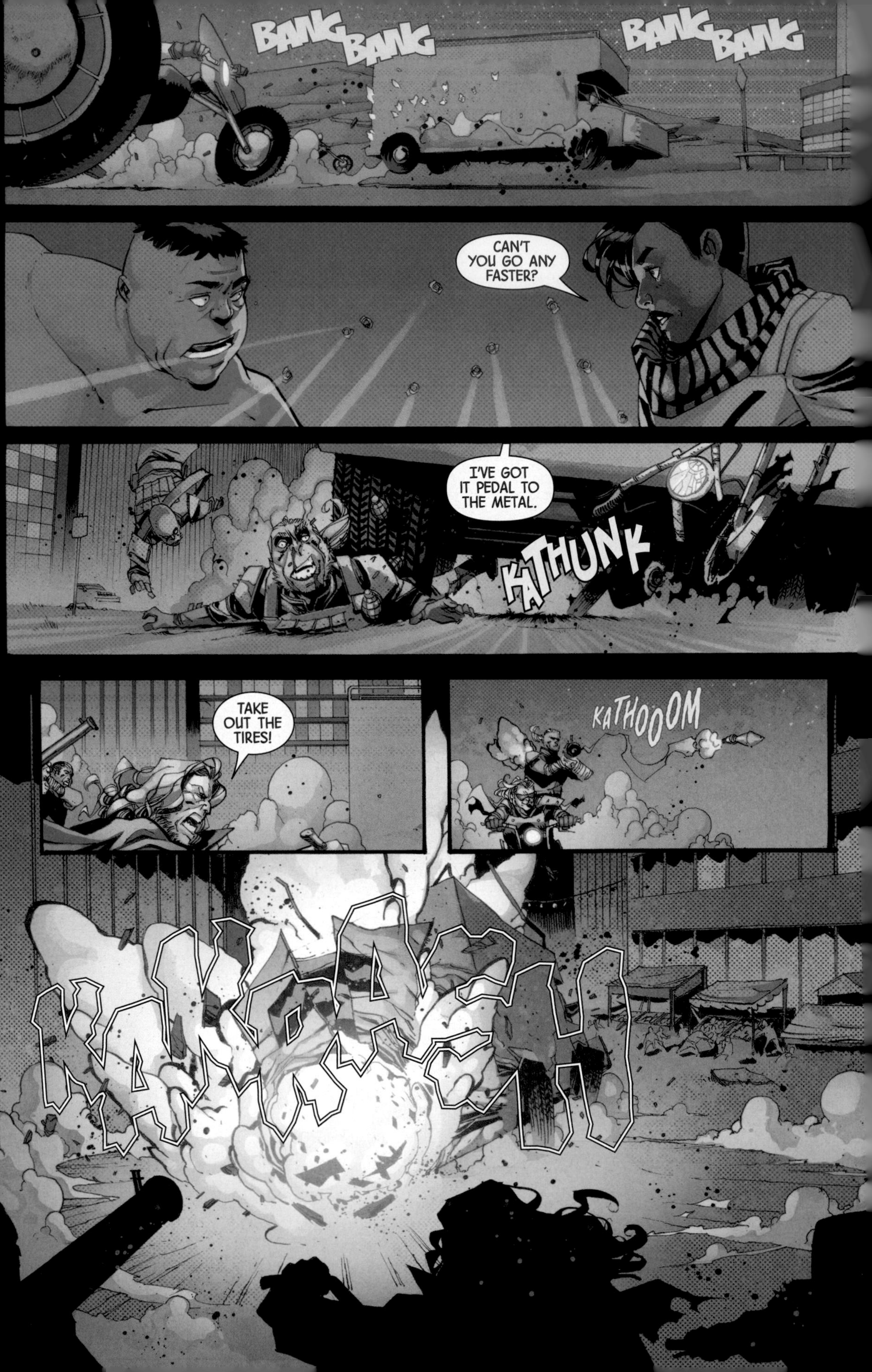
BANG BANG
BANG BANG
CAN'T YOU GO ANY FASTER?
I'VE GOT IT PEDAL TO THE METAL.
KATHUNK
TAKE OUT THE TIRES!
KATHOOOM

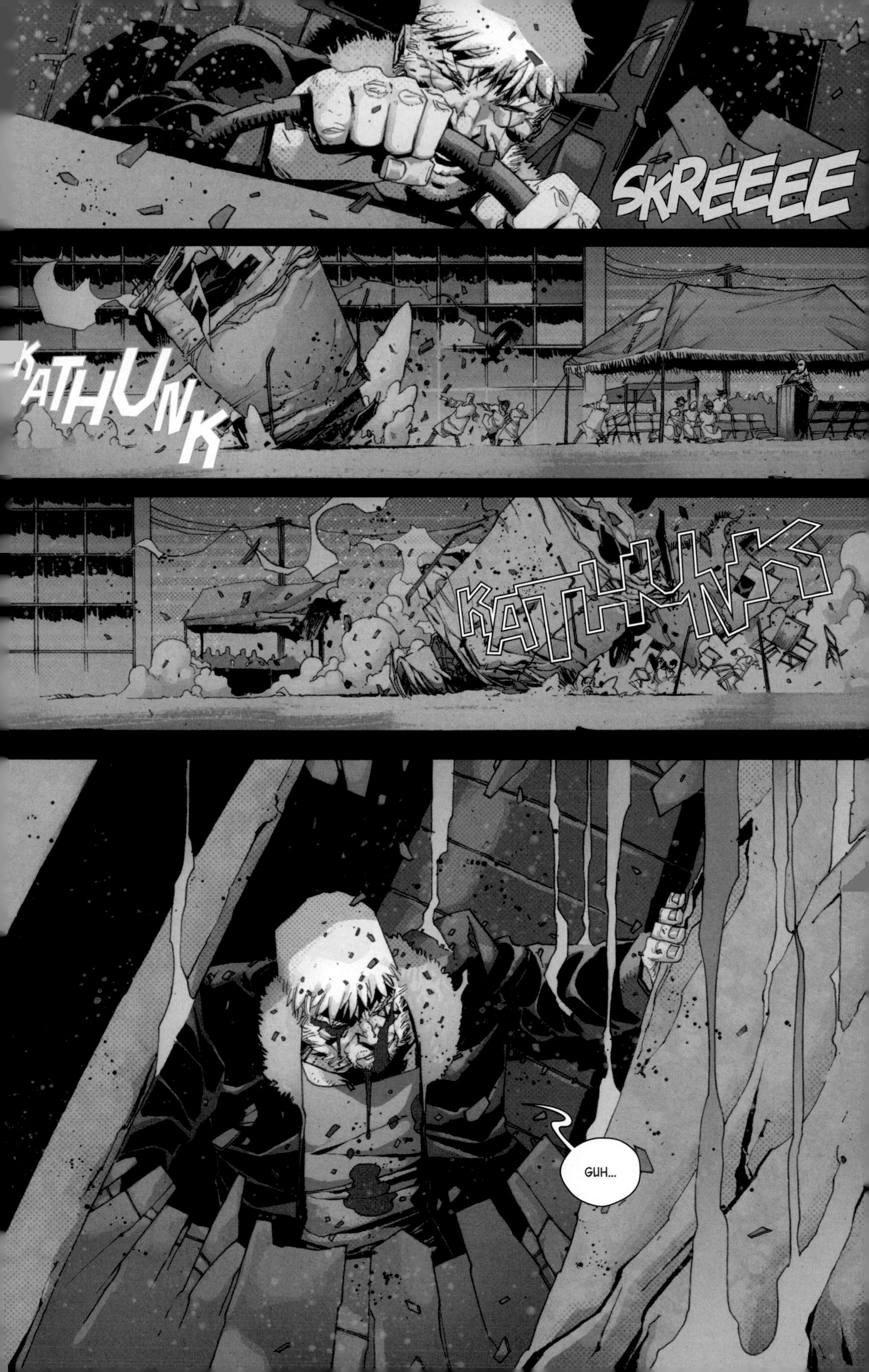
SKREEEE
KATHUNK
KATHUNK
GUH...

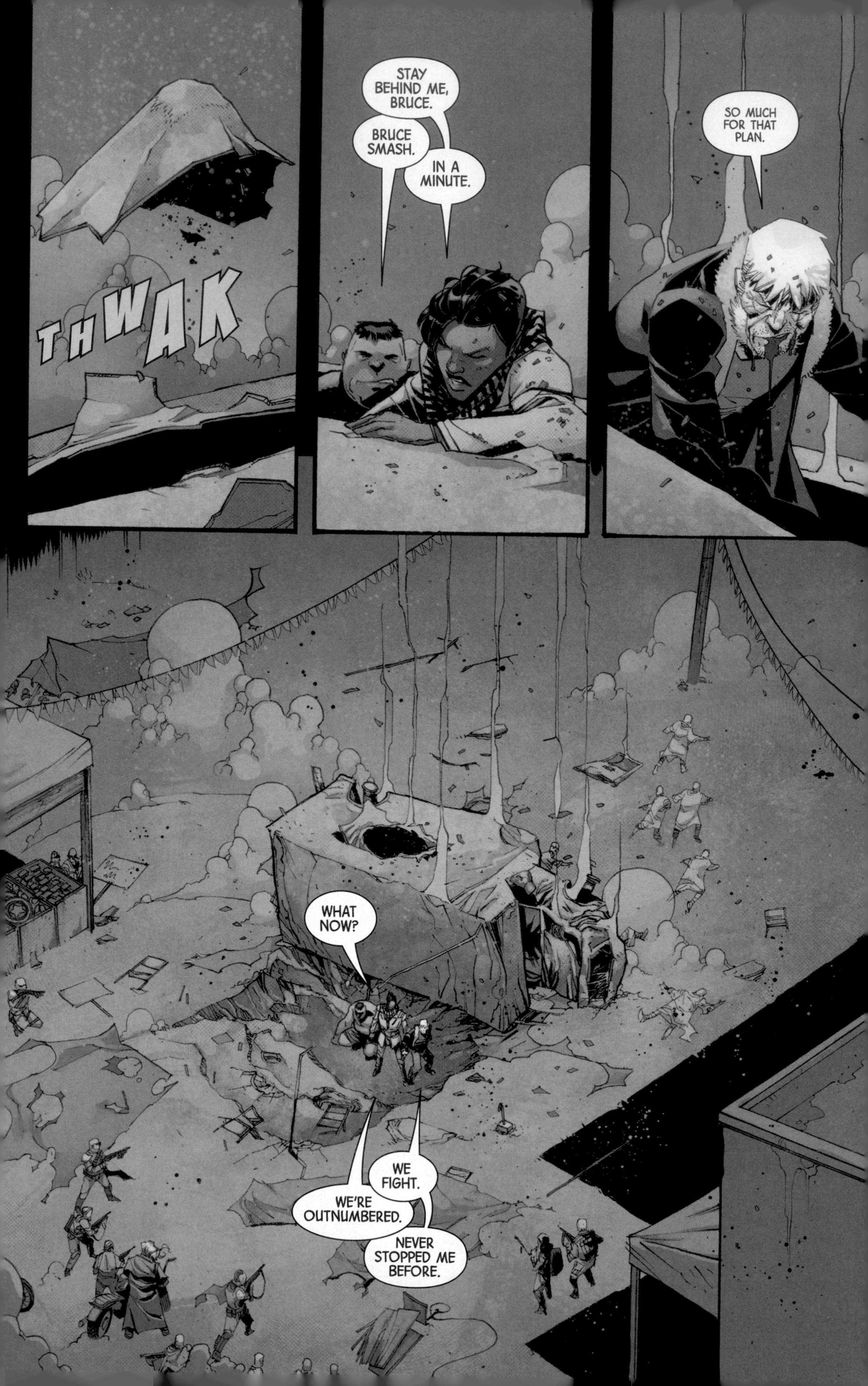
THWAK
STAY BEHIND ME, BRUCE.
BRUCE SMASH.
IN A MINUTE.
SO MUCH FOR THAT PLAN.
WHAT NOW?
WE FIGHT.
WE'RE OUTNUMBERED.
NEVER STOPPED ME BEFORE.

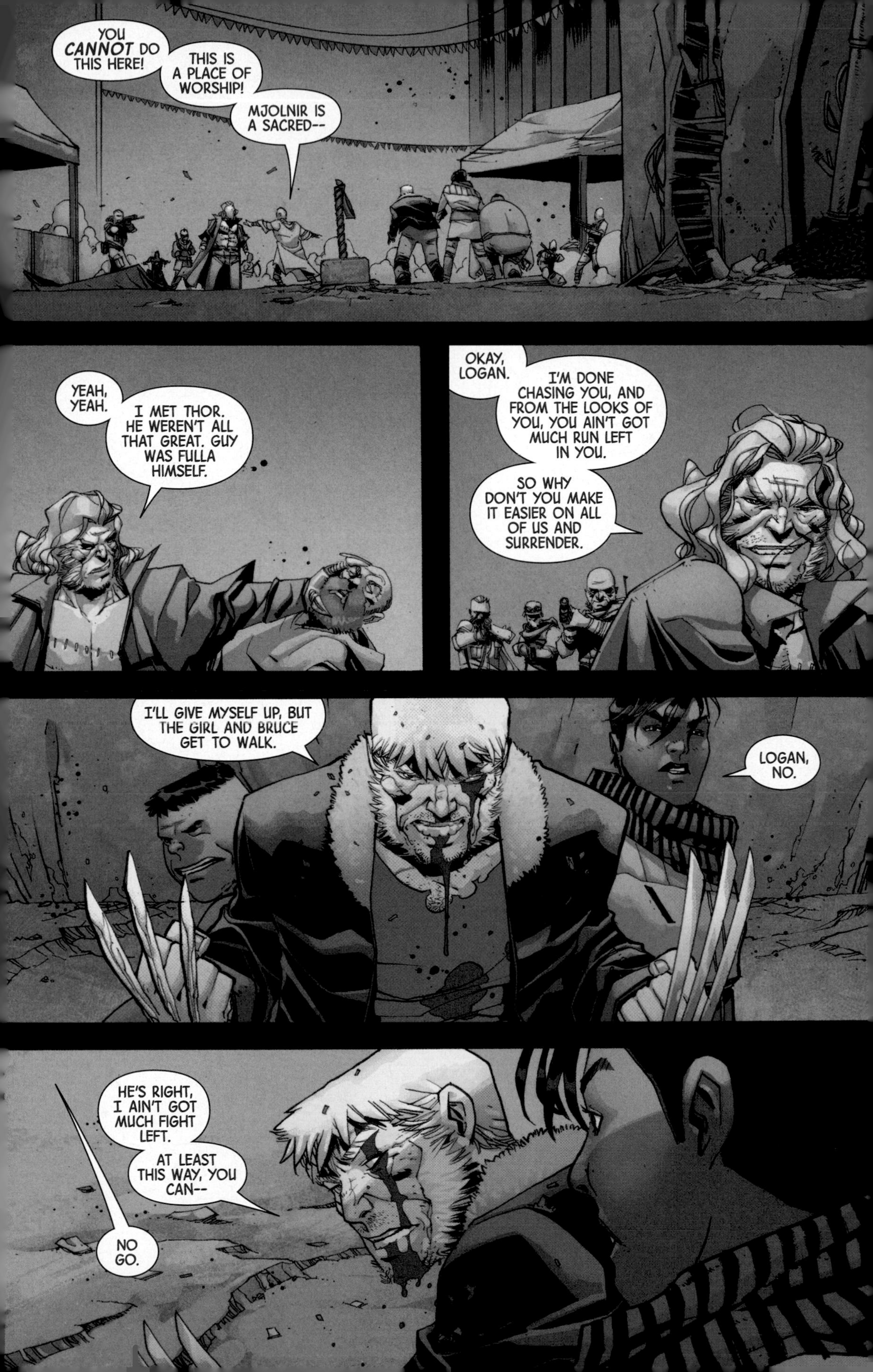
YOU CANNOT DO THIS HERE!
THIS IS A PLACE OF WORSHIP!
MJOLNIR IS A SACRED--
YEAH, YEAH.
I MET THOR. HE WEREN'T ALL THAT GREAT. GUY WAS FULLA HIMSELF.
OKAY, LOGAN.
I'M DONE CHASING YOU, AND FROM THE LOOKS OF YOU, YOU AIN'T GOT MUCH RUN LEFT IN YOU.
SO WHY DON'T YOU MAKE IT EASIER ON ALL OF US AND SURRENDER.
I'LL GIVE MYSELF UP, BUT THE GIRL AND BRUCE GET TO WALK.
LOGAN, NO.
HE'S RIGHT, I AIN'T GOT MUCH FIGHT LEFT.
AT LEAST THIS WAY, YOU CAN--
NO GO.

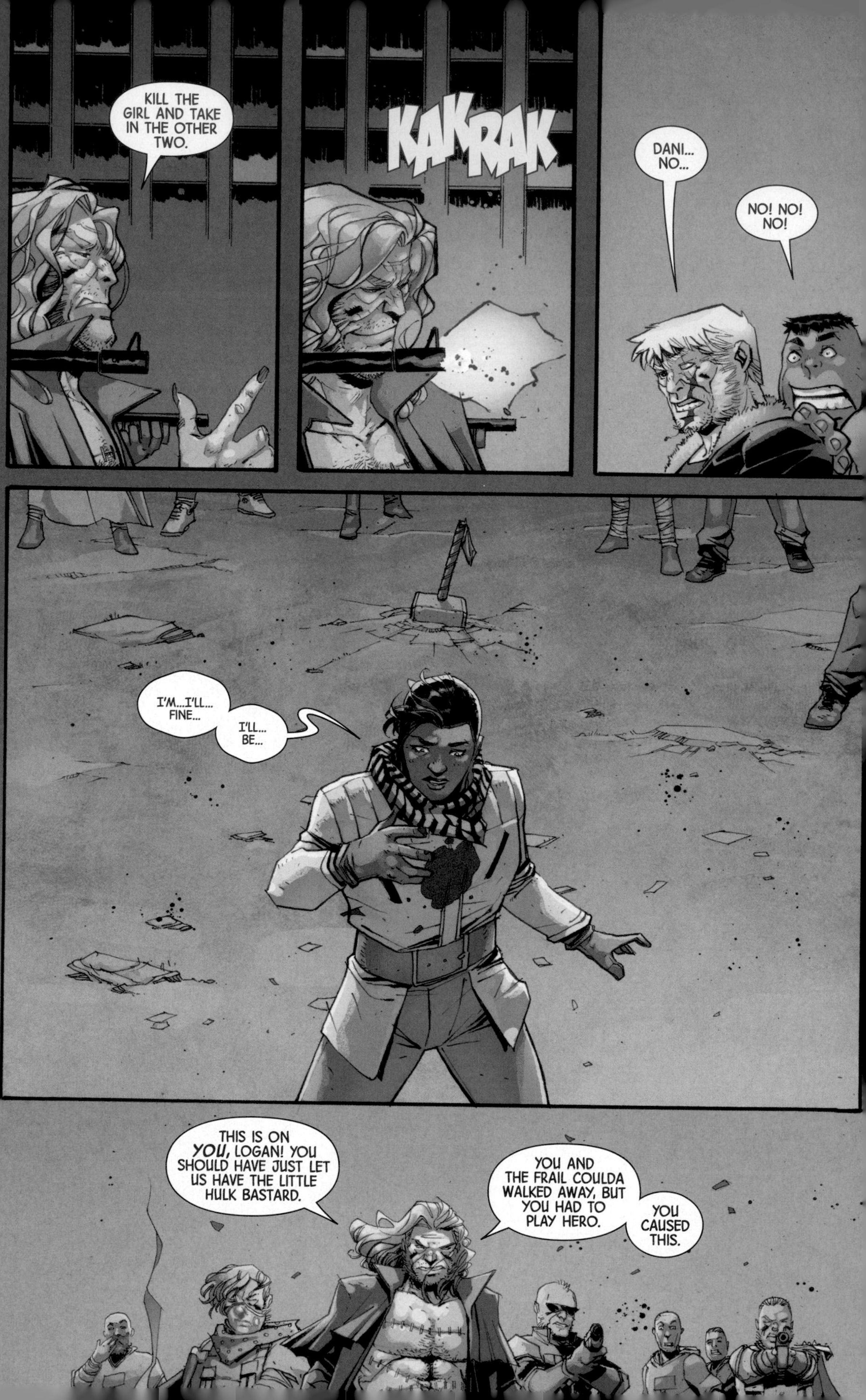
KILL THE GIRL AND TAKE IN THE OTHER TWO.
KAKRAK
DANI... NO...
NO! NO! NO!
I'M...I'LL... FINE...
I'LL... BE...
THIS IS ON YOU, LOGAN! YOU SHOULD HAVE JUST LET US HAVE THE LITTLE HULK BASTARD.
YOU AND THE FRAIL COULDA WALKED AWAY, BUT YOU HAD TO PLAY HERO.
YOU CAUSED THIS.

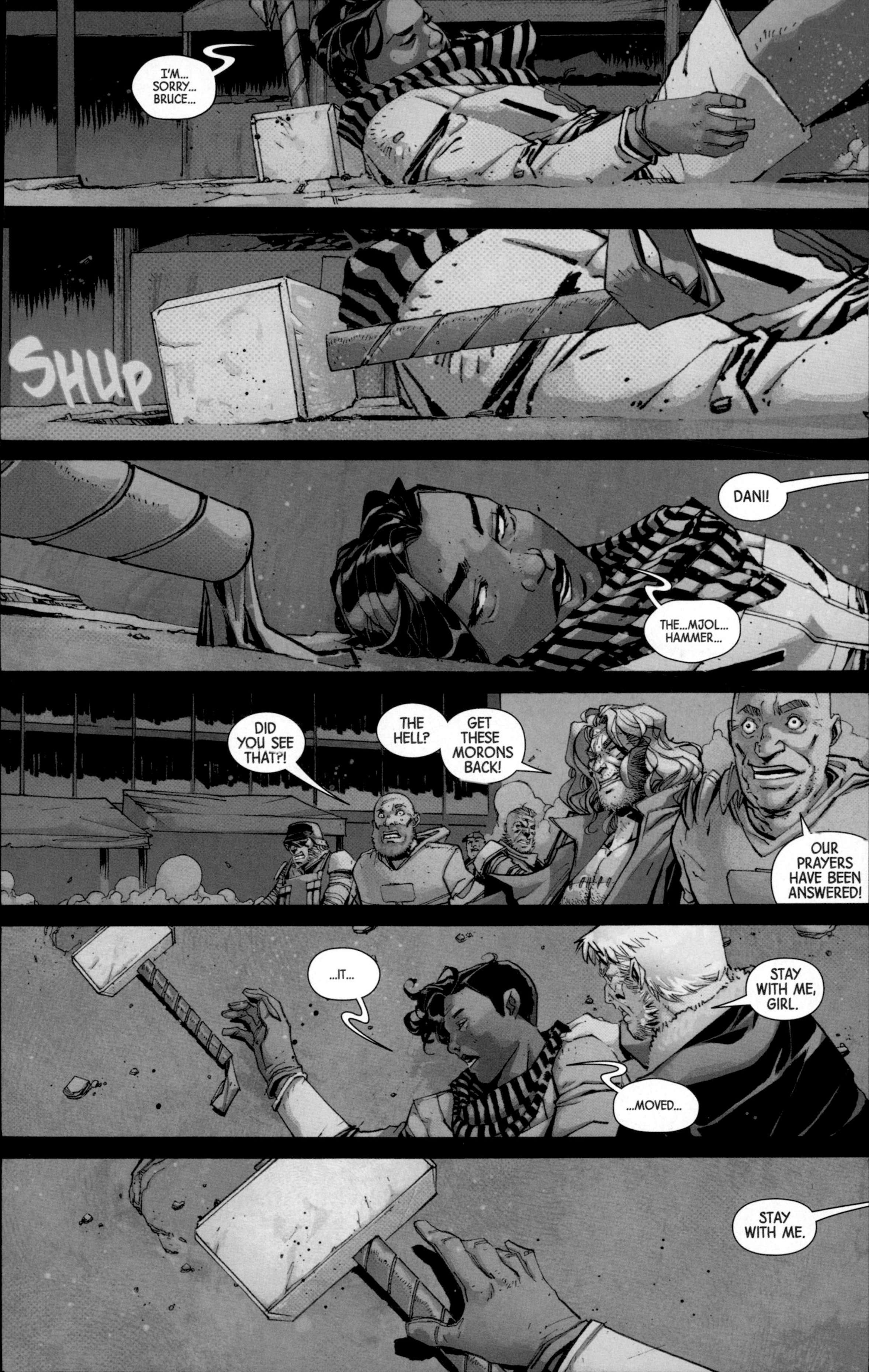
I'M... SORRY... BRUCE...
SHUP
DANI!
THE...MJOL... HAMMER...
DID YOU SEE THAT?!
THE HELL?
GET THESE MORONS BACK!
OUR PRAYERS HAVE BEEN ANSWERED!
...IT...
STAY WITH ME, GIRL.
...MOVED...
STAY WITH ME.

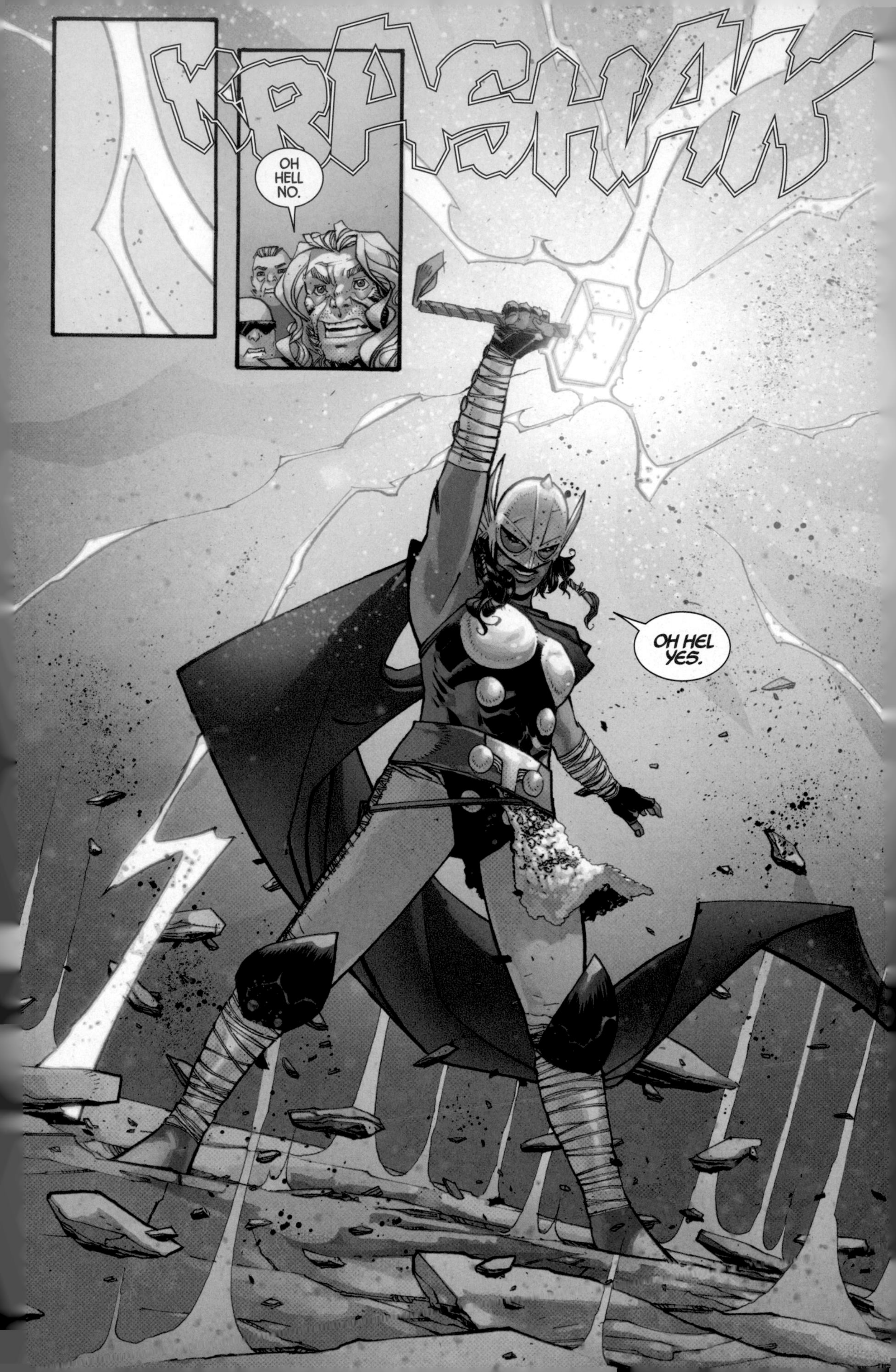
OH HELL NO.
OH HEL YES.

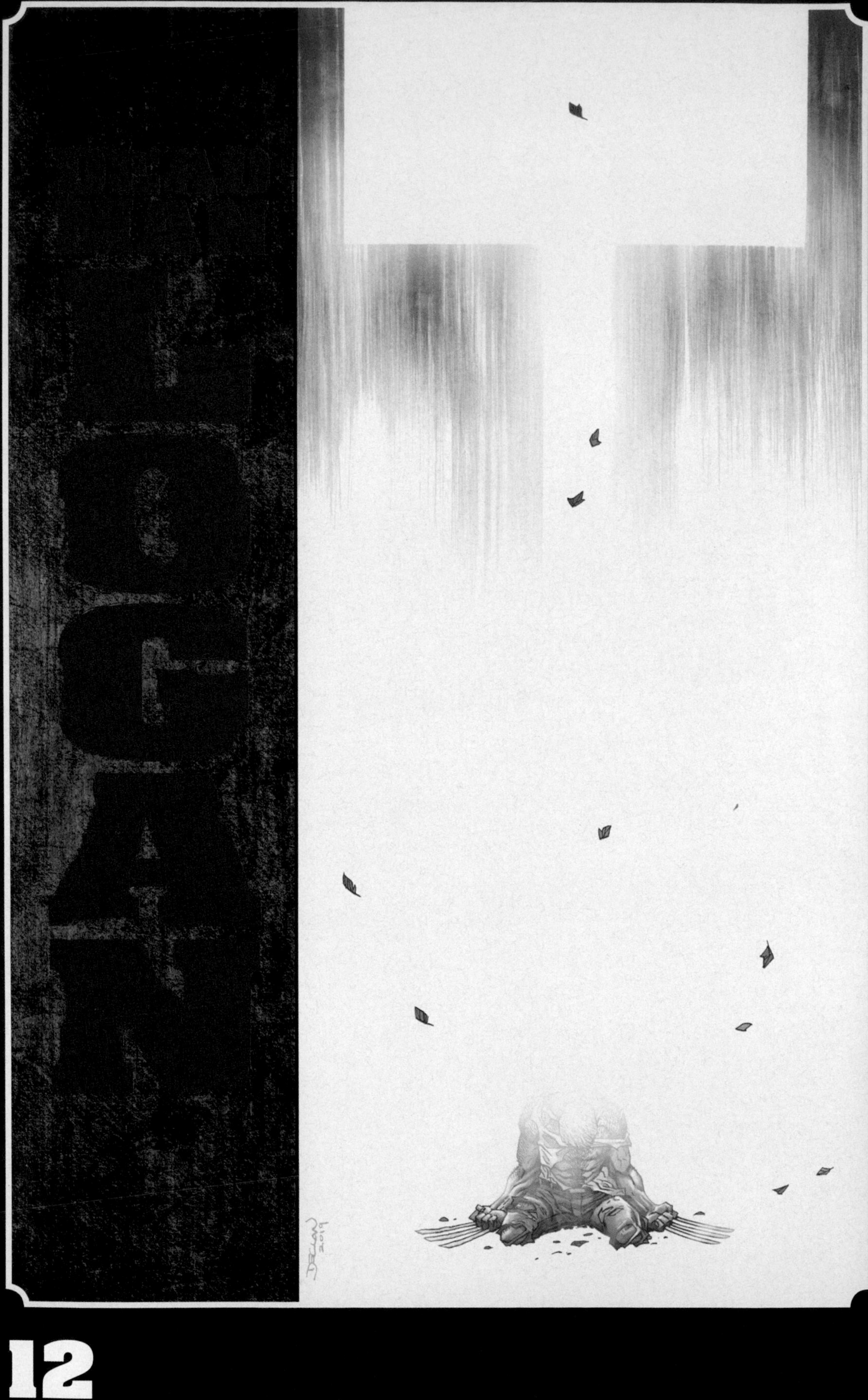

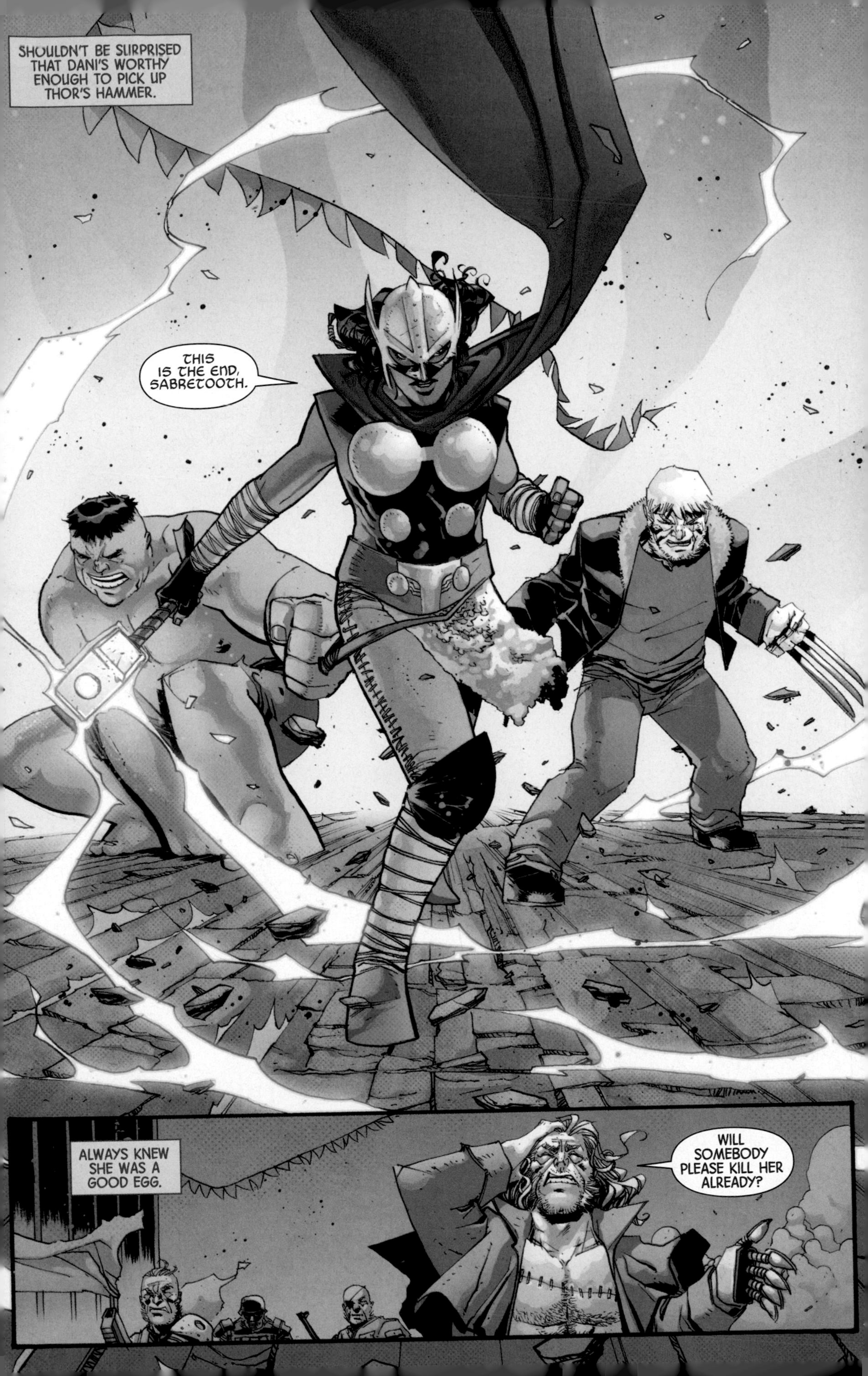
SHOULDN'T BE SURPRISED THAT DANI'S WORTHY ENOUGH TO PICK UP THOR'S HAMMER.
THIS IS THE END, SABRETOOTH.
ALWAYS KNEW SHE WAS A GOOD EGG.
WILL SOMEBODY PLEASE KILL HER ALREADY?

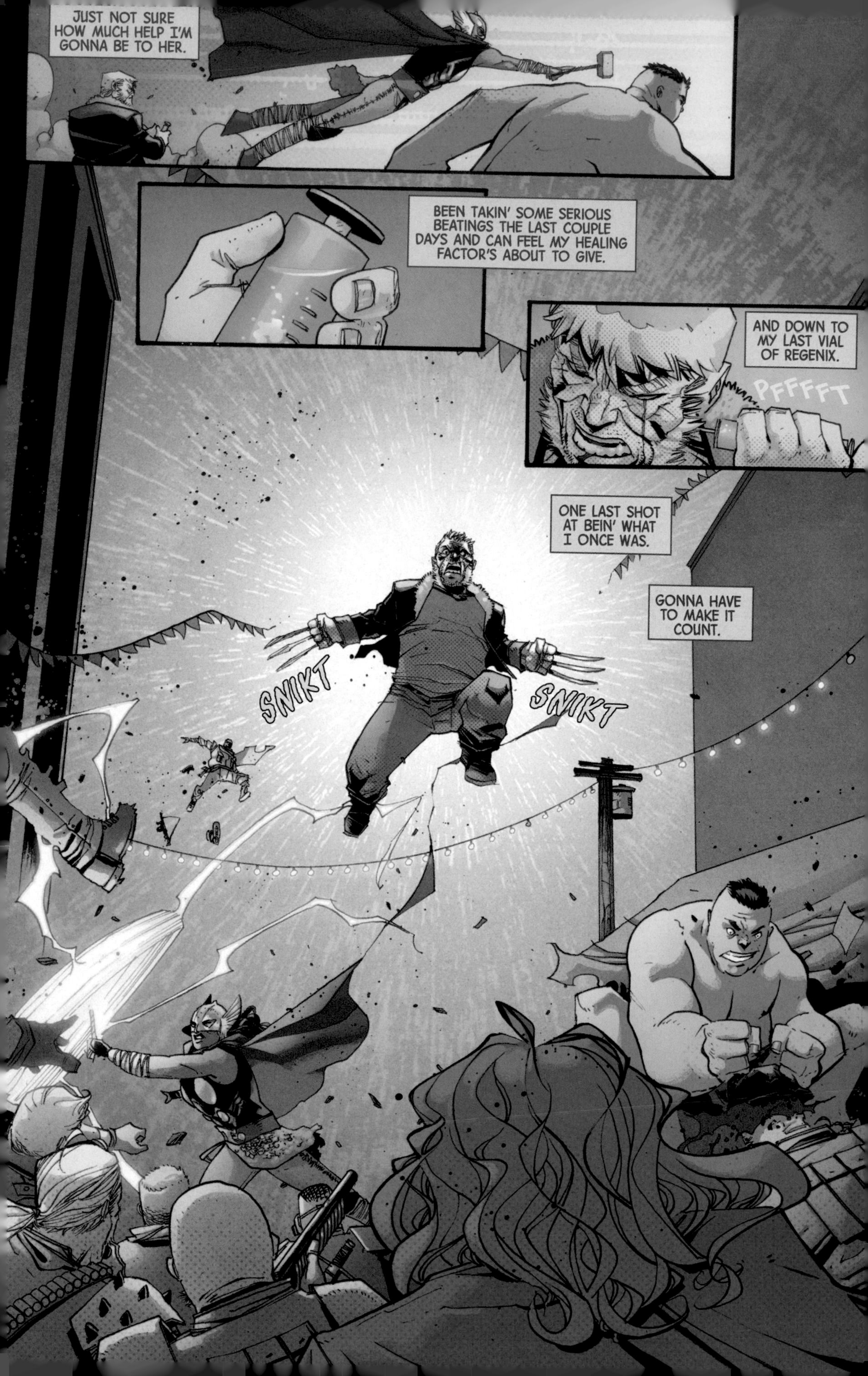
JUST NOT SURE HOW MUCH HELP I'M GONNA BE TO HER.
BEEN TAKIN' SOME SERIOUS BEATINGS THE LAST COUPLE DAYS AND CAN FEEL MY HEALING FACTOR'S ABOUT TO GIVE.
AND DOWN TO MY LAST VIAL OF REGENIX.
PFFFFT
ONE LAST SHOT AT BEIN' WHAT I ONCE WAS.
GONNA HAVE TO MAKE IT COUNT.
SNIKT
SNIKT

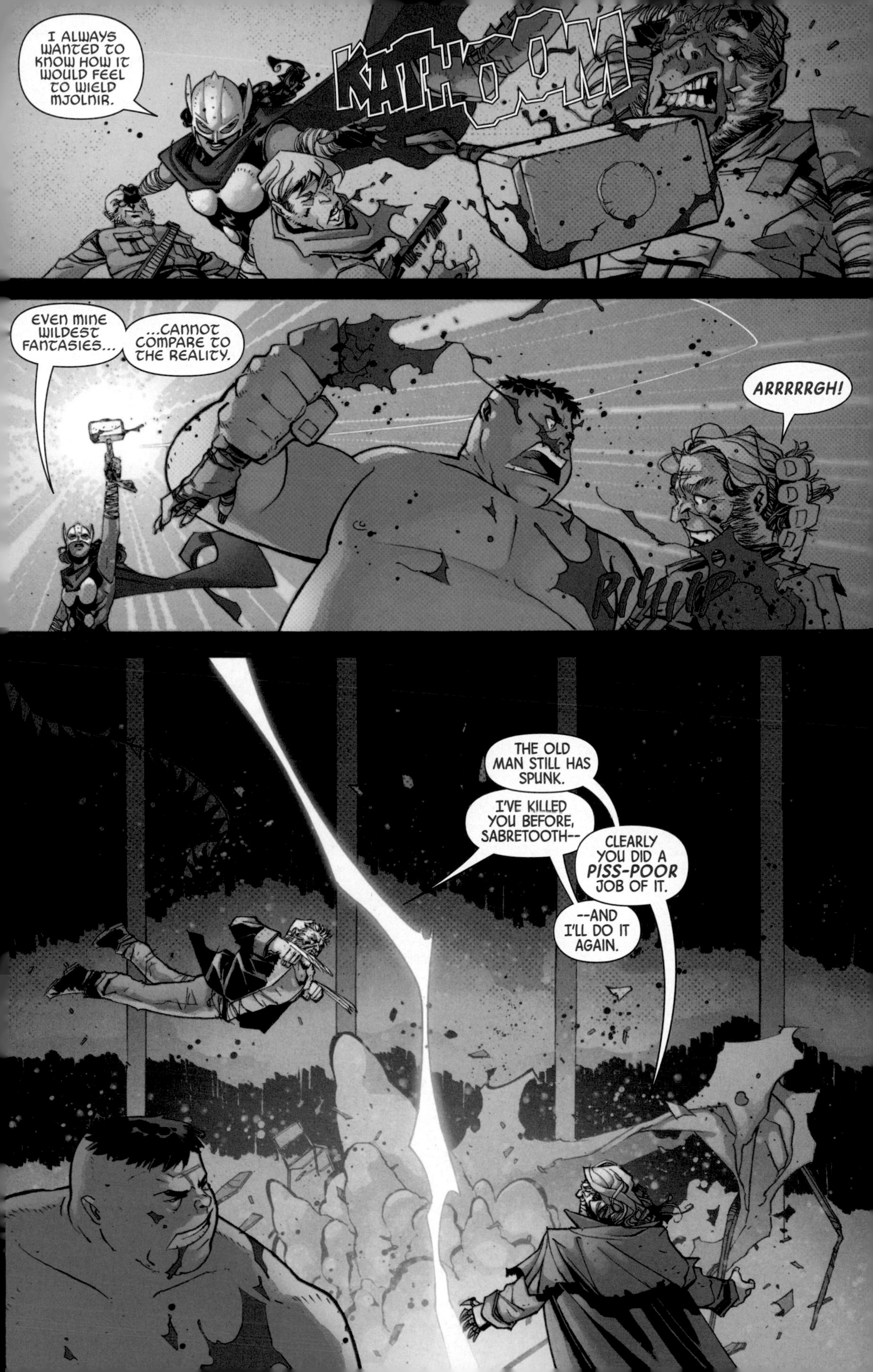
I ALWAYS WANTED TO KNOW HOW IT WOULD FEEL TO WIELD MJOLNIR.
KATHOOM
EVEN MINE WILDEST FANTASIES...
...CANNOT COMPARE TO THE REALITY.
ARRRRRGH!
THE OLD MAN STILL HAS SPUNK.
I'VE KILLED YOU BEFORE, SABRETOOTH--
CLEARLY YOU DID A PISS-POOR JOB OF IT.
--AND I'LL DO IT AGAIN.

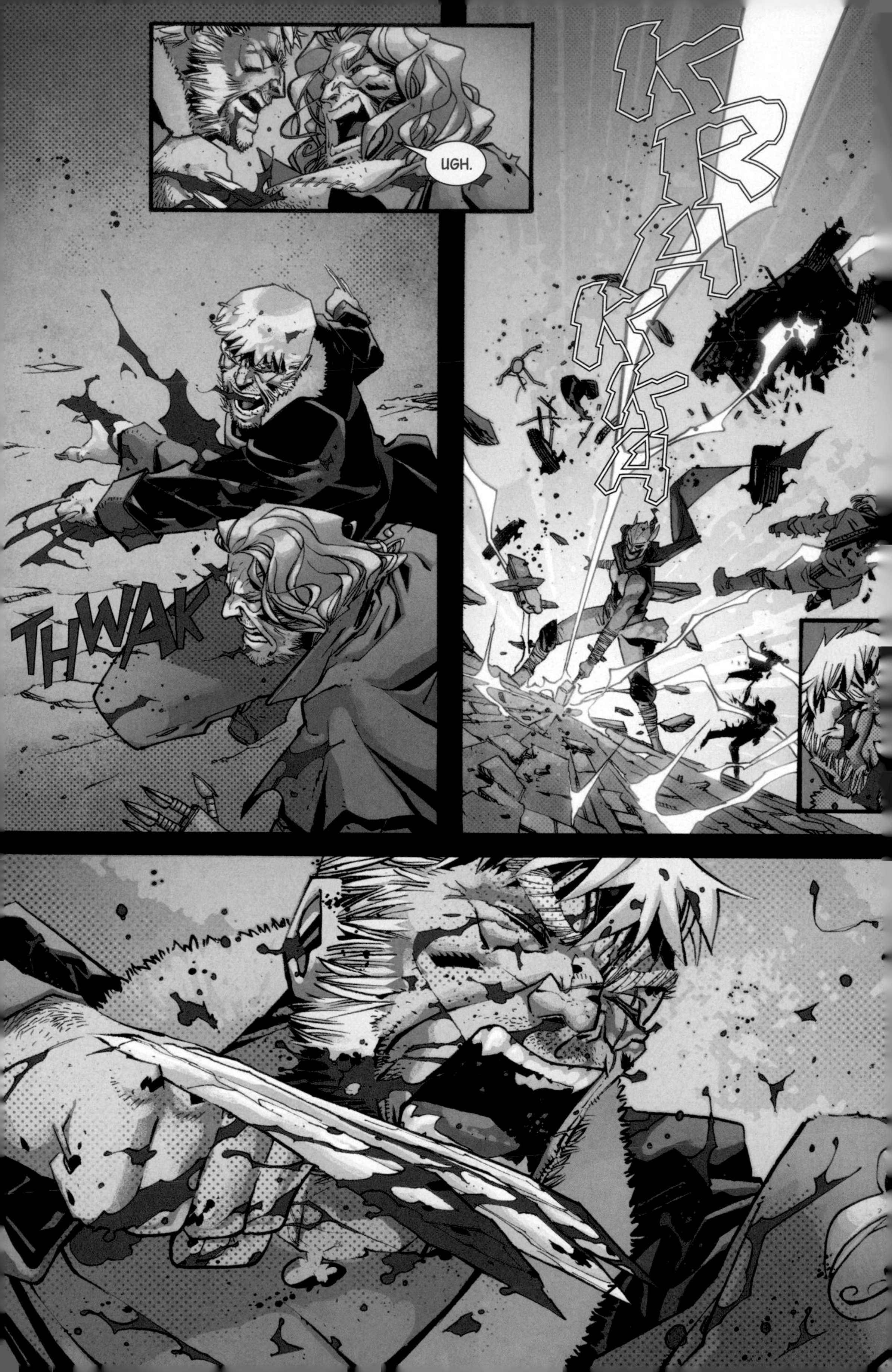
UGH.
KRAKKA
THWAK

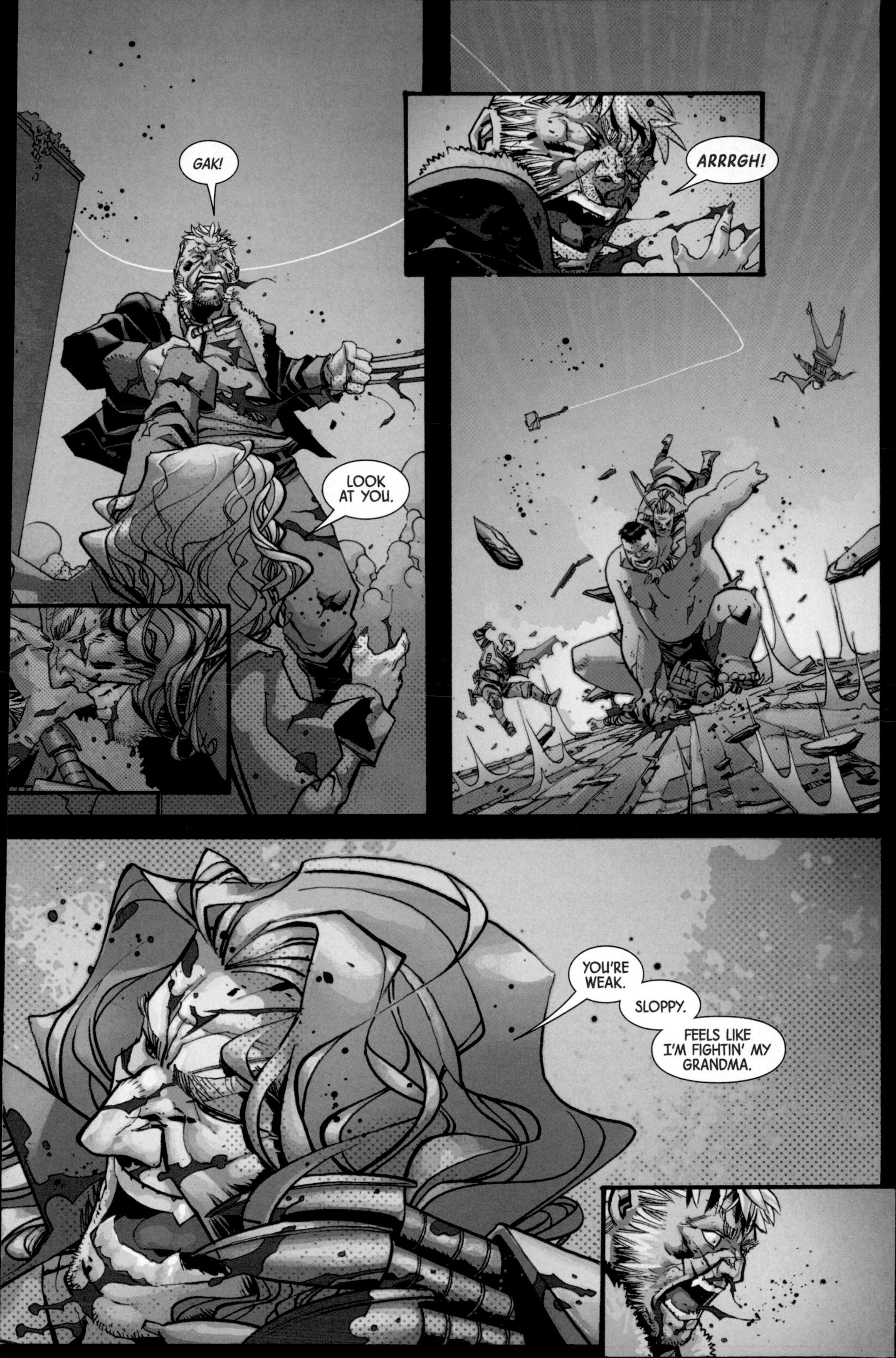
GAK!
ARRRGH!
LOOK AT YOU.
YOU'RE WEAK.
SLOPPY.
FEELS LIKE I'M FIGHTIN' MY GRANDMA.

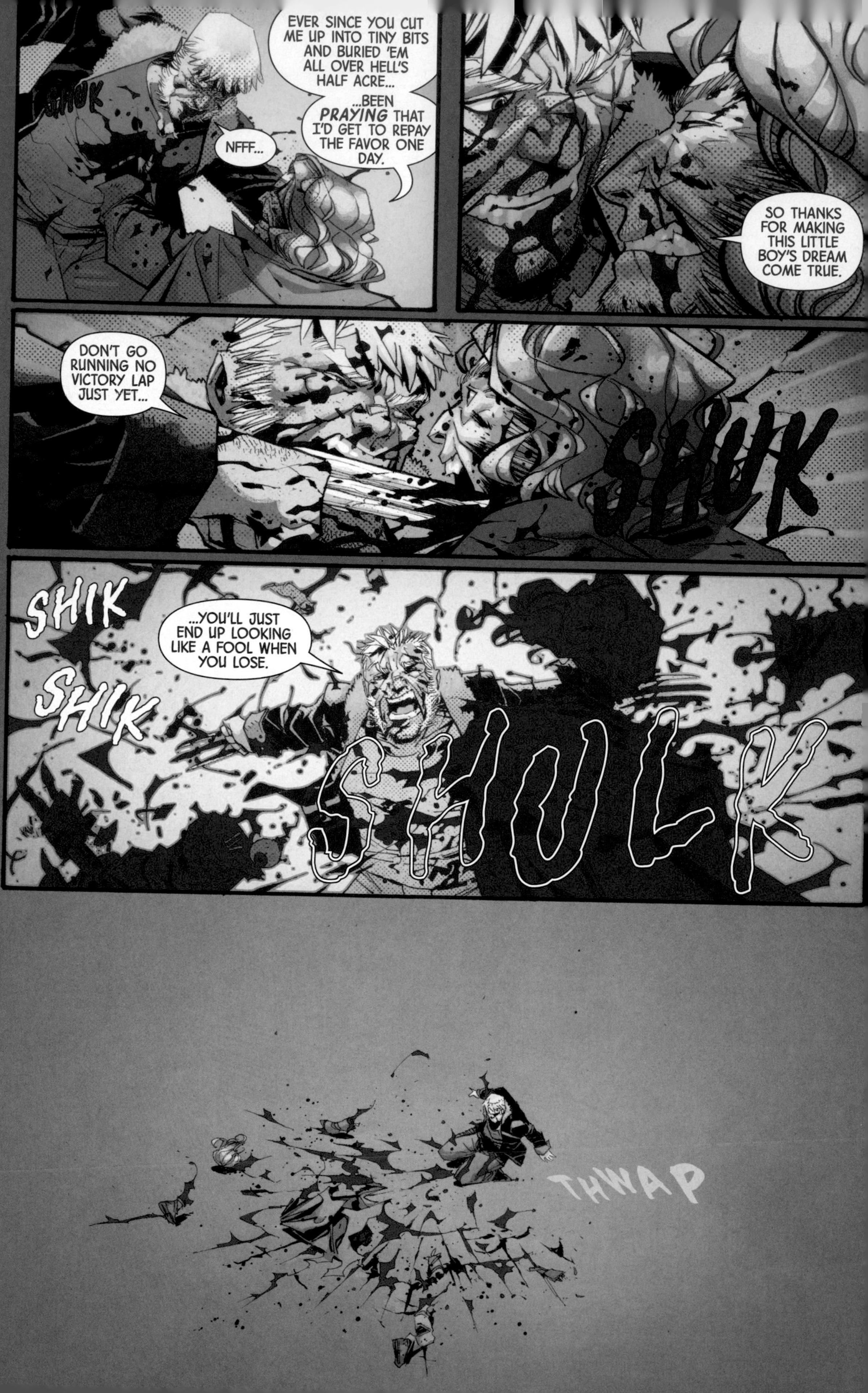
SHUK
EVER SINCE YOU CUT ME UP INTO TINY BITS AND BURIED 'EM ALL OVER HELL'S HALF ACRE...
...BEEN *PRAYING* THAT I'D GET TO REPAY THE FAVOR ONE DAY.
NFFF...
SO THANKS FOR MAKING THIS LITTLE BOY'S DREAM COME TRUE.
DON'T GO RUNNING NO VICTORY LAP JUST YET...
SHUK
SHIK
SHIK
...YOU'LL JUST END UP LOOKING LIKE A FOOL WHEN YOU LOSE.
SHULK
THWAP

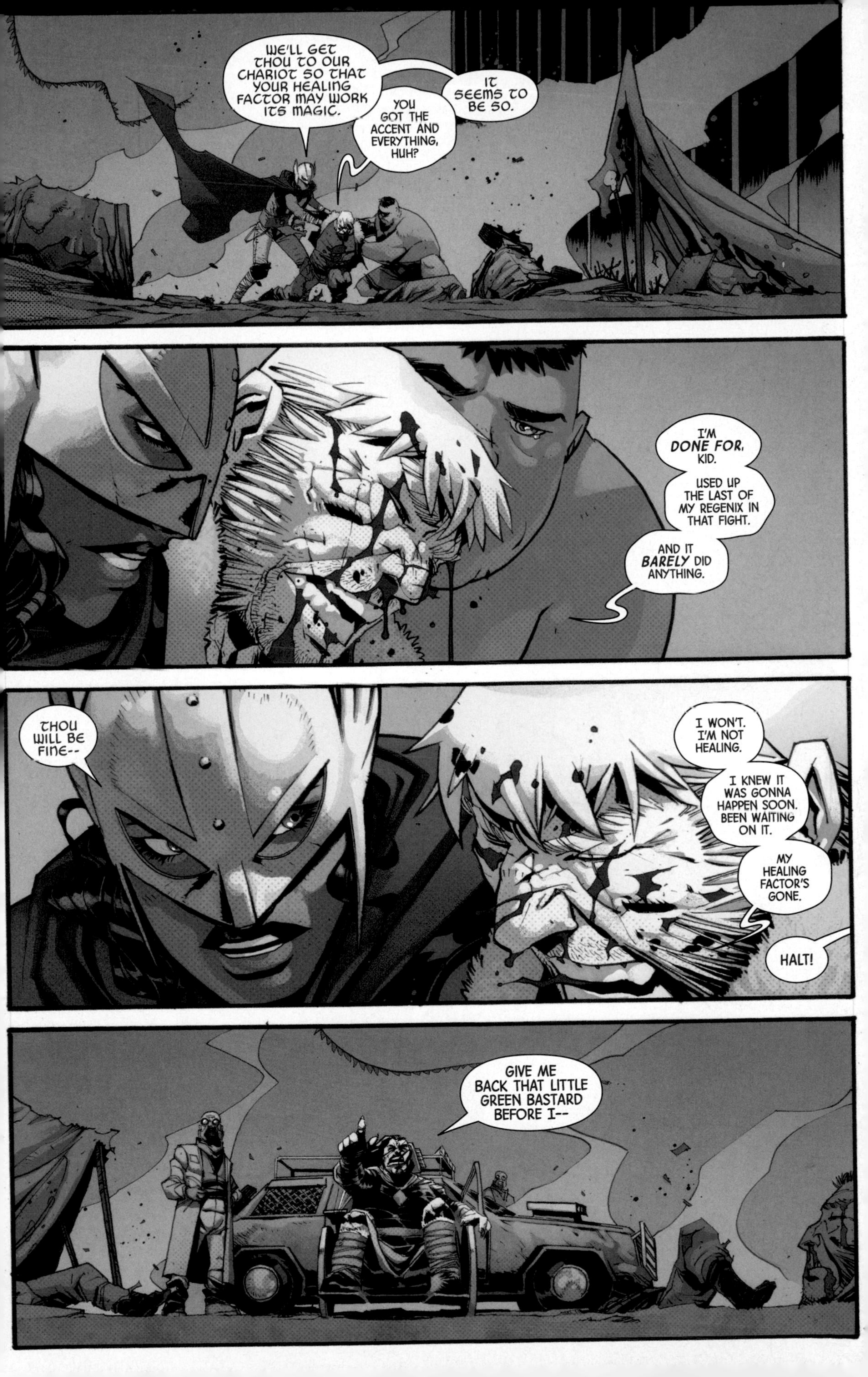
WE'LL GET THOU TO OUR CHARIOT SO THAT YOUR HEALING FACTOR MAY WORK ITS MAGIC.
YOU GOT THE ACCENT AND EVERYTHING, HUH?
IT SEEMS TO BE SO.
I'M DONE FOR, KID.
USED UP THE LAST OF MY REGENIX IN THAT FIGHT.
AND IT BARELY DID ANYTHING.
THOU WILL BE FINE--
I WON'T. I'M NOT HEALING.
I KNEW IT WAS GONNA HAPPEN SOON. BEEN WAITING ON IT.
MY HEALING FACTOR'S GONE.
HALT!
GIVE ME BACK THAT LITTLE GREEN BASTARD BEFORE I--

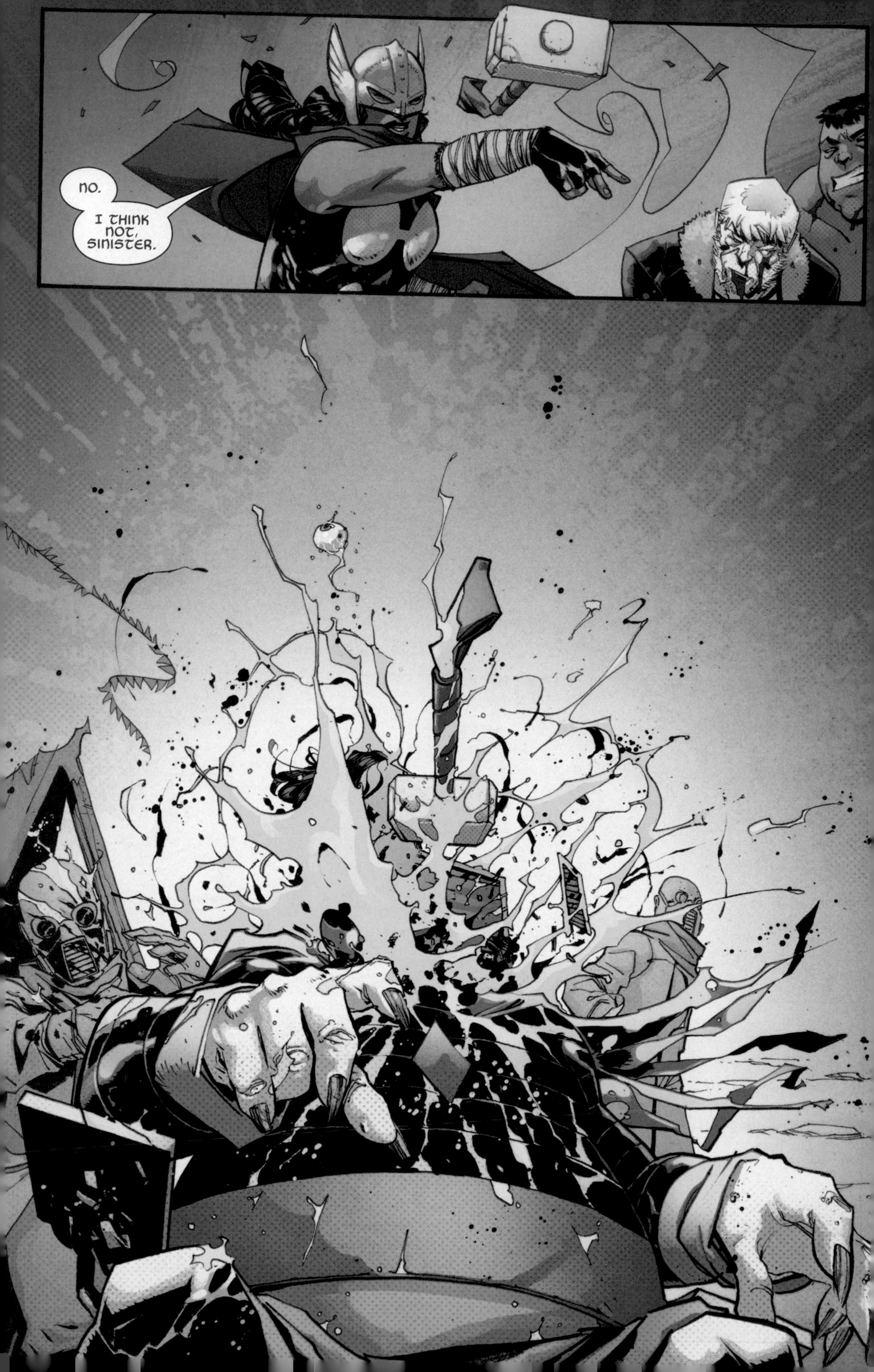
NO.
I THINK NOT, SINISTER.

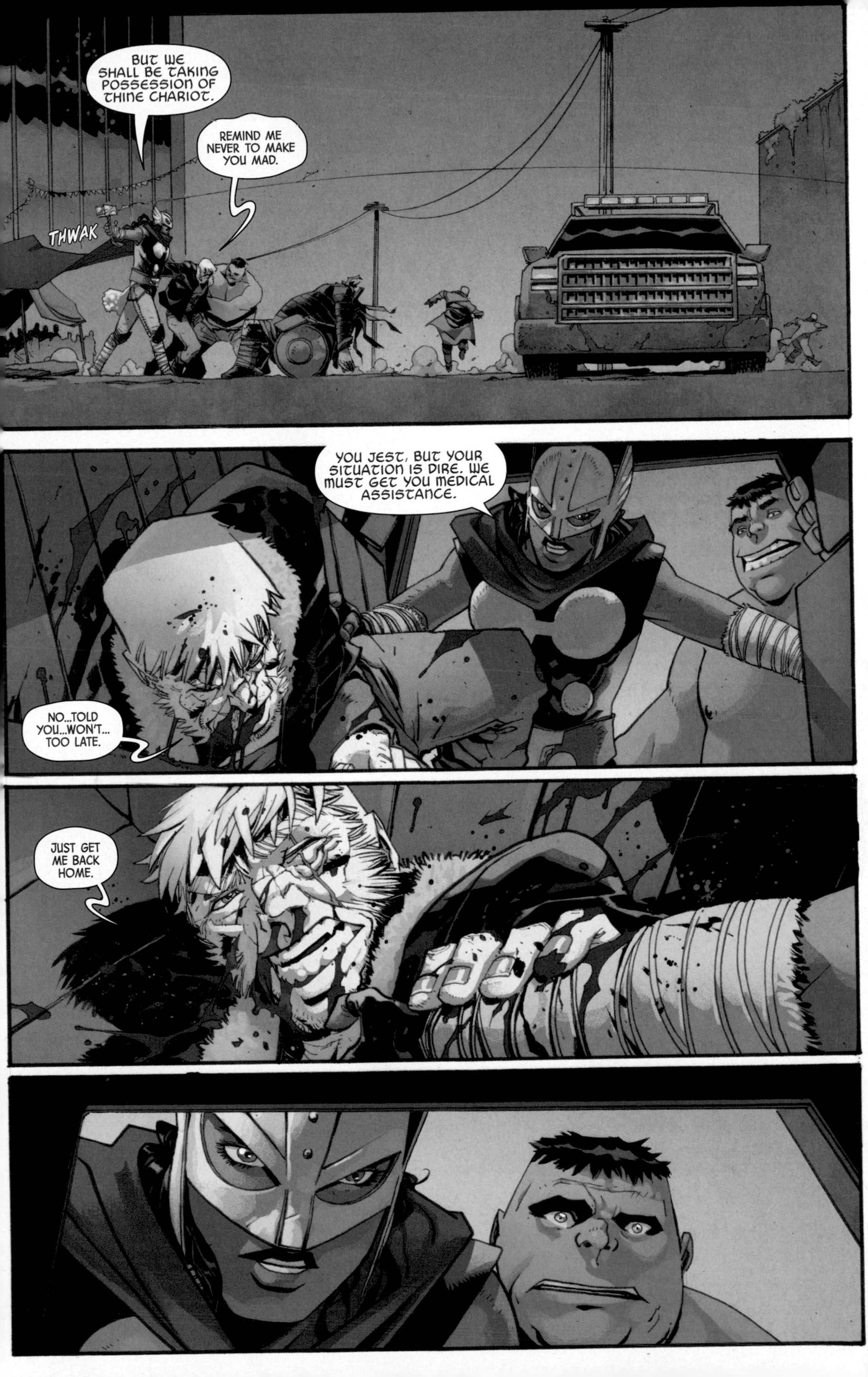
BUT WE SHALL BE TAKING POSSESSION OF THINE CHARIOT.
REMIND ME NEVER TO MAKE YOU MAD.
THWAK
YOU JEST, BUT YOUR SITUATION IS DIRE. WE MUST GET YOU MEDICAL ASSISTANCE.
NO...TOLD YOU...WON'T... TOO LATE.
JUST GET ME BACK HOME.

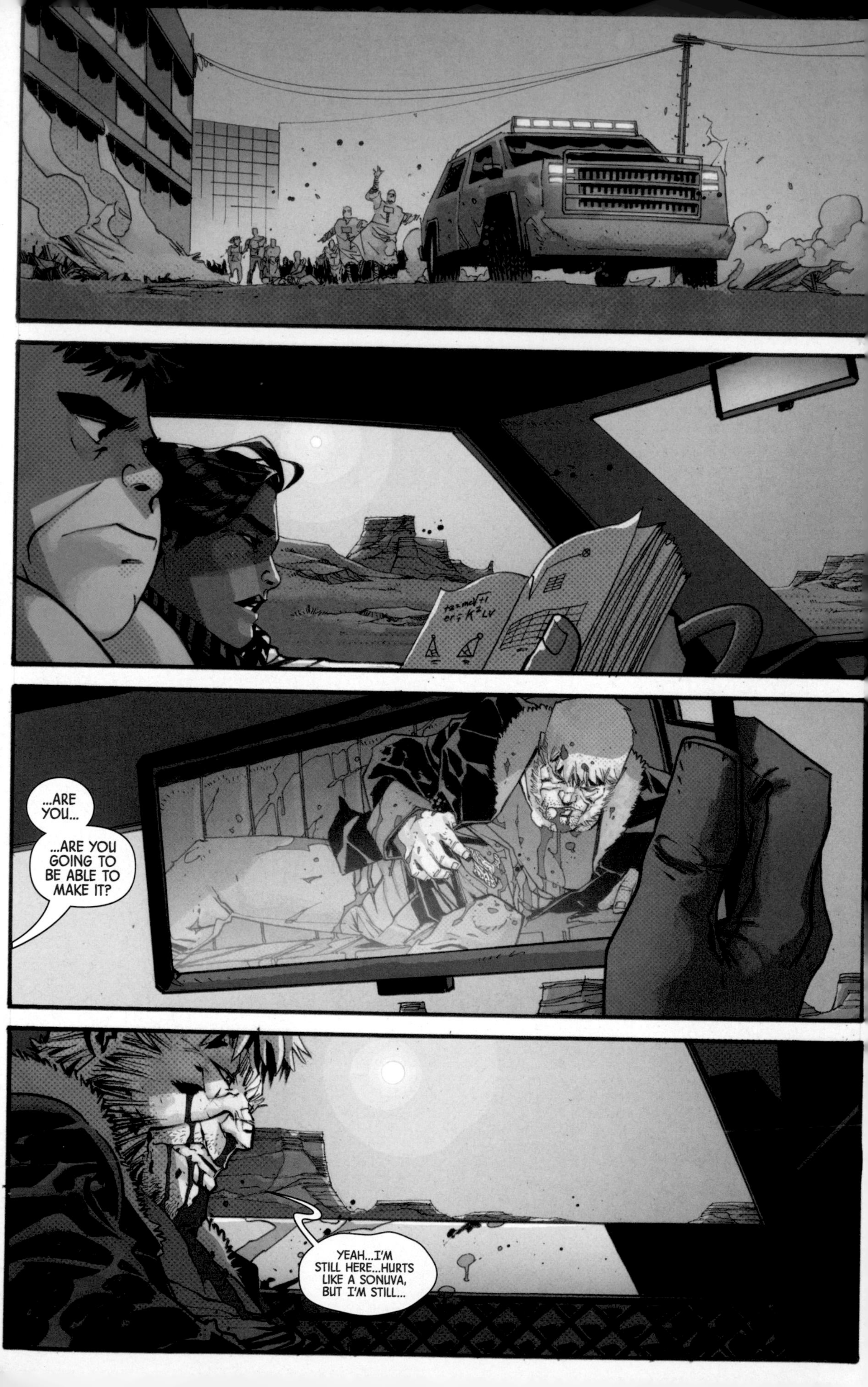
...ARE YOU...
...ARE YOU GOING TO BE ABLE TO MAKE IT?
YEAH...I'M STILL HERE...HURTS LIKE A SONUVA, BUT I'M STILL...

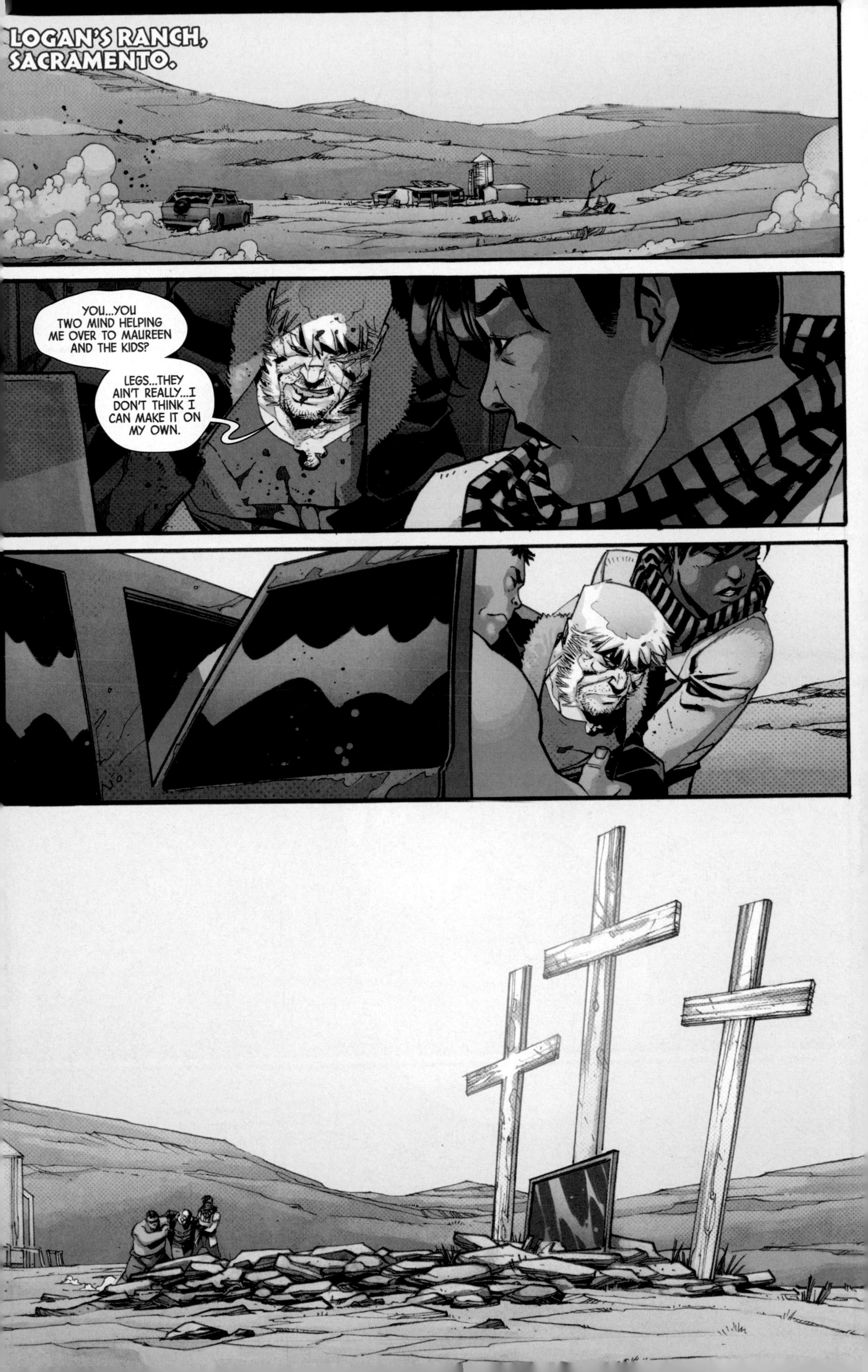
LOGAN'S RANCH, SACRAMENTO.
YOU...YOU TWO MIND HELPING ME OVER TO MAUREEN AND THE KIDS?
LEGS...THEY AIN'T REALLY...I DON'T THINK I CAN MAKE IT ON MY OWN.

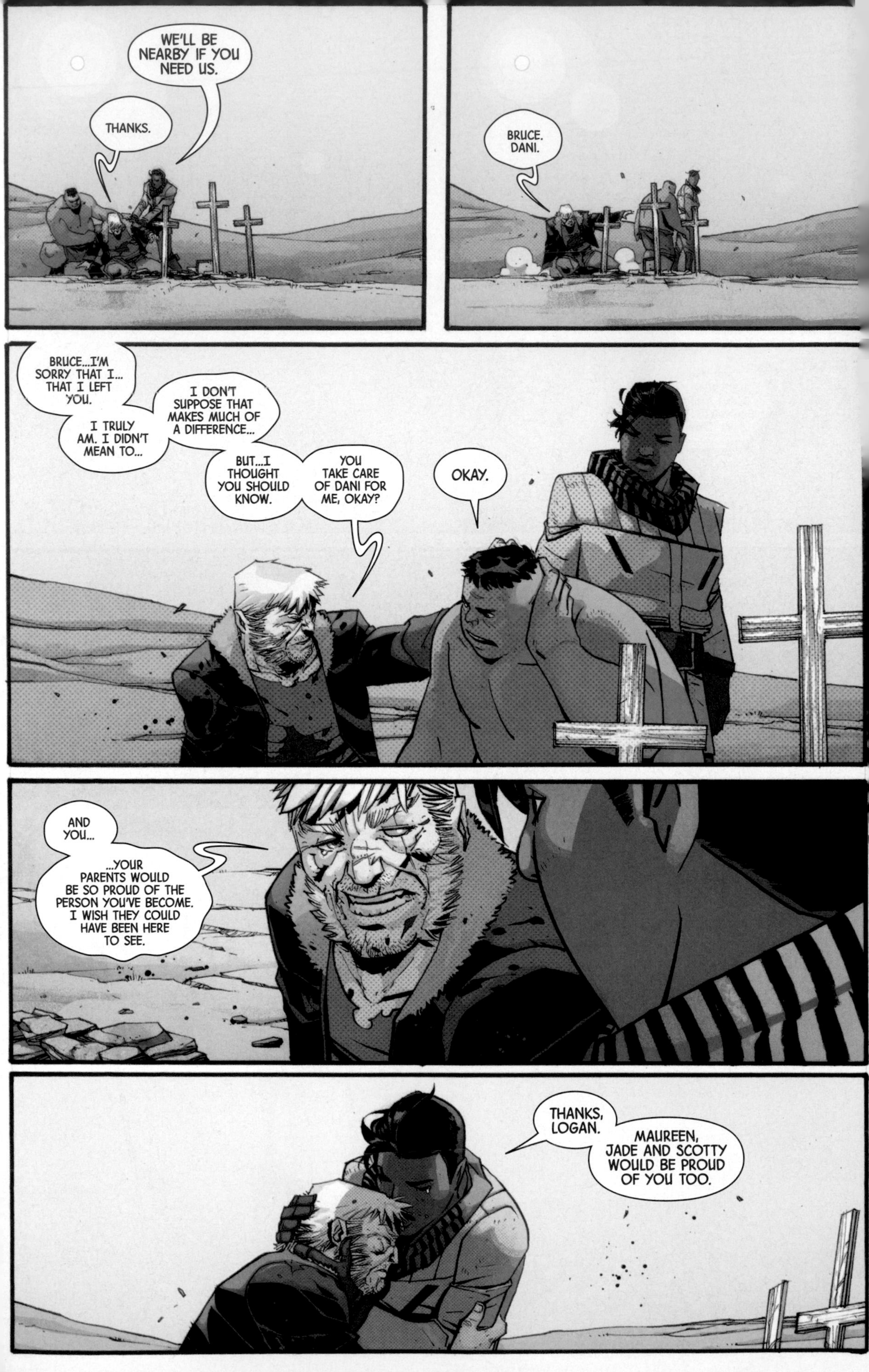
WE'LL BE NEARBY IF YOU NEED US.
THANKS.
BRUCE. DANI.
BRUCE...I'M SORRY THAT I... THAT I LEFT YOU.
I TRULY AM. I DIDN'T MEAN TO...
I DON'T SUPPOSE THAT MAKES MUCH OF A DIFFERENCE...
BUT...I THOUGHT YOU SHOULD KNOW.
YOU TAKE CARE OF DANI FOR ME, OKAY?
OKAY.
AND YOU...
...YOUR PARENTS WOULD BE SO PROUD OF THE PERSON YOU'VE BECOME. I WISH THEY COULD HAVE BEEN HERE TO SEE.
THANKS, LOGAN.
MAUREEN, JADE AND SCOTTY WOULD BE PROUD OF YOU TOO.

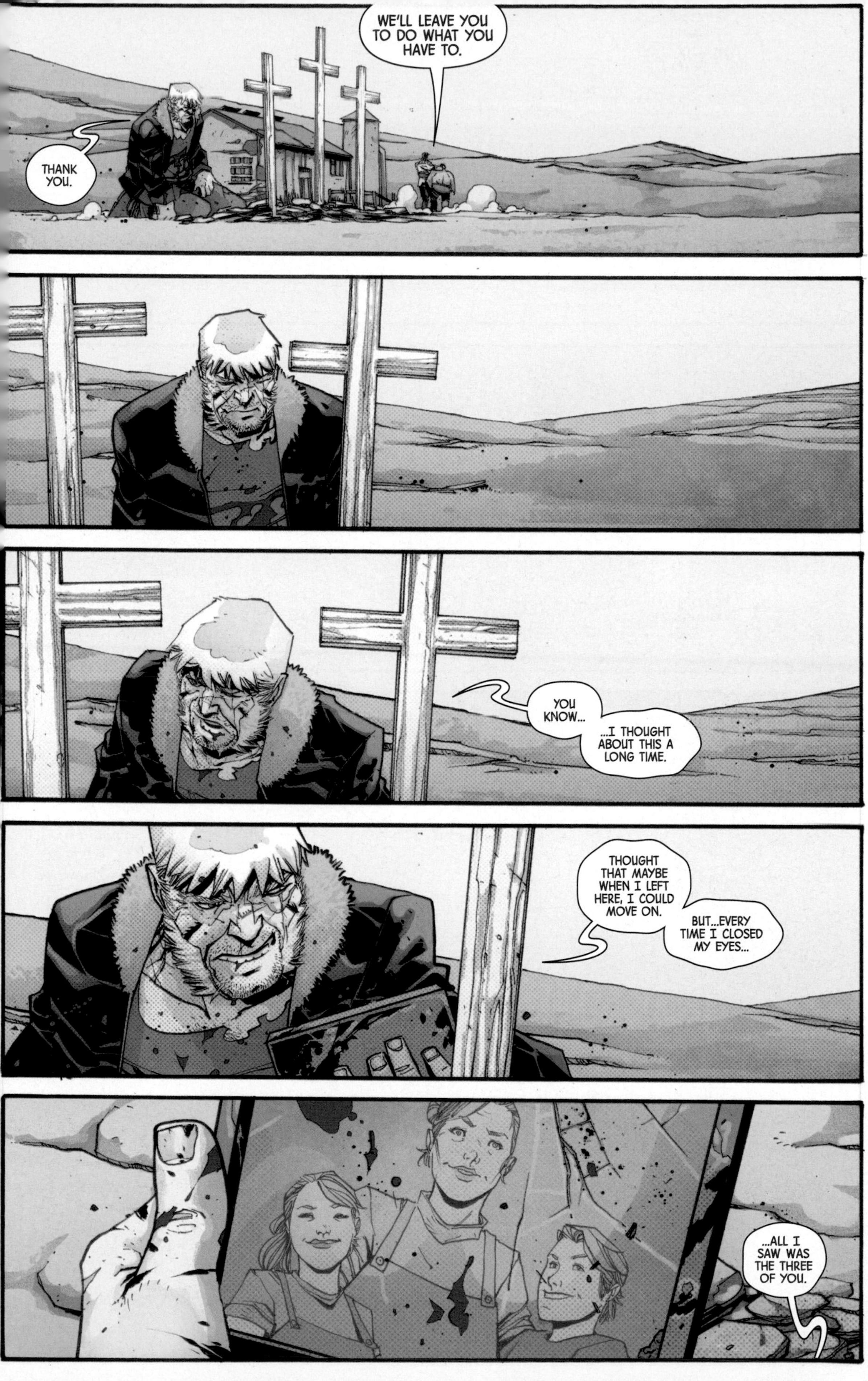
WE'LL LEAVE YOU TO DO WHAT YOU HAVE TO.
THANK YOU.
YOU KNOW...
...I THOUGHT ABOUT THIS A LONG TIME.
THOUGHT THAT MAYBE WHEN I LEFT HERE, I COULD MOVE ON.
BUT...EVERY TIME I CLOSED MY EYES...
...ALL I SAW WAS THE THREE OF YOU.

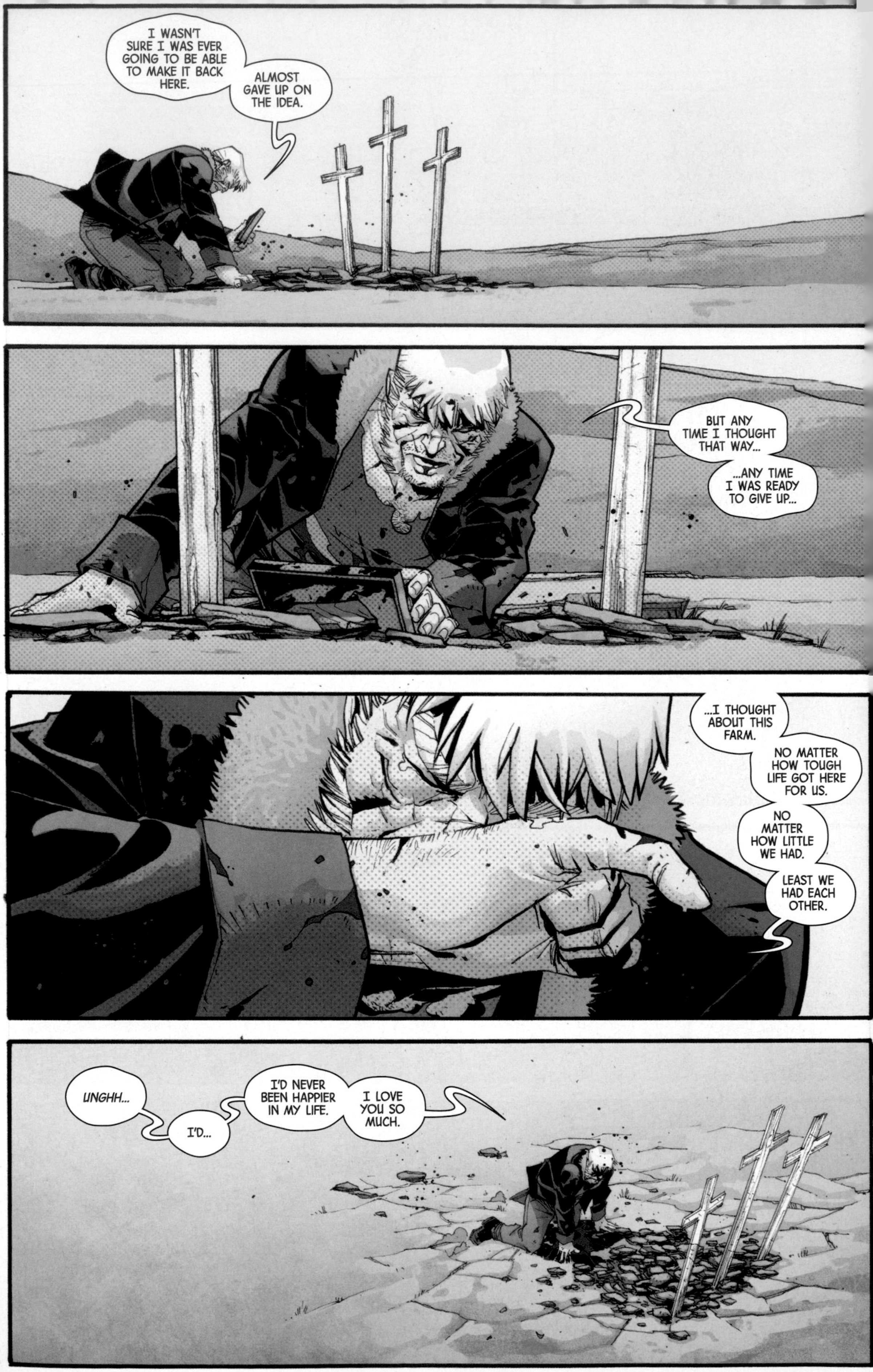
I WASN'T SURE I WAS EVER GOING TO BE ABLE TO MAKE IT BACK HERE.
ALMOST GAVE UP ON THE IDEA.
BUT ANY TIME I THOUGHT THAT WAY...
...ANY TIME I WAS READY TO GIVE UP...
...I THOUGHT ABOUT THIS FARM.
NO MATTER HOW TOUGH LIFE GOT HERE FOR US.
NO MATTER HOW LITTLE WE HAD.
LEAST WE HAD EACH OTHER.
UNGHH...
I'D...
I'D NEVER BEEN HAPPIER IN MY LIFE.
I LOVE YOU SO MUCH.

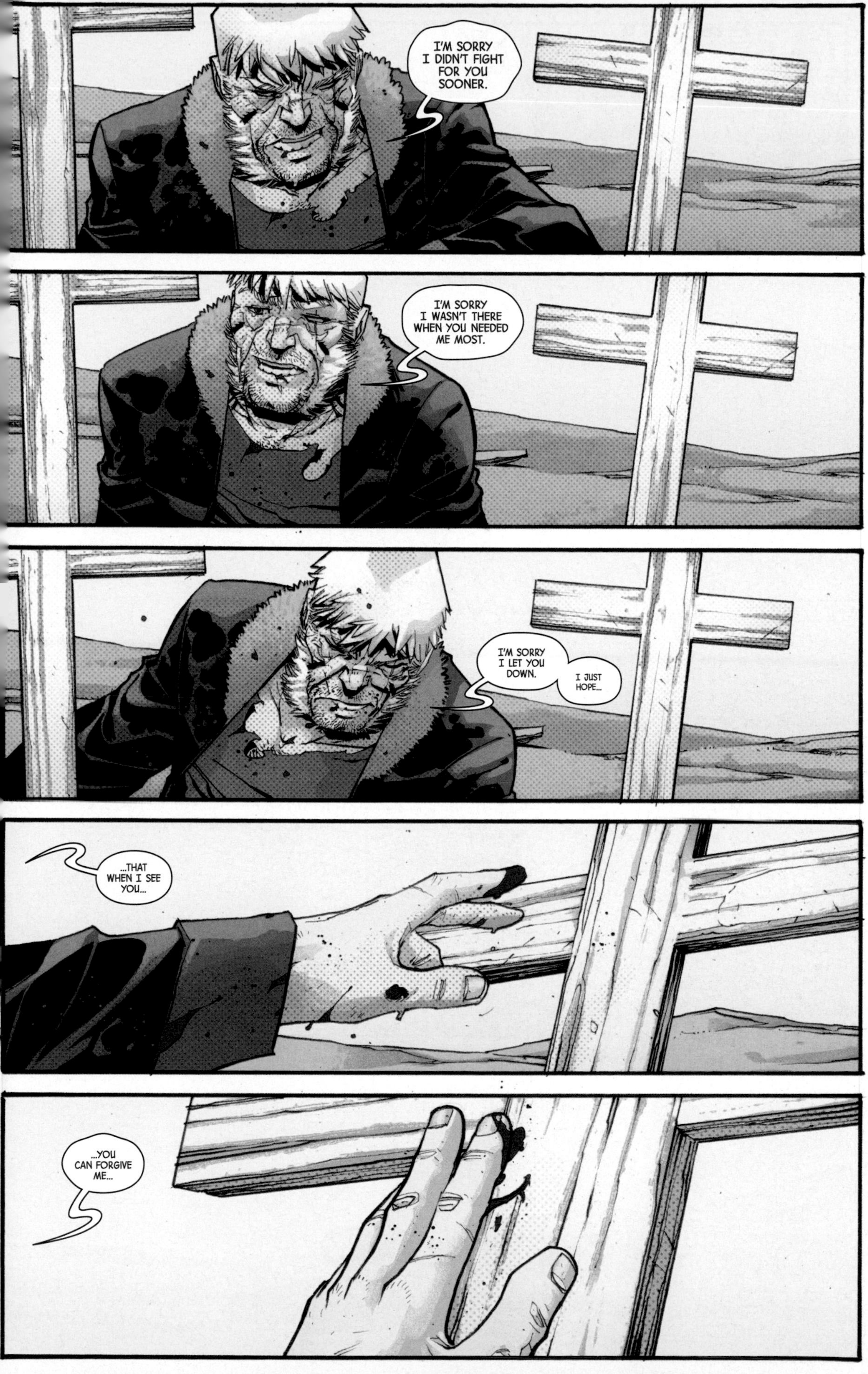
I'M SORRY I DIDN'T FIGHT FOR YOU SOONER.
I'M SORRY I WASN'T THERE WHEN YOU NEEDED ME MOST.
I'M SORRY I LET YOU DOWN.
I JUST HOPE...
...THAT WHEN I SEE YOU...
...YOU CAN FORGIVE ME...

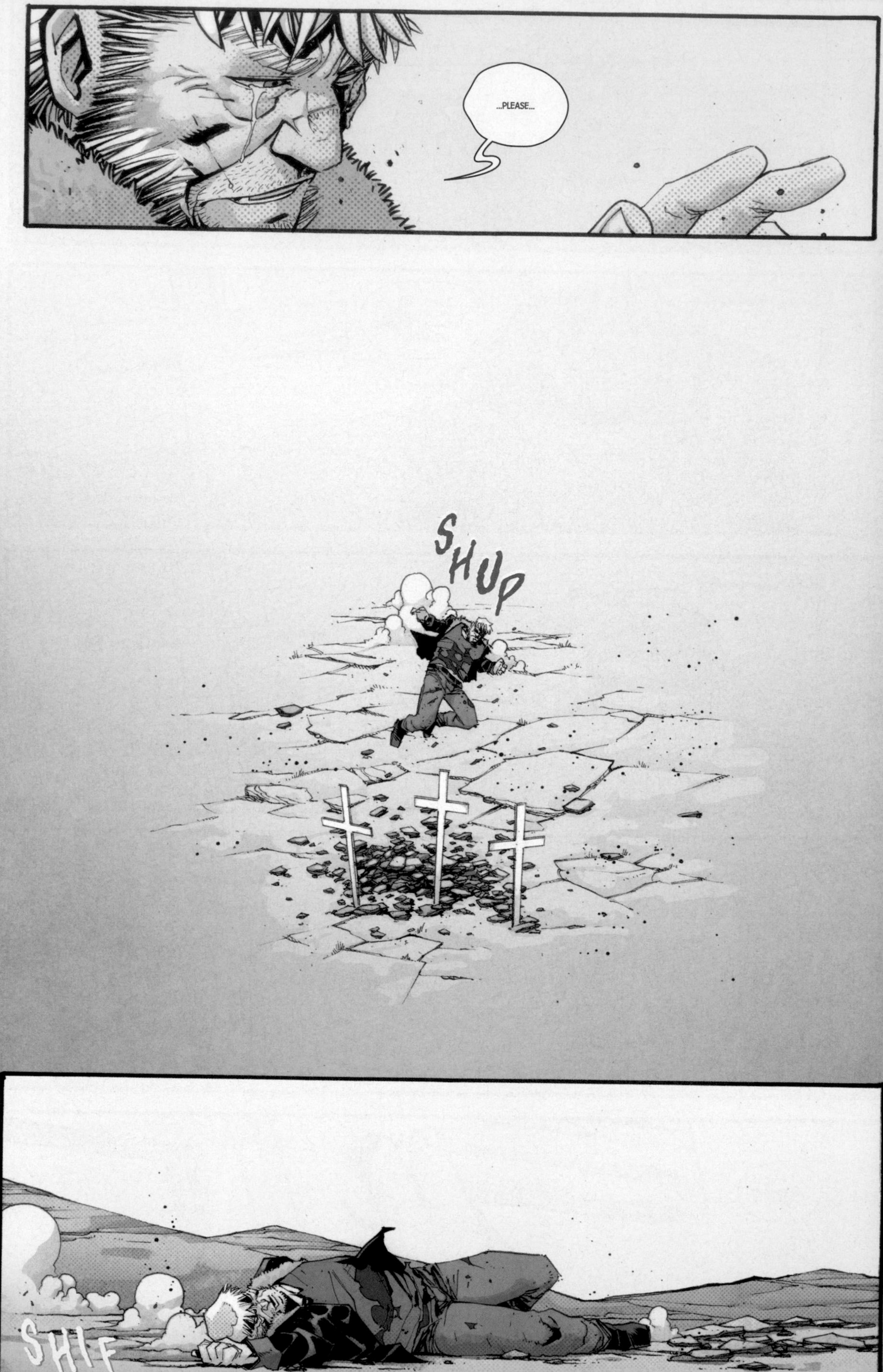
...PLEASE...
SHUP
SHIF

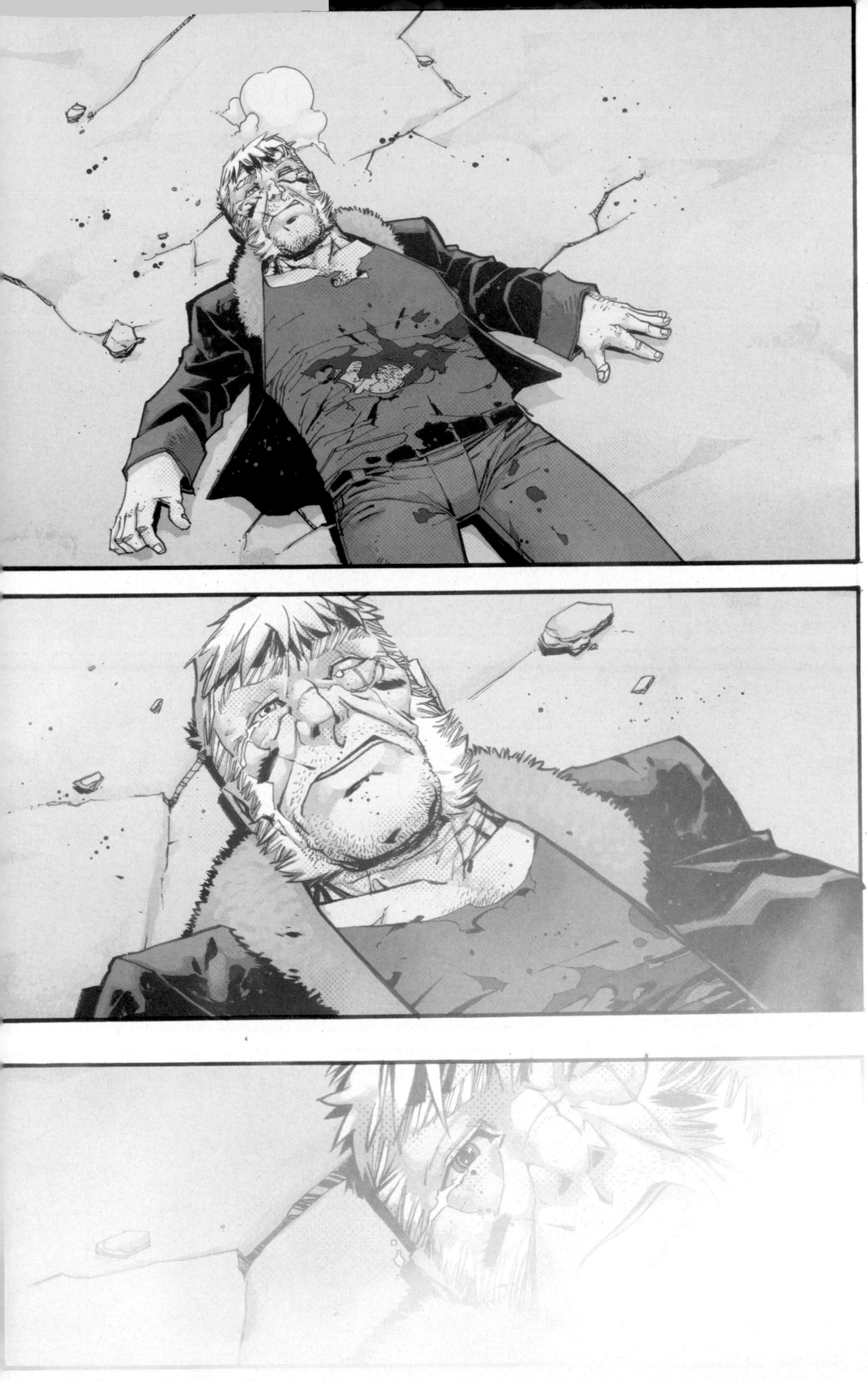

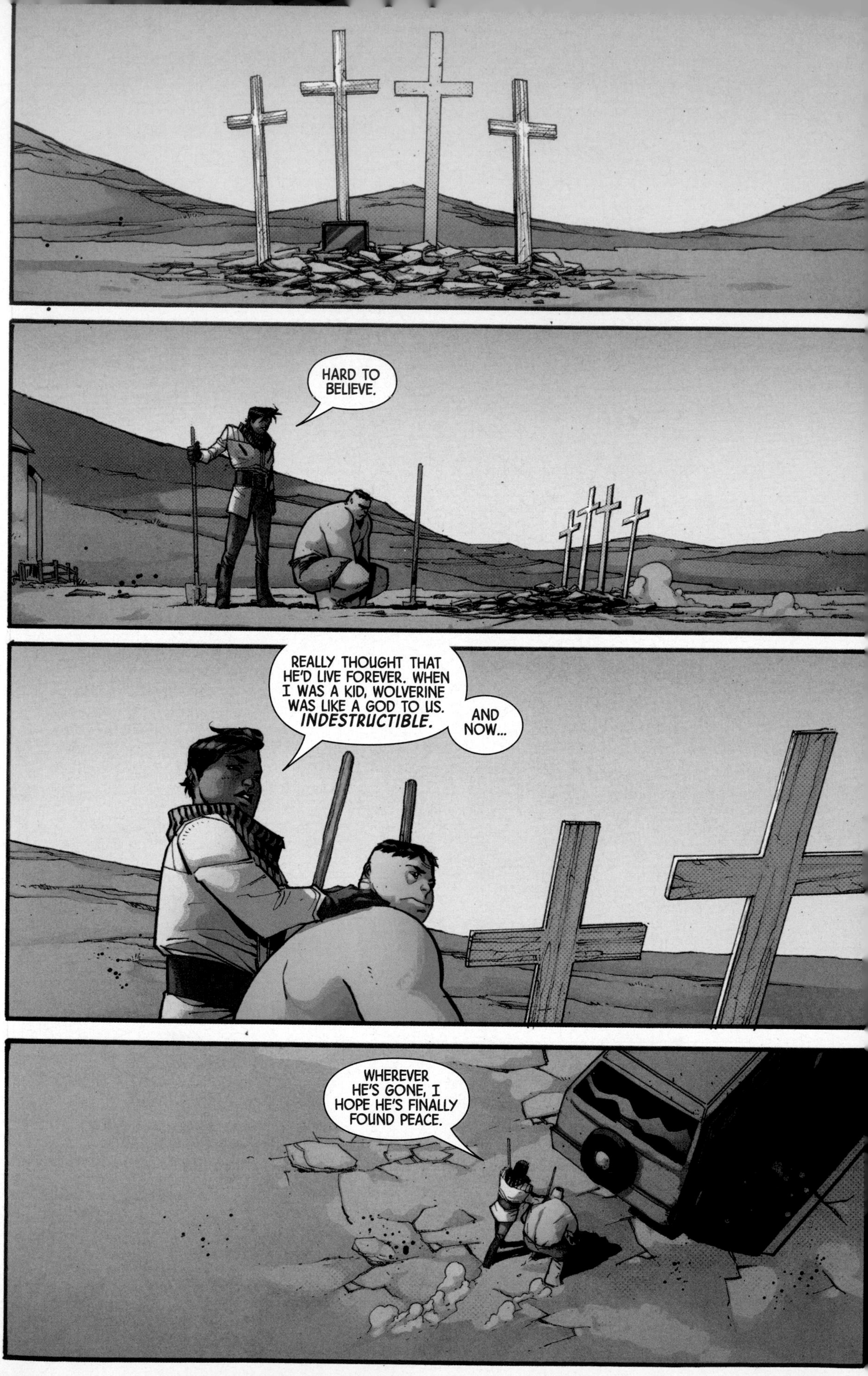
HARD TO BELIEVE.
REALLY THOUGHT THAT HE'D LIVE FOREVER. WHEN I WAS A KID, WOLVERINE WAS LIKE A GOD TO US. *INDESTRUCTIBLE.*
AND NOW...
WHEREVER HE'S GONE, I HOPE HE'S FINALLY FOUND PEACE.

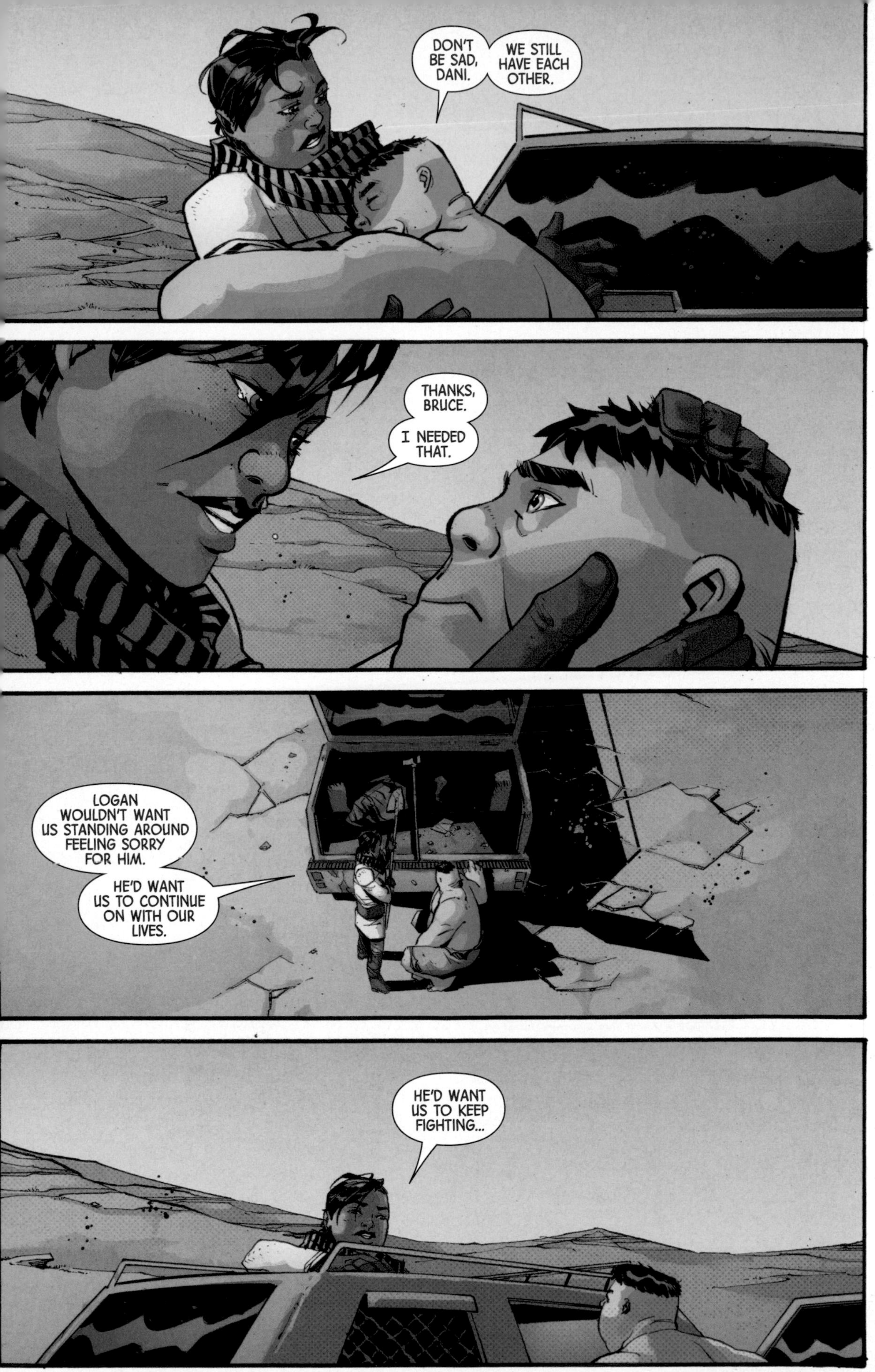
DON'T BE SAD, DANI.
WE STILL HAVE EACH OTHER.
THANKS, BRUCE.
I NEEDED THAT.
LOGAN WOULDN'T WANT US STANDING AROUND FEELING SORRY FOR HIM.
HE'D WANT US TO CONTINUE ON WITH OUR LIVES.
HE'D WANT US TO KEEP FIGHTING...

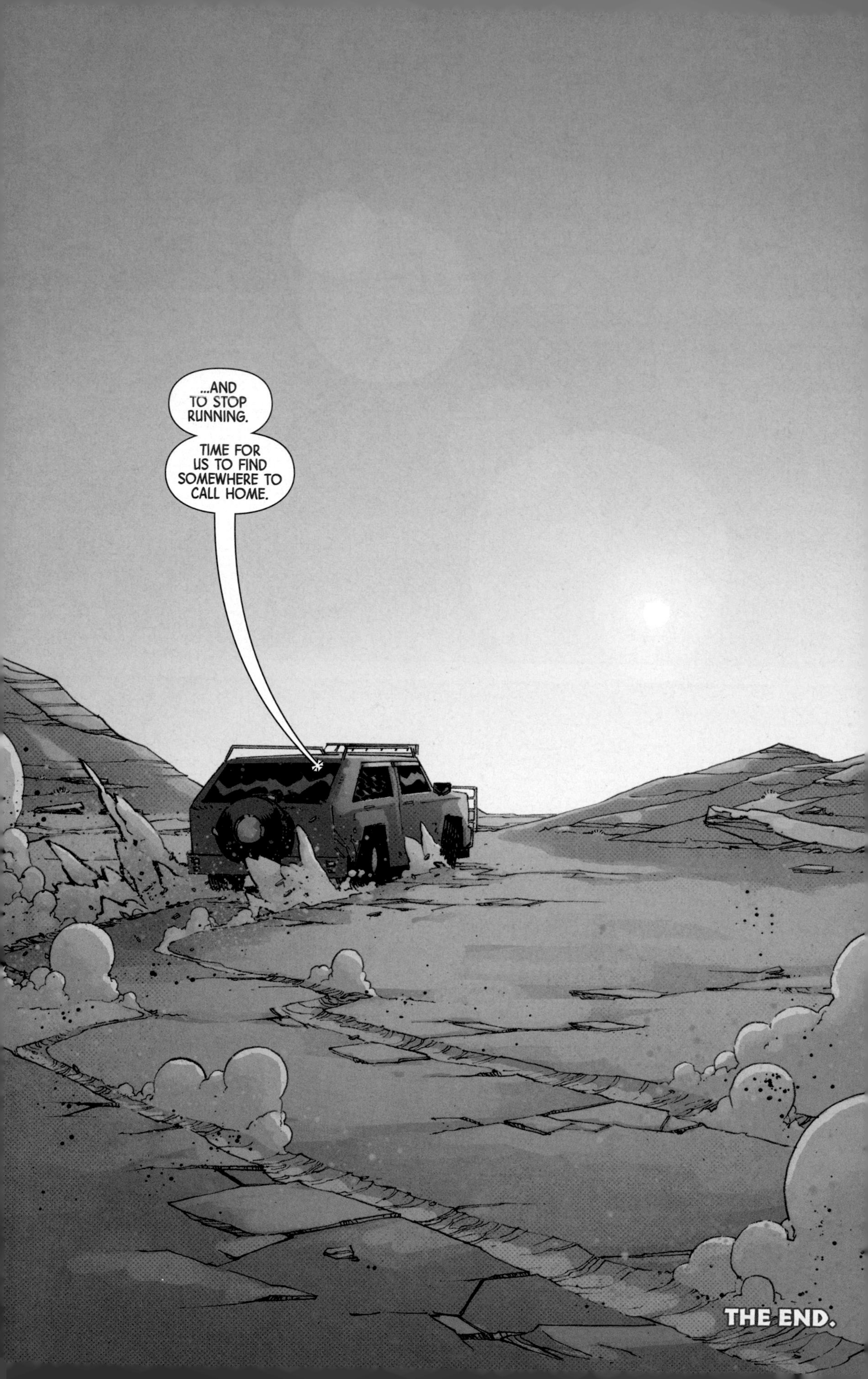
...AND TO STOP RUNNING.
TIME FOR US TO FIND SOMEWHERE TO CALL HOME.
THE END.

DAILY  BUGLE

MANHATTAN'S FINEST DAILY NEWSPAPER

IN MEMORY OF
RED SKULL

(Reporting by Christopher Holmes as told by Red Skull's former bodyguard)

"**H**err Skull was the most obsessed man I have ever met. He succeeded in killing all of the world's heroes and yet he still moved with urgency and purpose. But that determination made him crazy. He no longer cared about Hydra but instead began trying to unlock the secrets of the trophies he collected. He even scoured the country in search of Captain America's old shield. He would walk around in Captain America's mask, try to befriend the Cloak of Levitation and fly the cosmos using the Nova helmet. It was too much power, and it changed him.

That is why the Wolverine was able to kill him so easily. He couldn't master those items, and they ended up taking advantage of him. He was always talking to himself in his trophy room, languages I couldn't understand. But beyond the crazy, the evil that was the Red Skull remained."

DAILY ✄ BUGLE

MANHATTAN'S FINEST DAILY NEWSPAPER

IN MEMORY OF
GIANT-MAN

(Reporting by Christopher Holmes as told by Dwight Barrett)

"A lot of people come down here to Pym Falls. It's one of those things that's impossible to believe until you actually see it. It's amazing to think that there were people like this just walking around, and he was a hero at that. He had to be about ten stories high. I think I know why the villains leave him there like that. It's a reminder. If they can knock him down...they can knock anyone down. When I come out here to see it, I like to imagine what the age of heroes must have been like. It must have been great... I wonder if the people back then appreciated them while they were still here. Without the heroes this world has lost its hope. It'd be nice to get some of that back. The thing is, I think any of us could be Giant-Man. Any of us could be a hero. I'm just not sure how many out there want to be anymore."

DAILY BUGLE

MANHATTAN'S FINEST DAILY NEWSPAPER

IN MEMORY OF KINGPIN

(Reporting by Christopher Holmes as told by Jimmy the Finger)

KINGPIN

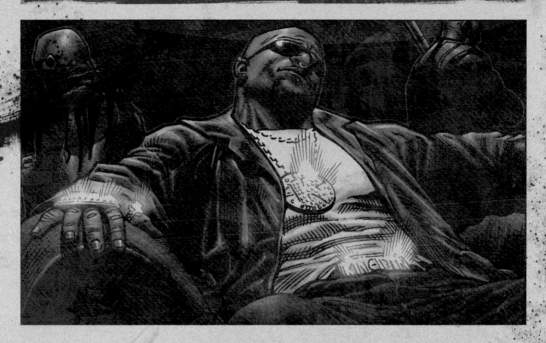

"Yeah, I worked for Kingpin. Nah, he wasn't the original—Wilson Fisk—but he treated us well enough. He's crazy, though, that one. He used to pack everybody in the football stadiums and put on these damn gladiator shows! Ha! Dude was a trip, man. Sometimes, he'd even dress them up as the old classic heroes and just torture them in front of everybody. The crazy thing is the people cheered! I thought they liked the heroes. This world is backwards, man, I'll tell you that much. They cheer the villains and boo at the heroes. He got killed though... by some girl dressed up as Spider-Man. Cut his head clean off. She took over his whole territory too. Someone dressed as Spider-Man took over the Kingpin's territory...I told you, man, the world is backwards."

#9 KINGPIN OBITUARY

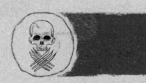

DAILY ✪ BUGLE

MANHATTAN'S FINEST DAILY NEWSPAPER

IN MEMORY OF
RHINO

(Reporting by Christopher Holmes, as told by a member of the Cheyenne Reservation)

" When the Rhino gang came to attack, they didn't know we had a shaman protecting us. He called himself Forge, but we in the community had another name for him. I will not tell you what it is because the English translation does not capture the meaning. Our shaman was a genius, and he built this reservation from the ground up...and protected it. Those monsters razed all of Dakota before coming here. They underestimated my people... it wouldn't be the first time that that has happened. Our shaman, Forge, made them pay for that mistake. He encased himself in metal armor, and he destroyed them. I was told that the Rhino was supposed to be an unstoppable force, but Forge ended him. When they came, they didn't stand a chance; he made an example of them in case anyone else wanted to come with evil intentions. We haven't seen Forge in a while, but with his actions we've been able to make this place a safe haven for people of all walks of life. He used to say, 'this is what Xavier would have wanted.' I don't know who that is, but he must have meant a lot to Forge."

DAILY BUGLE
MANHATTAN'S FINEST DAILY NEWSPAPER

IN MEMORY OF
TURK BARRETT

(Reporting by Elizabeth Bescherer, as told by Dwight Barrett)

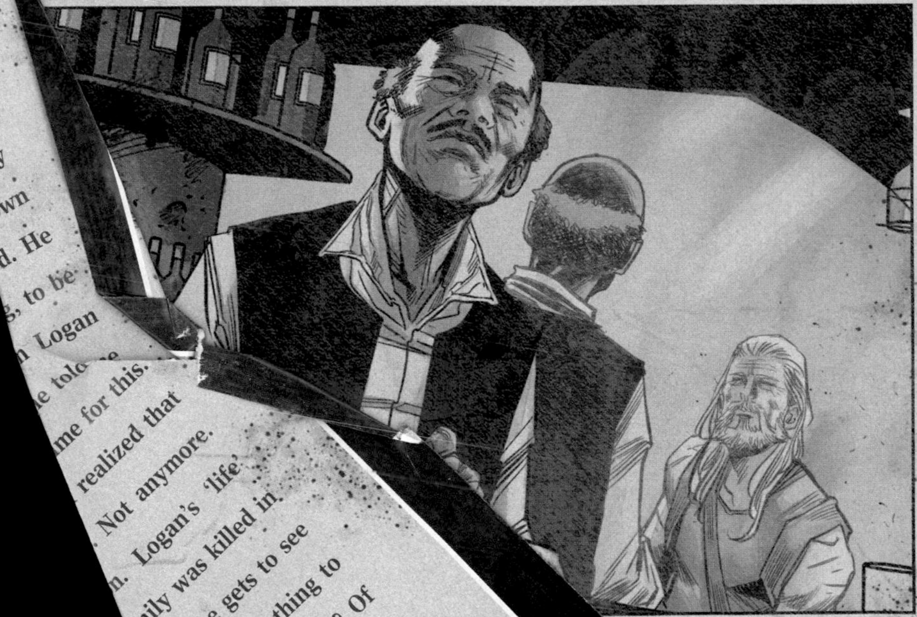

He
wn.
ably
down
od. He
g, to be
n Logan
ne told
me for this.
realized that
Not anymore.
n. Logan's 'life'
amily was killed in.
nally, he gets to see
me, that's nothing to
I gonna miss him? Of
of people are. He was the
rine! He was Logan...the
was."

ln't want to, though. I
ts to help him and
aybe if Uncle
be okay. I
I still
et

2 OLD MAN LOGAN OBITUARY

DAILY BUGL

MANHATTAN'S FINEST DAILY NEWSPAPER

IN MEMORY OF OLD MAN LOGAN

(Reporting by Jonathon Ellis, as told by Danielle Cage)

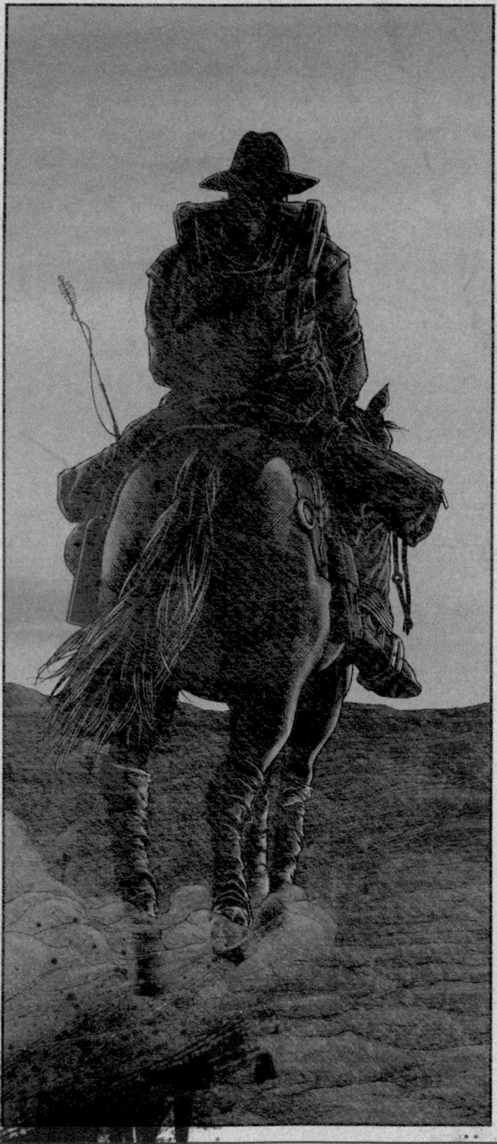

"Logan had his faults. No secrets there
He was brash, abrasive and stubborn. H
was also the best man I've ever know
He'd never admit it. Hell, he'd prob
snap at me for saying so, but...deep
I think that's what made him so go
always tried to prove himself wron
better than he was before. Whe
was suffering, toward the end, h
that he'd been waiting a long ti
Waiting to die. That's when I
this, for Logan, wasn't life
This was duty...obligatio
ended the moment his f
cold blood. But now, f
them again. You ask
get upset over. An
course I am, a lot
freaking Wolve
best there eve

DAILY  BUGLE

MANHATTAN'S FINEST DAILY NEWSPAPER

IN MEMORY OF
TURK BARRETT

(Reporting by Elizabeth Bescherer, as told by Dwight Barrett)

"Uncle Turk was grumpy a lot. He yelled at me for having my ants all over the place. But he never let anybody kill the ants because he knew I would get upset. That was nice. He said that the bar was the safest place to be, that's why Mom let me stay with him. The bar never really got customers... except for Mr. Barton. And I don't think any place is safe with Mr. Barton anymore. They only came because of him. When they were fighting, Uncle Turk kept telling me to go to the cellar. I didn't want to, though. I thought I could use the ants to help him and Mr. Barton defeat them. Maybe if Uncle Turk went to the cellar, he would be okay. I don't like thinking about how he died. I still get nightmares. I wish I'd gotten my helmet to work sooner."

DAILY 📯 BUGLE

MANHATTAN'S FINEST DAILY NEWSPAPER

IN MEMORY OF
OLD MAN LOGAN

(Reporting by Jonathon Ellis, as told by Danielle Cage)

"Logan had his faults. No secrets there. He was brash, abrasive and stubborn. He was also the best man I've ever known. He'd never admit it. Hell, he'd probably snap at me for saying so, but...deep down I think that's what made him so good. He always tried to prove himself wrong, to be better than he was before. When Logan was suffering, toward the end, he told me that he'd been waiting a long time for this. Waiting to die. That's when I realized that this, for Logan, wasn't life. Not anymore. This was duty...obligation. Logan's 'life' ended the moment his family was killed in cold blood. But now, finally, he gets to see them again. You ask me, that's nothing to get upset over. Am I gonna miss him? Of course I am, a lot of people are. He was the freaking Wolverine! He was Logan...the best there ever was."